# JEDIDIAH MORSE AND NEW ENGLAND CONGREGATIONALISM

# JEDIDIAH MORSE AND NEW ENGLAND CONGREGATIONALISM

*Joseph W. Phillips*

Rutgers University Press
*New Brunswick, New Jersey*

**Library of Congress Cataloging in Publication Data**

Phillips, Joseph W., 1948–
  Jedidiah Morse and New England Congregationalism.

  Bibliography: p.
  Includes index.
  1. Morse, Jedidiah, 1761–1826. 2. Congregational
churches—Clergy—Biography. 3. Clergy—New
England—Biography. 4. Congregational churches—
New England—History—18th century. 5. Congregation-
al churches—New England—History—19th century.
6. New England—Biography.    I. Title.
BX7260.M57P44  1983    285.8'32'0924  [B]    82–13133
ISBN 0-8135-0982-3

FRONTISPIECE. *Jedediah Morse [sic]* painted by S. F. Morse. Yale
University Art Gallery. Gift of Miss Helen E. Carpenter.

*To my parents*

# Contents

# *Preface*

Jedidiah Morse is a familiar figure to historians of the early republic, but he is mainly known only as a hysterical reactionary who issued fantastic charges during the French-American crisis at the close of the eighteenth century. This depiction of Morse, while not inaccurate, unfortunately slights other aspects of his long and active career. Morse, by no means a heroic figure, was an important leader of New England Congregationalism during a difficult transition period when it had to come to terms not only with democracy but with a host of social changes caused by an expanding national society. In fact, Morse's influence reached beyond New England, as he made important contributions to the general development of nineteenth-century evangelical Protestantism. He was a transitional figure between the traditional parish minister of the eighteenth century and the evangelical organizer of the nineteenth. Most important, despite his elitist biases and fear of democracy, Morse realized the power that public opinion would wield in American society and managed to forge tools of communication and organization with which to mold evangelical opinion and bring it to bear in the United States.

Neither William Buell Sprague's, *The Life of Jedidiah Morse* (New York, 1874) nor James King Morse's, *Jedidiah Morse: A Champion of New England Orthodoxy* (New York, 1939), the two previous biographies of Morse, present a full picture of his career or really explain it in the context of the development of evangelical Protestantism. This is what I have attempted to do. Probably I have not drawn a more appealing personal portrait of Morse than the generally accepted one. My main concern

ix

has been to explain his contributions to American religious life of his time.

I am indebted to the staffs of the manuscript divisions of the Yale University Library, the New York Public Library, the New York Historical Society, the Historical Society of Pennsylvania, and the Connecticut Historical Society for the aid they provided me in examining Morse's correspondence. I was also greatly assisted by the staffs of the Speer Library of the Princeton Theological Seminary, the manuscript division of the Rutgers University Library, and the newspaper and microfilm room in the Doe Library at the University of California, Berkeley.

I also wish to thank Lawrence Witalis, Winthrop D. Jordan, Ernest L. Tuveson, and Steven J. Novak for reading and commenting on several earlier versions and drafts of this book. Most of all, I want to thank Henry F. May for sharing generously both his time and knowledge of early American history.

# Introduction

More than any other Congregational leader of the Second Great Awakening, Jedidiah Morse attained prominence as a result of entrepreneurial ability. Unlike Lyman Beecher or Nathaniel William Taylor, he left no mark as either a preacher or a theologian. Above all an organizer, Morse articulated his orthodox Congregationalist colleagues' greatest concerns and organized campaigns to deal with them. He led New England Congregationalists in responding to the vast changes the United States underwent in the early years of its national existence.

It is hardly surprising that Morse recognized and attempted to deal with the political and social forces transforming New England and the nation. As the foremost geographer of the United States when "human geography" was as much a part of his subject as the physical environment, he was an attentive, if not impartial, chronicler of social developments for more than forty years. Moreover, no one among the Congregational clergy believed more strongly than he that this order of men had the responsibility of shaping the national culture.

This notion of course extended back to the beginning of New England, when ministers were expected to work in co-operation with civil authorities in ensuring that the Puritans made good their "errand into the wilderness." Within his parish the minister was an imposing figure who played a large role in the affairs of the village. Still, declension did set in, as both the original sense of religious purpose and the commitment to a cohesive society weakened. Economic and social change eroded the power of the Congregational clergy. New

Englanders became more and more worldly and increasingly individualistic. Less concerned with communal welfare, they questioned the right of the parish minister to intrude into their lives for the good of the community. In addition, by the mid-eighteenth century, in large part because of the Great Awakening, the Congregational clergy faced theological divisions within their ranks, the opposition of many church members, and even new denominations which rejected both the Standing Order's social and religious authority.[1]

Though diminished when the new federal government was inaugurated in 1789, the Congregational clergy's power within their parishes was still real, and by no means had they rejected the idea that they had an important role to play in public life. Only a few years before, during the revolutionary crisis, Congregational ministers had proved a potent force in aiding the causes of independence and republicanism. With the Revolution achieved, they faced the task of dealing with new forces in American society.

One of these forces was democracy. The clergy had worked zealously in behalf of independence and had supported the creation of a republic, but it was an elitist republic they envisioned. Out of their Puritan past they adhered to a hierarchical, ordered view of society. They were willing to accept a democratic element in the republic, but they believed that too much democracy was socially unsound and dangerous. Morse and the majority of Congregational ministers set themselves against the rising democratic political aspirations the American Revolution had released.

The growing democratic spirit affected society generally, not just politics, and these changes, too, alarmed the clergy. The Revolution had released new social forces and weakened some old restraints. The convulsion of the war had opened the way for some men to rise to new economic and social positions, and even more hoped to do the same. The Revolution had delivered a heavy blow to the notion of a static, hierarchical society. The men of the revolutionary generation were even less apt than those before them to accept their rank in society as fixed, and they were less deferential toward the well-born and those in authority. The clergy, part of the traditional New England elite, saw in this a threat to their social position.[2]

The Revolution had also had a damaging effect on New England religious life. The struggle with Britain preoccupied many people. Religious attendance dropped to a new low, and religious indifference was widespread. In addition, there was a good deal of dissatisfaction with the Calvinism of most of the Congregational clergy, and even infidel attacks on Christianity itself found an audience among New Englanders. The prospect of infidelity running wild seemed real to Morse and many of his colleagues.

Moral life also grew more lax after the Revolution. Now, more than ever, people gambled and drank excessively. Congregational ministers had long condemned such practices but were particularly unable to control them during the war, and they spread widely. Assessing New England's moral and religious life, the clergy feared that New Englanders were becoming another people, unworthy of their Puritan past, degenerate and disorderly in many respects.

The Congregational clergy also perceived danger from outside New England. By 1790 a new era in American expansion set in, as vast numbers flocked to the frontiers of Kentucky and Tennessee, of New York and Ohio. Morse was not the only Congregational minister who realized the power of the West and who feared that social conditions there would play a large part in determining the character of the new nation. New England could not be quarantined. If the agencies of decency and order, if churches and schools, did not keep pace with settlement, ministers felt that irreligion, barbarity, and chaos would reign and threaten to contaminate older regions of the country. New England must either be deeply shaken by the changes taking place elsewhere or exert itself to see that it imposed its stamp on the rapidly developing areas.

While there were these fears, there was also the hope that forces that were potentially unsettling and corrupting might

3

be harnessed to make the United States the leading nation in all history. The source of the Congregational clergy's optimism was their millennial outlook. By the mid-eighteenth century many ministers had come to accept the notion that a new era was in the offing, that biblical prophecies of universal piety, peace, and happiness were soon to be fulfilled. They felt that America would play a leading role in bringing Protestant Christianity to all men. This faith that their country had a providential mission to fulfill accounted for much of their support of independence. They regarded independence for America as part of a larger movement that would uplift the spiritual and secular lives of all mankind. Ministers hoped that the United States would serve as a powerful example and help to bring on the political and religious transformation of the world. Despite the disappointments of the 1780s, this hope did not die. If a correct, sober republicanism took hold and Americans took seriously their religious and moral duties, the United States might still fulfill its providential mission.

With Morse often leading the way, the Congregational clergy embarked on schemes and programs to realize their vision. Their efforts were not all marked by clear forethought and direct implementation. There was a good deal of innovation and unescapable adaptation, and also a number of serious errors. The most serious one was the alliance forged with the Federalist party during the 1790s. This grew out of the shared values of the party and the Congregational clergy, especially their mutual fear of democracy and their support of elitism. The clergy had long been fighting to preserve their elite position in New England society. Easily and almost naturally they fell into their political stance of the 1790s. But after the Revolution the struggle in behalf of elitism was tougher than ever before and proved to be a losing battle, given the new values and sensibilities of most Americans. Elitism cost the Federalist party control of the national government and destroyed it as a national party. Elitism was also costly to the Congregational clergy, though they managed to survive the debacle and live on to launch more successful projects.[3]

Through the Second Great Awakening, orthodox Congre-

4

gationalists were able to reach many people, but in doing so they had to accommodate themselves to American realities and adapt to some of the conditions which alarmed them. To a great extent they were ultimately successful because they held a good deal in common with other denominations. Overcoming resentment over the competition these groups represented, Congregationalists could join with them in a system marked by both competition and cooperation. The Second Great Awakening in New England was but part of a national religious movement. The affinity between Congregationalism and Presbyterianism is well known, attested to by the Plan of Union of 1801, under which the two denominations agreed to cooperate in evangelizing the frontier. Congregationalists also shared some important religious and social values with the Methodists and Baptists, the groups which were to grow enormously during the Second Great Awakening.[4]

All these denominations were committed to evangelical Protestantism, especially to its central tenet: that the sinful person had to come to an acceptance of Christ as a redeemer through a conversion experience. The evangelical denominations were also united by their belief that church members and even the larger society had to follow a pattern of behavior the denomination leaders considered the only one consistent with true religion and morality. Though Congregationalists like Morse were unique in their emphasis on elitism, they were able to form ties and alliances with other denominations likewise committed to making the United States evangelical in religion and behavior. The support these values received from all the denominations gave them enormous power.

The evangelical denominations shared common techniques as well as common values. They regarded the revival as the prime method of attracting church members, and they depended on religious organizations, called benevolent societies, to spread their values in American society. Though there were differences among the denominations over certain aspects of revivalism and also over the emphasis they gave to benevolent societies, there was a common acceptance of both.

These common values and methods would have meant little,

of course, if they had had little impact on the public. In fact, they proved extremely effective in winning people to the churches and to the support of the denominations' objectives. Evangelical Protestantism gave a sense of order to people who lived in a period of conflict and often alarming change. Above all, it was a time of fierce international war, which might well have overwhelmed the United States, and also of bitterly divisive political contention which threatened to undermine the republic from within. Moreover, internal migration surged during these years, bringing thousands to the anonymity of the city and many more thousands to the loneliness of scattered frontier settlements. While an industrial, urban America lay in the future, that future was rapidly being advanced by ongoing transportation and commercial revolutions that were uniting Americans in the perils, as well as the benefits, of a new market economy.

The conversion experience, whether wrought in a sober Connecticut meetinghouse or a boisterous Kentucky camp meeting, provided a sense of place and purpose outside the disorder of everyday life. Participation in benevolent societies provided a sense of community of the highest sort when the idea of an organic community had all but disappeared. In the values and instruments of evangelical Protestantism, the clergy of various denominations found the means of meeting the deepest concerns of hundreds of thousands of Americans.

Congregational success was achieved only at the price of adaptation. The denomination had to come to terms with the reality of voluntarism in American religious life. Congregational hegemony in New England had disappeared by the time of the Revolution, and it could not be recaptured. Other denominations, with other emphases and organizational strengths, held greater appeal for far more people, as the Baptists and Methodists demonstrated, and they had to be accepted. Even while Congregationalists were fighting long, losing battles in behalf of their establishment by law in Connecticut and Massachusetts, they were forced to accept voluntarism and find means to compete against the Baptists and

Methodists outside of those states. While failing to win the most members, Congregationalists did manage to establish a solid foothold in the northern frontier areas. They retained an elite position of a kind, for they tended to win the better educated and solidly middle-class, and they controlled colleges and benevolent societies with power beyond the size of the denomination. Moreover, their falling behind other denominations in numbers could not obscure the fact that a common evangelical Protestantism had become a powerful force in American society, driving infidelity, once the great threat in the minds of Congregationalists, into total disgrace. When the establishment fell in Connecticut in 1817, there were few who mourned its passing for very long, and evangelical Congregationalists even had a hand in bringing down the establishment in Massachusetts in 1833.

The acceptance of evangelical pluralism was but one of the major changes Congregationalism underwent. The ministerial role was also transformed. As appealing as was the idea of the Congregational minister as an elite figure who directed the affairs of a united, organic community from a position of unquestioned authority, it could not be reestablished, for more than religious pluralism prevented it. The democratization of American life had to be reckoned with. The minister no longer could lead simply because of his position. The success of revivals and benevolent societies proved, however, that the minister could establish a new kind of authority if he could win converts through his preaching and organize the religious-minded in benevolent societies. The minister's effectiveness—not his office—became the basis upon which he had to rely.[5]

The practical theology of Congregationalism also changed as a result of the Second Great Awakening. The orthodox clergy had not set out intending to dilute Calvinism, but that had happened. Before Nathaniel William Taylor summarized and defended this new system of "operational Arminianism," it had gradually taken shape. The spirit of Calvinism was weakened by Congregational participation in the Awakening, by

7

competition for members, the practical consideration of getting as many converts as possible weighing heavily. During revivals, ministers fell into stressing human ability as they urged their congregations to turn from sin to God and to make a new heart for themselves. Never openly repudiated, the Calvinist doctrines of election and predestination lost real meaning. Evangelical Protestantism effectively replaced Calvinism as the theology of most orthodox Congregationalists. Certainly the idea of sinful man winning salvation through the mediation of a divine savior was retained. This was the heart of evangelical Protestantism, which was more practical-minded but theologically simpler than Calvinism.[6]

One of the major episodes of the Second Great Awakening in New England—the orthodox assault on Unitarianism, which Morse did so much to bring about—is often described as a defense of Calvinism. It was not actually that. Many orthodox ministers were not serious Calvinists, having drifted far from that system in spirit and emphasis. When Morse called for them to break off from their Unitarian Congregational brethren, his standards of orthodoxy were decidedly evangelical rather than Calvinistic. He was not so much calling on the orthodox to stand up for the faith of their Puritan forefathers as he was calling for them to rally to the evangelical faith that was emerging during the early years of the nineteenth century and providing the basis for cooperation with denominations throughout the nation in the growing benevolent empire.

As a result of the emergence of this network of associations and Congregationalists' place within it, they felt far more comfortable with American society by 1825 than they had in 1790. Not only had the infidel threat been wiped out, but never before had so many Americans or such a large proportion been church members. Moreover, the wheels were in motion —through Congregational and interdenominational benevolent societies—to carry evangelical Protestantism to all Americans and finally all men. Now more than ever, as missionaries, Bibles, and tracts were finding their way to distant places, it seemed that the millennial era of universal piety and morality was near at hand.

By 1825, Congregationalists like Morse were even comfortable with democracy. Experience had taught these men, once so fearful of democracy, that a large portion of the public could be organized to support their religious and moral causes. The evangelical clergy in general were vocal supporters of the American system of republicanism, predicting that with the coming millennium it would spread throughout the globe. Faith in America's political institutions became a corollary, if not a part, of evangelical Protestantism.

Congregational ministers also gave whole-hearted support to the economic changes fast advancing industrialization and urbanization. There was no dramatic shift in their economic outlook as there was in their political thought. Early on, they had supported new inventions and means of transportation, citing the role these played in the growth of the American economy. Many ministers also believed that these also played an important role in bringing on the millennium. Closer commercial and transportation ties linked people together, they argued, and helped to spread religious truth more rapidly. These ministers even considered a much higher standard of living rendered possible by economic development as one of the blessings to be enjoyed during the millennium. The transition from an agricultural, rural society to an urban, industrialized one was not easy, but the clergy doubtlessly eased the anxieties of many evangelical Protestants, assuring them that the coming economic order was but part of a glorious new religious era.

In fact, evangelical Protestantism and the new economic order tended to bolster each other. Evangelicals openly admired the foresight and efficiency of the entrepreneur and attempted to operate their benevolent societies on the same principles. At the same time, by emphasizing the importance of sobriety, prudence, and industry, evangelicals helped to inculcate values important for American industrial development.

9

Though Morse did not live to see the formation of the Whig party, it was to provide a new political home for many of his evangelical cohorts. Both their faith in the beneficence of economic development and their emphasis on self-culture made the party congenial to them. As has recently been suggested, they constituted one strain of Whiggery, as they strove within the party to promote their moral concerns in American society.[7]

Whether or not Morse might have taken this step, he did play a major role in shaping evangelicalism among New England Congregationalists. To be sure, he was not a theologian or even a skillful revival preacher. As a man concerned with practical results rather than theology, he did move in the direction of evangelical Portestantism, but he left it to Taylor and others to expound and defend the theological shift in Congregational preaching. Similarly, Morse also accepted the revival, but he was a largely ineffective preacher, far below Taylor and Beecher in ability.

Morse's contributions to the Second Great Awakening were as an organizer, a promoter, a battler. In thought and opinion he was generally representative of the majority of evangelical Congregationalists, but he was unique in his tireless efforts to put these into action. Through his efforts Morse helped to define new ministerial roles and was, in fact, a transitional figure between the traditional parish minister of the eighteenth century and the religious organizer and editor of the nineteenth. These roles were foreshadowed in his work to organize all kinds of benevolent societies to promote evangelical values and in his involvement with the *Panoplist* and other forms of media to spread the evangelical message.

Only Lyman Beecher can be compared to Morse as an organizer of the Second Great Awakening in New England. As president of Yale, Timothy Dwight did much to bring into being the nineteenth-century evangelical college, but compared to Morse and Beecher his labors were restricted. Both these men performed the same sort of wide-ranging, activist ministry, though Beecher, arriving on the stage just a few years after

Morse and living well beyond him, operated in ever broader circles. In the end, Beecher was probably the more successful of the two, although he encountered disappointment and frustration as the united evangelical front, of which he and Morse dreamed, eluded him. Still, Morse's failure was of a more personal nature. As a transitional figure between two different sorts of ministries, he fell and failed somewhere in between. While he was shaping new ministerial roles, he was still responsible for fulfilling the responsibilities of the traditional one and finally lost his pulpit after many years of not meeting them. Nonetheless, Morse did play a major role in the development of evangelical Protestantism, which, by the time of his death, had become a pillar of nineteenth-century American culture, exerting tremendous influence on the attitudes and habits of millions of Americans.

# Chapter 1

---

# The Making of a Ministry

Jedidiah Morse was born in 1761 in Woodstock, Connecticut, a small, rather poor Windham County town settled in 1686 by people from Roxbury, Massachusetts. Both of Morse's parents had been born in Woodstock, his mother Sarah in 1724 and his father, also named Jedidiah, in 1726. His father especially had a lasting influence on him, setting examples of piety, industry, and dedication to public service.[1]

The elder Jedidiah had also been born into a pious household. Both of his parents were church members, and their home was a center for religious meetings during the Great Awakening. Attending religious conferences with other young people during this period of religious excitement, he had come to acknowledge his depraved condition and submit to a gracious Savior. As he later recalled, at that time he resigned himself and all he had "to His sovereign will and pleasure, and to [be] wholly at His dispose, both in this and the coming world." He did not immediately take up church membership but waited until 1747, several months after his marriage. At that time, with the encouragement of his wife, who was already a member, he joined the First Society of Woodstock.[2]

Jedidiah Morse, senior, went on to play major roles in both church and public affairs. Like his son later, he was dutiful and deferential toward his father, letting him lead in the church and town. Morse began his public career in 1752 when

13

he was elected surveyor of highways, and he occupied a number of other minor offices until 1763. That year, with his father seriously ill and soon to die, he was elected one of the two deacons in the church.[3]

Deacon Morse was also elected to his first important civil office in 1763 when he was chosen selectman, an office he filled for eighteen years. The next year, he was elected representative to the Connecticut General Assembly, the first of thirty-one regular and special sessions he attended. These were the most important offices in which he served, but he held others: town clerk for more than twenty-seven years, clerk and treasurer of the First Society for twenty years, and justice of the peace for more than twenty-five years. He calculated that "were I to have served in but one of the aforesaid capacities in one year, it would have required 280 years to have gone through the whole." In a brief account of his life, which he wrote in 1810, Deacon Morse said that as a young man he had resolved "to do as much good in my day and generation consistent with my talents, ability and time as I was able." In addition to his duties in church and government and tending his farm, Deacon Morse practiced the trade of farrier for fifty years and recalled having "castrated upwards of 1,700 horses and mules, and, no doubt, more than three times that number of smaller creatures; and but four horse kind of that number have died by means of the operation, to my knowledge." As a result of hard work, Deacon Morse prospered during his lifetime, becoming one of the town's fifteen highest tax payers by the end of the century.[4]

Holding the number and variety of offices that he did, Deacon Morse influenced every aspect of Woodstock's development in the latter half of the century. Most important, he was one of the leaders of the patriotic cause in the town and county. Windham was one of the two counties in Connecticut that most vigorously resisted the enforcement of the Stamp Act. It continued its opposition when Parliament approved the Townshend Acts in 1767. Towns in the county endorsed the radical

Boston town meeting's call for nonimportation, and they created committees of correspondence to put it into effect. In 1774 Morse, serving as a representative in the General Assembly, cast his vote with the majority in opposing the Intolerable Acts and insisting that the colonists could be taxed only by their own representatives in the colonial assemblies. At a town meeting in June 1774, Morse was accorded Woodstock's thanks for his vote: The meeting also endorsed the calling of the Continental Congress and the continuation of nonimportation. Deacon Morse was one of five men appointed to a committee of correspondence.[5]

Later that year the Windham towns voted their support of the Continental Congress's call for halting imports immediately and for stopping exports to Britain by September 1775. They also began making preparations for hostilities. In December a town meeting in Woodstock created a committee of inspection to see that the nonimportation pledge was obeyed, and it levied a penny rate to purchase arms. Many men from Windham County volunteered for military duty in the spring of 1775, most of them serving in Connecticut's Third Regiment, which fought at Bunker Hill.[6]

Throughout the war the people of Woodstock and the other towns of Windham County continued to provide men, food, and clothing at considerable hardship to themselves, as even in time of peace the area was not prosperous. Deacon Morse remained in Woodstock, directing town and church affairs and helping to provide for the families of enlisted men from the town.[7]

It was against this background of resistance and revolution that Jedidiah Morse, born in August 1761, grew up. Little is known of his childhood. He was the eighth of ten children, five of whom died in infancy. As a boy he was sickly and not physically capable of labor on a farm. For this reason and because he was fond of books, his father decided to provide him with a college education. After preparing for a year at an academy in Woodstock, Morse entered Yale College in 1779.

He had been drafted into the Connecticut line, but Deacon Morse intervened with Governor Trumbull to have his son exempted because of his poor health.[8]

Morse's correspondence with his father while he was a student at Yale offers the first view of his personality. He was close to his father, probably the favorite child because he was the youngest of the five who lived to adulthood. Morse wrote his father often and frequently asked for more letters from home. Their letters show that the father, as one might expect of a deacon, had observed religion within his home and instilled in his son an attachment to a Calvinist religious outlook and also to order. Morse wrote with alarm of the profanity of many of the students, and in 1782 he expressed his support of President Stiles's decision to expel forty students who had broken some windows during a riot: "This I am glad to see & shall do my endeavour to promote—for in such a Multitude of Youth were there not severe discipline kept up, Jargon & confusion would soon be introduced, & instead of being a School of Learning, we should be a Seat of Discord."[9]

Morse also took his religious duty seriously, writing to his father that the death of one of the professors showed the "uncertainty of life" and the need "to get prepared for so great & solemn a change." With his friend Abiel Holmes, who was also from Woodstock, Morse visited Stiles to prepare himself for church membership. Both young men decided to make their Christian professions in February 1781 and the next month took communion for the first time in the college chapel. Writing his father of his decision Morse expressed his hope that he had "an Interest in the Merits of a Crucified Saviour, & that I have had a Desire to forsake all & follow him."[10]

This decision placed him among a small minority of Yale students. Stiles's diary shows that no more than thirteen of one hundred sixty students took communion in 1781. Within a month of his profession Morse felt "exposed to the ridicule of an ungodly multitude: One false step is of dangerous consequences. Those that mean to be advocates for Religion have need to be clad with the whole Armour of God, & to rely

upon Jesus for their guide & Protector." As a Calvinist he recognized that men ignore religion because of their depraved
nature: "The greatest Enemy Mankind have to encounter, is
his own corrupt Heart. This invincible Enemy . . . can only be
conquered by *Him* who formed it." In response to his father's
complaints about inattention to religion in Woodstock, he argued that sinners were incapable of helping themselves on
their road to destruction; there is "nought but the infinite
Love & Mercy of God that keep them from it . . . 'tis God
alone that can soften the hard heart of the Sinner."[11]

Morse shared not only his father's Calvinism and attachment to order (perhaps a strange quality for a revolutionary
but one common among Connecticut's revolutionaries) but his
industry. Years after his days at Yale one of Morse's class-
mates recalled that he was known "not more for good talents
than for vigorous application." During at least one college
vacation he taught a singing class in Woodstock, and in his last
year at Yale he taught one in a town close to New Haven. After his graduation in September 1783 Morse remained in New
Haven, where he taught at a girls' school in the daytime and
also gave classes in singing, arithmetic, and geography in the
evening.[12]

All the while he began preparing for the ministry by studying divinity with Jonathan Edwards, Jr. of North Haven and
Samuel Wales, the Yale professor of divinity. Morse had little
time to devote to his study of theology. He blandly wrote a
friend about reading the works of the elder Jonathan Edwards and said that he approved of them. He spoke more enthusiastically of his study to his father, who was concerned
that he was not paying adequate attention to it. Morse assured
his father that his study delighted him and that he wanted
"nothing so much as to be able to attend to it without inter-
ruption." Morse received his first two invitations to preach in
the spring of 1784, but he declined, preferring to teach once
again at the girls' school, to which the leading New Haven
families sent their daughters.[13]

One end to which Morse applied himself as a student and

afterward, one which was very different from any to which his rustic father ever devoted his energies, was the task of making himself a gentleman. He sought out genteel company. During summer vacations Morse and his college friends spent their evenings visiting the daughters of the prominent families in the Woodstock area. A diary from 1782 records his going boating and having tea with some young women from New Haven. He was also an active member of the Phi Beta Kappa society at Yale and of another secret society, the Linnonian Society, whose members presented dramatic exhibitions. Perhaps one of them was a short play Morse wrote, a sentimental piece about a young woman whose husband, shortly after their marriage, proves to be an unfeeling monster.[14]

This playwriting was part of a program of self-improvement Morse undertook as a student. The major part of this effort consisted of his keeping a letter book in which he attempted to develop an easy, graceful style. Surprisingly, he also studied Philip Chesterfield, *Elements of a Polite Education,* a book condemned by many religious people for advising young men to be disingenuous. Morse learned from it how to converse and conduct himself in polite society.[15]

As a result of his efforts Morse developed a style which he brought to his later ministry. The Reverend John Todd, who as a boy regularly heard Morse preach, remembered him for his manners and his "uncommon conversational powers." One of the most striking things about his preaching was his smooth, pleasant voice, with which he sought "to win, draw, and persuade, rather than to overwhelm with argument, or drive by the awfulness of manner or matter."[16]

While he was teaching in New Haven, Morse also wrote his first geographical work, *Geography Made Easy.* The book began simply as some lessons for his students, but some friends who read the manuscript encouraged Morse to enlarge it and have it published. Ignoring his theological studies for the last three months of 1784, Morse had the book ready for publication in December. It was an immediate success. Within several weeks it sold more than three hundred copies, and in March 1785

Morse wrote a friend that it was selling "beyond my expectations." Finding that he had "hit upon a popular subject" even
before it was published, Morse asked his readers to assist him
in preparing a second edition, for which he began laying
plans.[17]

Despite the time his various labors took from his preparation for the ministry, by the summer of 1785 he felt it was
time for him to begin his career as a preacher. In September
he was licensed to preach by the New Haven County Association. He accepted an offer in Norwich, where he was also to
teach school. He began preaching in the winter of 1785 and
was popular enough to be asked to continue. He also received
invitations from churches in Farmington, Greenwich, and
New Haven and from Deerfield in Massachusetts. Uncertain
about what to do Morse asked his father's advice and accepted
it, agreeing with him that he was "too young in preaching, too
ignorant—too imprudent to settle yet." Instead he decided to
return to Yale where he had been appointed a tutor.[18]

In June 1786 Morse took up his position at the college, one
which allowed him more time in preparing his geography
than a new ministerial office would have. In July he made a
tour of New England, going as far as Portsmouth and collecting information for the next edition. By September Morse
worked out a plan with his friend Holmes, who was then
preaching in Midway, Georgia, that they temporarily exchange positions so that Holmes could recover his health in
Connecticut and Morse could collect information for his geography while traveling to Midway. In asking his father what he
thought of this scheme, Morse made it seem that the idea was
not of his making but that he was "not wholly averse to a proposal of this kind." Writing to a friend, however, Morse expressed his plans more strongly: "I am determined on a tour
to Georgia. . . . My design in retiring from College . . . is to
supply Brother Holmes Chh, and Congregation at Midway
in Georgia,—and to collect such Geographical information
as shall enable me to accuratize my Geography in a 2
Edition."[19]

With these plans made, Morse decided to postpone the new edition until he could incorporate findings from his travels. This decision was also strongly influenced by economic conditions. Though *Geography Made Easy* sold well, Morse complained to his father that he could not collect the money owed him. Despite his industry and the regard for his work, the prevailing scarcity of money blocked his success. This was just one aspect of a distressing time father and son sometimes discussed in their letters. Deacon Morse complained of postwar conditions in Woodstock—inattention to religion and a new level of litigation, which he found especially distressing as a justice of the peace. Morse wrote of the common opinion in New Haven that the Confederation government was too weak. In the summer of 1786 he wrote of his fear that Shays Rebellion would spread from Massachusetts to Windham County. With this threat of mob rule in mind, he felt that it became "the firm friend to good Government to be peculiarly active & assiduous in preserving peace."[20]

Morse was ordained in New Haven on November 9, 1786 and within a few days began his southern journey. Carrying a letter of introduction from Stiles, his first stop was New York City, where he visited the Reverend John Rodgers, the respected minister of the Collegiate Presbyterian Churches. Rodgers was sufficiently impressed with Morse to provide him a letter of recommendation addressed to members of the Synod of New York and Pennsylvania, suggesting that they avail themselves of Morse's preaching talents if they had occasion to use them. Passing through New Jersey, Morse met Gov. William Livingston, who promised his assistance in providing materials on his state for the geography. He also met John Witherspoon and Samuel Stanhope Smith, president and vice-president of Princeton College, and other Presbyterian leaders. In Philadelphia Morse informed Benjamin Franklin of his geographical plans, and he preached in the Reverend John Ewing's church, one of the most important Presbyterian churches in the city. The high point of the trip was his visit to Mount Vernon, where he dined with General Washington

who, he wrote his father, "entered into a free Conversation respecting the Insurrections in Massachusetts & appeared deeply interested in their issue."[21]

Morse arrived in Midway in January 1787 and preached there for six months. Morse was surprised to find that the people there were not irreligious, as his prejudices and his travel suggested most southerners were. Morse was well received at the Midway church and in several others at which he also preached. He received calls from three South Carolina churches, one of them in Charleston. Morse spent a month in that city, collecting geographical information and meeting prominent men. By the end of August Morse completed his return trip to New Haven.[22]

Morse had doubtlessly put his study of Chesterfield to good use, making favorable impressions on prominent men in public life, the church, and science, and these impressions served him later. Aside from the information he gathered during the trip and his stay in the south, his travels had two important effects for him. He established contacts through whom he could be supplied correct information on the different states, and his name became associated with the project of an accurate, thorough American geography. By the beginning of 1788 the Reverend Jeremy Belknap, Geographer General Thomas Hutchins, and Postmaster General Ebenezer Hazard, all authorities, abandoned the field to Morse.[23]

Once back in New Haven Morse set upon assembling the information he had compiled. He was quick to acknowledge that the strength of the work would derive from "the accuracy & judgment with whh it is *compiled,* rather than from the genius with whh it is composed." For this reason he issued broadsides which were printed in newspapers throughout the country requesting that people send him information.[24]

Morse's plans at this time were very ambitious. He intended to publish a much larger work than *Geography Made Easy,* giving the different states greater attention and also enlarging the sections on the eastern hemisphere to make the book a world geography. In addition, he wanted to prepare a gazetteer, a book in which geographical units (towns, rivers, mountains . . .) are listed alphabetically. With the Constitution moving toward ratification at the time, however, friends began to counsel Morse to concentrate on preparing an American geography. They also advised him that the geography should be delayed to wait for ratification, of which it should take account. Acting on their advice, Morse decided that he would publish a volume devoted to America and postpone his treatment of the eastern hemisphere to a second volume.[25]

When Morse came to this decision in the spring of 1788, he was preaching at the Collegiate Presbyterian Churches in New York City. In January the Reverend Rodgers had invited him there to fill a vacancy. Ebenezer Hazard, a fellow geographer and a church member who had befriended Morse, advised him to come preach there, telling him that he could use his free time to improve the geography while waiting for the Constitution to be approved. Morse accepted the position, writing Rodgers that New York was an excellent place to obtain accurate information needed for his book and that it was close to the town in New Jersey where he planned to have it printed. This candor surprised Rodgers, and he told Morse that he was among those who thought that he should not make so much of his geographical labors, "at least not make so much a business of it, as thus wholly to neglect your ministry." Morse began preaching in New York in March and continued through August 1788. He made a favorable enough impression to be considered for settlement, but the congregation was divided between him and another candidate.[26]

Shortly before Morse left for New York an opening presented itself in Charlestown, Massachusetts, which Belknap thought Morse might fill. Belknap, a Boston Congregationalist minister and another geographer, asked Hazard about Morse's abilities as a preacher. Hazard replied that Morse was a capable Calvinist but emphasized most his personal qualities: "As a *man*, I am charmed with him. He is judicious and sensible, decent and modest in his deportment, a cheerful companion, who prettily supports the dignity of the clergyman in the midst of friendly affability."[27]

Hazard probably stressed Morse's personal qualities because his theological views placed him in a different camp from Belknap. By this time, though they were not fighting, there were two broad groups within Congregationalism, orthodox and liberals. The division had become apparent in the two groups' reactions to the Great Awakening. The liberals, much affected by the rational spirit of the age, had reacted in horror to the Awakening. To them it was sheer enthusiasm and delusion. The convulsions of the movement convinced them that true religion was a matter of sound understanding and upright morals, not of self-abasement and claims of spiritual union with God. In 1788 liberals were firm Arminians and were drifting even further from Calvinism. Almost all of them preached in churches in eastern Massachusetts, and the heart of the movement was in Boston.

In opposition to the liberals were the orthodox, who had given general though not unqualified support to the Awakening. As Calvinists, they supported the theology of the Awakening—especially the idea that sinful man could be saved only through the mercy of God and that human efforts alone were unavailing. In 1788 the majority of Congregational ministers were still orthodox, as the liberals had made almost no gains in western Massachusetts or Connecticut. It was natural for Morse to fall into the orthodox camp because of his upbringing and his education at Yale, which was solidly orthodox.

Despite the fact that all the orthodox considered themselves Calvinists, they were divided into two parties, the Old Calvinists and the New Divinity. The New Divinity men, sometimes also called Consistent Calvinists or Edwardseans, took theology more seriously than the Old Calvinists. A good number of them put in long hours in their libraries, trying to follow up on Jonathan Edwards's insights, constructing a solid edifice of pure Calvinism, untainted by even the slightest trace of Arminianism. Also like Edwards, they wanted to remove practices from the church which they felt were tainted by Arminianism, and this brought them into conflict with the Old Calvinists. New Divinity ministers rejected the Half-Way Covenant because it opened the church to some who lacked faith.

The Old Calvinists could not accept this position. They argued that to limit membership to only those who could provide convincing testaments of a conversion experience was unacceptable. They felt that it was often difficult and sometimes impossible to determine who had experienced real conversion. It simply could not be the only standard for church membership. Moreover, the Old Calvinists took very seriously the notion that the church had the duty of inculcating morality in the people. If it set standards too high, it would exclude people who might benefit from membership and would fail to fulfill its social role. Thus, though both factions of orthodoxy claimed loyalty to Calvinism, the New Divinity emphasized the purity of the church while the Old Calvinists emphasized its social role.

When Morse was invited to the Charlestown church, he was among the Old Calvinists. While he was still a student at Yale, he had written in support of the Half-way Covenant, and he had preached in behalf of it in Midway, Georgia. No doubt his commitment was influenced by Ezra Stiles, who was contemptuous of the restrictive practices of the New Divinity. But Morse's own temperament, more than anything else, made him an Old Calvinist. Theology, which was so important to New Divinity ministers, was not of great interest to him. He had slighted it in preparing for the ministry. Of a more practical than speculative bent, Morse was responsive to the Old Calvinist concern that the church fully live up to its social responsibilities. In addition, his piety perhaps fell short of New Divinity standards. His conversion experience had not been the self-abasing ordeal New Divinity men believed it must be, as a person recognized his unworthiness and utter dependence on God. Indeed, Morse's letters to his father indicate that his experience led him to speculate more on a sinful nature of other men than to dwell on his own unworthiness. His faith is not to be doubted, but he seems not to have lived a particularly rich interior spiritual life. Consistent with the Old Calvinism of his early ministry and also the evangelical Protestantism toward which he was to drift, Morse expressed his faith outwardly in efforts to build up the church. Less attractively, his faith was sometimes expressed aggressively against those who in his mind represented sin and religious error.[28]

But all this lay in the future. Belknap was satisfied with Hazard's recommendation of Morse, certainly not suspecting that in time this affable young minister would make war on liberals like himself. Belknap worked in Morse's interest with the Charlestown church, helping him to win an invitation to preach there. Still caught up in preparing his geography, Morse had to postpone his visit until November, but then he preached almost every day for two weeks. He was so well liked that both the parish and the church voted for him unanimously. Morse accepted the call but had to postpone his settlement for several months because he was still involved in the final stages of the preparation of *The American Geography*.[29]

The spring of 1789 was an eventful season for Morse. On April 30, 1789 he was installed over the Charlestown First Society. Belknap preached the installation sermon. Deacon Morse and the Reverend Eliphalet Lyman were present, representing the Woodstock First Society, one of the churches invited to participate in the ceremony.[30]

Several weeks later Morse returned to New Jersey to marry Elisabeth Ann Breese, whom he had met and become engaged to while preparing his geography for the press during the winter. She was the daughter of a judge and the granddaughter of Samuel Finley, a recent president of the College of New Jersey. Their family began taking shape in 1791 as Elisabeth Morse gave birth to their first child, Samuel F. B. Morse, who, in time, was to invent the telegraph. She bore ten other children, but only three survived infancy. Morse explained his and his wife's feelings about their children, when he wrote his father about a three-month-old daughter who was "very forward, sprightly & engaging" but who was to die before her first birthday: "We have had sufficient warning not to place our affections inordinately on enjoyments of so precarious a nature. I hope it is our endeavour to possess this & every other temporal blessing as though we possessed not." Besides

Samuel, the surviving children were Sidney, who was born in 1794, and Richard, born in 1796. Morse was both an affectionate and a controlling parent, much as his own father had been.[31]

Morse's installation and marriage coincided with the inauguration of the new federal government. Morse was a supporter of the Constitution in the hope that the new government would put an end to the dislocations of the Confederation. A stronger government, he hoped, would make for peace and stability, ending the dangers of mobs and the inconveniences and frustrations of a weak economy. While preaching in New York in the summer of 1788, he was concerned with the debate over ratification there, fearing that if New York rejected the Constitution, the result would "be dreadful—nothing less, it is believed here, than a cruel civil war." He praised the Constitution as "a grand machine constructed by wise men, & I hope & trust that by the blessing of heaven it will diffuse peace, harmony, prosperity & happiness throughout our land."[32]

The inauguration of the new government was also important in a personal sense, for it helped to establish Morse's career. He made it the occasion for the publication of *The American Geography*, which came out in the spring of 1789. The new Union became a natural market for the book, which described in great detail the states now joined under the Constitution. Morse's interest in geography made Charlestown attractive to him because it was close to Boston, where he could easily continue his writings. It was such a pulpit which Morse desired, one near a cosmopolitan center. Then, too, the Charlestown office carried such benefits as a seat on the Harvard Board of Overseers.[33]

There was, however, another reason why Morse accepted the call from Charlestown. As his son Sidney later said, Morse "sought his father's counsel, shaped his plans to meet his approval, and even was influenced in accepting the call to Charlestown by the desire that the two might be near each other."[34] Morse's Charlestown ministry was founded on these two elements: ambition to establish himself more fully as a geographer and allegiance to his father, which involved in it an attachment to certain values his father supported.

Some of the values Morse adopted from his father are reflected in his geographical writings, in *Geography Made Easy, The American Geography,* and *The American Universal Geography* of 1793. These values are the norms by which Morse evaluated the various states. In 1784 Morse asserted in *Geography Made Easy* that New England's settlement by men seeking religious freedom gave rise to the characteristics that distinguished that section: simple manners, moral purity, industry, personal independence, and a fairly equal distribution of land. This was the common image New Englanders had of themselves, and probably nowhere was it better exemplified than in Woodstock. Deacon Morse's public career testifies to conditions that made it possible for a common man of industry to distinguish himself on a local level.[35]

Measuring the other states against these standards, Morse found them all wanting. He complains, for example, that New Yorkers are too luxurious and dissipated. But it is the southern states that stand most in contrast to New England and fare the worst in his judgment. Slavery is the principal cause of the South's shortcomings. It is an evil practice which breeds laziness on the part of whites. It also gives rise to a great inequality of wealth, creating two classes among whites, a rich, haughty upper class and an ignorant lower class.[36]

These were his judgments in 1784, several years before his southern trip and at a time when he had not traveled outside of New England. Prejudices that these were, they were confirmed by his tour. Passing through Virginia, he wrote his father that he missed the closely settled New England countryside, that he found the sparsely populated southern landscape lonely and depressing. He added that his trip provided "great opportunity to learn human Nature. I am extremely sorry to find it so extremely depraved." In Alexandria and Baltimore he calculated how many people did not attend church, an inquiry that led him to record in his almanac,

"How different from New England. Thrice happy is Connecticut in this respect." By the time that his stay in the South was nearly at its end, he concluded that the difference between southerners and New Englanders rested on slavery: "so long as the impolitic inhuman practice of Slavery continues—Industry among the white people will never be fashionable—for Idleness grows on Slavery."[37]

In 1789 Morse provided a more developed image of New England in *The American Geography*. He emphasizes the homogeneous quality of life there, the fact that most of the people, unlike those in the states to the south, are of English ancestry. To this he credits their greater attention to education. He claims, in fact, that New Englanders are the best educated people in the world. Because of their education the people are assertive, independent, and jealous of their rights, though perhaps too suspicious and litigious. Education allows men of ability to rise by means of personal distinction and their improvement of opportunities open to all. Such men "are the channels of political information to the lower class of people; if such a class may be said to exist in New England, where every man thinks himself at least as good as his neighbour, and believes that all mankind are, or ought to be equal." Men are able to distinguish themselves by their talents because of the equality of wealth which prevails, because there are no "overgrown estates, with rich and ambitious landlords, to have undue and pernicious influence in the election of civil officers." This general economic equality also fosters a republican spirit in that it does not permit luxury and forces men to be industrious. The reward of their industry and frugality is an independent spirit, for they know that they rely on no man. As a result, their manners are "plain, simple, and unpolished." These qualities reach their highest form in Connecticut, which "resembles a well cultivated garden," where the yeoman "toils cheerfully through the day—eats the fruits of his own labour with a gladsome heart—at night devoutly thanks his bounteous God for his daily blessings—retires to rest, and his sleep is sweet."[38]

Once again Morse develops in 1789 the unhappy condition of societies to the south, beginning with the middle states with their ethnically mixed populations.[39] Once again it is the slaveholding South that provides the great contrast. The mode of settlement—the spread-out plantations—makes social life—at least the kind that prevails in New England and centers around the meetinghouse and the town meeting—impossible. Slavery breeds insolence, pride, and dissipation in the slave owners, one consequence of which is that the South lags behind the rest of the nation in improvements. The South's lower class is given to habits of gambling, intemperance, and other forms of dissipation. The inequality among whites is reflected in public affairs, as in Virginia, where a few men constitute the political leadership "so that their government, though nominally republican, is in fact, oligarchal or aristocratical." Moreover, throughout the South great inattention to religion prevails.[40]

The image of New England by which Morse evaluated American society suggests that the best society is simple, homogeneous, and almost static, that it is one in which social and economic egalitarianism prevails, in which religion and education are strictly attended to, and in which a republican spirit coincides with a respect for order. Morse, however, does more than just look back to the values of Woodstock. *The American Geography* was in a sense a celebration of the Constitution. Morse praises the federal government and sees it helping to raise the United States to greatness, putting an end to the unrest and weakness of the past decade and promising to remove evils like slavery. He expresses his confidence that the new government will realize the hopes for which Americans struggled to achieve independence, spurring the development of a new republican civilization. Morse predicts that greater attention to education and improvements in farming will result in a new level of prosperity for agriculture and commerce. Technology and invention will spur the growth of American manufactures. Farms, linked together by canals and turnpikes, will checker the American landscape, making it resemble the pleasant state of Connecticut. The United States, he predicts four years later in *The American Universal Geography*, will develop a homogeneous population; "the language, manners, customs, political and religious sentiments of the mixed mass of people" will be assimilated and "all nominal distinctions shall be lost in the general and honourable name of AMERICANS." Toward the conclusion of *The American Geography* Morse expresses his confidence that the United States will spread across the continent, becoming the greatest, the culminating empire in the history of the world:

> Here sciences and the arts of civilized life are to receive their highest improvement. Here civil and religious liberty are to flourish, unchecked by the cruel hand of civil or ecclesiastical tyranny. Here Genius aided by all the improvements of former ages, is to be exerted in humanizing mankind—in expanding and inriching their minds with religious and philosophical knowledge, and in planning and executing a form of government, which shall involve all the excellencies of former governments, with as few of their defects as is consistent with the imperfection of human affairs, and which shall be calculated to protect and unite, in a manner consistent with the largest empire that ever existed. Elevated with these prospects, which are not merely the visions of fancy, we cannot but anticipate the period, as not far distant, when the AMERICAN EMPIRE will comprehend millions of souls, west of the Mississippi. Judging upon probable grounds, the Mississippi was never designed as the western boundary of the American empire. The God of nature never intended that some of the best part of his earth should be inhabited by the subjects of a monarch, 4000 miles from them.

In time the European colonies in the Americas will follow the United States's republican example and cast off their colonial rulers. By November 1789, with news of the fall of the Bastille, Morse saw the American spirit of civil and religious liberty working its way across the Atlantic, giving promise that the United States would lead all mankind to republicanism and Protestant Christianity.[41]

These expectations were informed by a millennial vision, the belief that in the scheme of world history the United States was to introduce a new order of things. Through her instrumentality, the Old Testament prophecies of universal peace, happiness, and holiness would be fulfilled. Thinking in these terms, the American and particularly the New England clergy had thrown their support behind the American Revolution, believing that the establishment of republican liberty in the United States was a first step toward bringing all men liberty and Protestantism. Stiles was one clergyman who accepted this outlook; it was the subject of his 1783 Connecticut election sermon *The United States Elevated to Glory and Honor*. Stiles, in particular, influenced the vision of the United States which Morse expressed in *The American Geography*.[42] But such beliefs were common among the clergy during the Revolution and took on greater force after the disappointing Confederation period with the adoption of the Constitution. They were further bolstered shortly afterward with the news that France was following the United States in the pursuit of liberty.

Within *The American Geography* there is a tension between Morse's view of the United States as a republican empire and harbinger of the millennium and his New England standards which emphasize order, not growth, and "mediocrity," not wealth. As a Calvinist, Morse maintained that man was sinful and, like his Puritan forefathers, he believed that social happiness could be secured only by maintaining established habits of control and order. Such habits had made New England's the best society since Eden. But he also thought that history was about to reach its culmination with the approach of the millennium, a time when man's depraved nature would be overcome and all men would be united under republicanism and Christianity in a world free of war, poverty, and ignorance. He conceived of this happy future in terms of liberation, expansion, and progress.

These contrasting outlooks were merged, though not reconciled, in the kind of ministry to which Morse dedicated himself. Although he accepted his father's parochial values, particularly his Calvinist orthodoxy and his concern for order and authority, he was not content to play the part of a small-town minister. He saw a new world coming into being which the United States was advancing with its values and physical growth. Morse wanted to chronicle that development in his geographical writings, and he also wanted to shape it. Morse enlarged the role of the parish minister. In *The American Geography* he emphasized the role the clergy had played during the Revolution, claiming that to them must be "ascribed no inconsiderable share of the success and victory that crowned the Americans." He assigned the clergy a large role in maintaining Connecticut's happiness by serving "as a check upon the overbearing spirit of republicanism." He even suggested that when ministers preached the annual election sermons in the New England states, they should submit histories of the events of the past year for reference in settling any political disputes and preventing the rise of political factions. Clearly Morse believed that the minister was someone who was to stand above society, imposing peace and order.[43]

Morse hoped that his geographical writings would play some role in the development of a national character. In 1793 in *The American Universal Geography,* he spoke of the formation of a national culture, of a time when all Americans would share "language, manners, customs, political and religious sentiments." He hoped that the moralizing in his geographies, such as his criticism of the New York Dutch for their reluctance to adopt agricultural improvements or his condemnation of slavery, would encourage reforms in these matters. In responding to St. George Tucker's attack on him for charging the town of Williamsburg, Virginia, with irreligion, Morse said that his only intention had been to awaken a concern for religion. As the eminent German geographer Christoph Ebeling, who was to figure in one of Morse's more important controversies, noted unhappily in 1796, Morse was not content just to describe geographical conditions in his writings. He "perhaps indulges too much in general reflections on people and their characters."[44]

In defining and preparing for the kind of ministry that he

did, Morse could not quite qualify for the more traditional ministerial role. His father and Rodgers expressed their irritation that he gave his geographical work priority over his ministerial concerns. Hazard, a friend, told him that his lack of theological preparation hurt him in the opinion of some of the congregation in New York. When Morse was installed over the Charlestown church, his friend Holmes expressed his hope that he would soon finish his geographical writings so that he could give his full energies to his ministry.[45] Morse, however, could not restrict his activities to a parish. He believed that his geographical writings served religious ends, and this was not an unjustified conclusion given his millennial expectations. No doubt, ambition and the success of his work also influenced his commitment.

*The American Geography* was an immediate critical and financial success. Stiles had it placed in the Yale curriculum soon after its publication, and it went on to become an accepted text in American colleges. Samuel L. Mitchill, outstanding American scientist and naturalist, spoke the opinion of the nation's men of letters when he praised the book, telling Morse that it "wipes away one of the spots on our national character, for it was truly reproachful, that we should be endebted to Europeans for the History of our own country." It was an important enough work for Thomas Jefferson to take the time to provide Morse with corrections. On the strength of *The American Geography* Morse was asked to prepare the article on America for the first encyclopedia published in the United States. The book was also significant, as Dartmouth's president, John Wheelock, wrote Morse, because "it communicates useful light, and will strengthen the union between the remote citizens of our States." Federal officials realized that and were cooperative in furnishing Morse assistance in his future editions, as were state officials who thought the work benefited the individual states.[46]

*The American Geography* was also well received outside the United States. An edition was published in England, and Morse was extremely pleased to receive a favorable notice from the British *Monthly Review*. As a result of the geography's popularity, Morse entered into correspondence with a number of British dissenting clergymen, the most notable of whom were Richard Price and Joseph Priestley. The geography was so well regarded by the University of Edinburgh that it awarded Morse an honorary doctor of divinity degree in 1794.[47]

With such encouragement Morse completed the series of geographical writings he had marked out for himself in 1786. In 1793 he published his major work, *The American Universal Geography*. The first volume of this work was an improved edition of *The American Geography*, and the second dealt with the eastern hemisphere. The second volume was compiled from geographical writings in English and so was much less impressive than the volume on the United States, which contained new information. Ebeling considered the second volume "too defective and erroneous" because Morse was unable to read German and French and so was unable to provide the American public with the best available information of Europe. In 1790 Morse published the second edition of *Geography Made Easy*. This was an abbreviated edition of *The American Geography* (its later editions would be based on *The American Universal Geography*) and was intended for use in schools and lower classes in academies. In 1795 appeared the first edition of *Elements of Geography*, an even briefer text taken from *The American Universal Geography* and intended for the use of children in lower school grades. Two years later *The American Gazetteer* was published. Morse himself did not do a great deal of work on this. He employed others to prepare the various articles by going through writings he provided them, among which was *The American Universal Geography*. Morse's contributions to the work were some stylistic improvements and his name.[48]

With the exception of *The American Gazetteer*, these writings sold very well, and all of them were corrected and published in new editions in the following years. Morse wrote Ebeling in May 1794 that up to that time he had sold 20,600 copies of his writings. This figure did not include the sales of *Elements of*

34

*Geography,* which probably became the best selling of his books because it was introduced as a text in schools.[49]

These sales provided Morse with a good income, in fact a very substantial one for a clergyman. Through his well-placed friend Ebenezer Hazard, Morse subscribed to a number of shares in the Bank of the United States in 1791. He also invested in other ventures, including the first Massachusetts Turnpike and the Middlesex Canal. Informing his father of the purchase of some notes, Morse declared, "The Country is flourishing, & all industrious and economical men will not fail to get a comfortable living." Certainly his circumstances had improved since the 1780s, when he could not collect money owed him.[50]

Still, the financial and critical success of the geographical writings did not prevent Deacon Morse from expressing his concern that his son, the "father of American geography," was misspending his time, ignoring his ministry. In reply, Morse sent a favorable British review of his book, hoping that it would relieve his father's "anxiety." He assured him that "I find my mind, after engaged in Geographical pursuits returns with ease & pleasure to my Theological studies.—I hope my Geog$^y$ had done & will do great good, & that it will appear in due time, that I have not misspent my time in writing it, whatever some good people may think to the contrary." This did not rest the deacon's fears that his son stood in danger of forgetting "that which is the conclusion of the whole matter to fear God; & keep his Commandments; which is the whole duty of man."[51]

Perhaps it was because of such misgivings on the part of his father that Morse dedicated himself so fervently to his greatest theological concern, the defense of the doctrines of the divinity of Jesus and the Trinity. In the first sermon he preached before his congregation the week after his settlement, he declared that "J Ch$^t$. & him crucified, or a crucified Saviour, shall be the *Alpha* & the *Omega* of all my preaching— He shall be the Great *Pole Star* to which my studies of whatever kind shall have an ultimate reference." He called the doctrine of the Trinity "the very foundation of the Christian System."[52]

True to his declaration Morse made the defense of the Trinity the subject of his sermons delivered at the Boston Thursday Lecture during 1790. This created something of a stir, for as a liberal minister noted in his diary, the "Clergy fear the controversy should be opened & yet the Orthodox will be meddling with it." Actually both the liberals (who, in 1790, preached as Arminians and only privately doubted the Divinity of Jesus) and almost all of the orthodox among the Congregational clergy sought to prevent a return to the divisiveness and debate of the Great Awakening when Charles Chauncy and Jonathan Edwards contended against each other, representing the two broad factions. Almost all of the clergy would have agreed with Belknap's call in Morse's installation sermon for a conciliatory spirit and for the toleration of differing religious opinions. Orthodox as well as liberal ministers feared that controversy would hurt all of the Congregational clergy without aiding the cause of religious truth.[53]

Morse, however, feared that the liberals would take the offensive against the Trinity. By the end of 1789 he had prepared a defense of Jesus' divinity, which he held ready for publication should the Trinity come under attack. In March 1790 an edition of Thomas Emlyn's *Humble Inquiry into the Scripture Account of Jesus Christ*, which denied Jesus' divinity, was published in Boston. It was probably Morse who anonymously addressed the men behind the publication, challenging them to reveal themselves so that he could meet them openly. Morse did not himself publish anything in retaliation but let a reprint of Aaron Burr (Sr.), *The Supreme Deity of Our Lord* suffice.[54]

By the end of 1790 Morse was engaged in a minor controversy with the Reverend James Freeman, rector of King's Chapel in Boston. Freeman was a nominal Episcopalian (significantly, not one of Morse's brethren among the Congregational clergy), so liberal that no bishop would approve his ordination and he had to be ordained by the church members. Freeman had assembled an edition of Watts's songs for children, which dropped all allusions to the divinity of Jesus. In one of the Boston papers, Morse attacked this as an act of willful misrepresentation, an attempt to propagate sentiments of which Watts would not have approved under the cover of his name. Freeman denied this charge, pointing out that he had not added a word. He found his opportunity for retaliation in 1793 when *The American Universal Geography* was published. Freeman issued a pamphlet that charged that the book was riddled with errors and marked by illiberal sentiments against the southern states and religious groups that differed from Morse in their outlooks. Again taking to the papers, Morse claimed that Freeman attacked him because he was a Calvinist.[55]

These exchanges, which illustrate Morse's early commitment to orthodoxy, were only a prelude to the later struggle between liberals and orthodox within Massachusetts Congregationalism. But they show a side of Morse's personality different from those charming, winning qualities that so pleased men like Hazard and Belknap and that had played an important role in bringing him success as a geographer and minister. This episode showed something of that aggressive spirit that Morse was to bring to later controversies and also of a tendency to see himself situated in a difficult, nearly solitary, defensive position, fighting a concealed enemy who sought to vanquish not only his cause but him. But in the 1790s the attention of Morse and much of the American clergy was focused on events taking place in France and their meaning for the causes of republicanism and Christianity in the United States and the world.

# Chapter 2

---

## Clerical Federalism and the French Revolution

When news of the French Revolution reached New England in 1789, most of the Congregational clergy reacted with joy. Morse was among that large majority. He said in his Thanksgiving Day sermon of November 1789 that the American "spirit of civil liberty & of religious toleration" had touched off the Revolution and that already it "was making rapid & Glorious devastations of tyranny, superstition, & ecclesiastical oppression." He was certain that it would help to usher in the millennium, "the Messiah's peaceful reign," when all people would enjoy liberty and embrace Protestant Christianity, "when redeeming love & its blessed fruits, will be known in all the earth."[1]

By the end of 1796, however, Morse and almost all the Congregational clergy no longer supported the Revolution. Their change of feeling was related to their emergence as firm, key supporters of the Federalist party but was not occasioned by it. The major political events of the 1790s, as the clergy perceived them through a set of political and social values to which they were deeply committed, moved them into the Federalist camp and convinced them that the Democratic-Republicans held out to the nation only the prospects of war and disorder. When they came to believe that France gave its sup-

39

port to their political enemies and was trying to raise them to power, their support of the French Revolution dissolved.

———— * ————

The millennial expectations of the New England clergy were also held, though perhaps not quite as intensely, by ministers and the Protestant public throughout the nation. Many Americans felt, as did Morse, that their own revolution had inspired the French, and they hoped for broad reforms in the French government and for the disestablishment of the Roman Catholic church. They believed that these changes would prepare the way for the spread of liberty and Protestantism throughout Europe and eventually the entire world and would finally culminate in the millennium.[2]

Two books written by New England ministers in the early 1790s show what the concept of the millennium meant to American Protestants. The authors were Samuel Hopkins, the leading New Divinity theologian, and Samuel Langdon, an Old Calvinist who criticized some of Hopkins's theological positions. Their differences did not extend to their views of the millennium. Both men accepted the position that it would begin with the destruction of the Roman Catholic church.[3] With the fall of the papacy, Satan would be bound for one thousand years. True religion would spread throughout the world, making it as it would have been had not Adam fallen, except that men would continue to be subject to disease and death. Both writers explained that Jesus would not reign personally; nor would the saints, the pious dead, rise from their graves to live again during this era.[4] Nature would continue to operate as before, but Satan's confinement and the prevalence of religion would make for an astounding transformation of the world. Hopkins said that it would be a time of "universal peace, love, and general and cordial friendship." There would be a vast expansion of human knowledge and the development of new inventions, making for material abundance so that men would work for no more than a few hours a day, no longer than necessary for their exercise. All mankind would speak one language, a new one better than any spoken before, which would speed the advancement of knowledge.[5] Hopkins argued, as had Joseph Bellamy and Jonathan Edwards, the previous principal American writers on the millennium, that the earth's population would increase so vastly during the holy era that, at its end, of all the humans who ever lived, "there will, on the whole, be many thousands of mankind saved to one that shall be lost."[6]

This happy state, Hopkins and Langdon agreed, would not last forever. (Nor in Hopkins's opinion would it be easy arriving there, because its beginning would be preceded by at least one hundred years of war and natural disasters, which would decimate all but those who turned to God. Most men would embrace infidelity, deism, and atheism and so would be destroyed.)[7] At the end of the one thousand years, God would unleash Satan, and men would again turn to him, reducing the church to its lowest point in history. Then Jesus would descend, destroy this world, and judge all mankind. The millennium, despite the piety and happiness that would prevail during it, would finally "show that the heart of man is naturally as full of evil as ever it was, and that all the good and holiness of the millennial state was the effect of the power of the Spirit of God."[8]

The millennium's gloomy conclusion, however, was hardly ever mentioned by the clergy, who dwelled on its coming. It did not abate Langdon's enthusiasm as he speculated whether the French Revolution would be followed by "events more and more remarkable, until all the nations of Europe shake off the yoke of ecclesiastical tyranny to which they have so long submitted, and assert the rights of nations and of conscience."[9]

The Revolution confirmed the belief of the American clergy that the United States would play the paramount role in introducing the millennium. Previously men like Morse and Ezra Stiles had stressed the physical growth of the United States, the establishment of an empire that recognized the civil and religious liberties of man, as the major process leading up to the millennium. They enthusiastically greeted France as the providential instrument for extending these principles, first recognized and established here. The Revolution bolstered their hope that their country would be the "medium through which religion, liberty and learning, shall be handed round creation."[10]

New Englanders generally, not just the clergy, warmly supported the Revolution. Both the *Massachusetts Centinel* and the *Independent Chronicle* praised it and expressed the hope that other European nations would follow the example of the French. In 1789 these Boston newspapers represented respectively the Stephen Higginson and John Hancock factions within Massachusetts politics, and with the development of early national politics they became the leading organs in New England of the Federalists and Democratic-Republicans. Both papers reported and expressed regret over the disorder and violence of the Revolution during its first several years, but they insisted that these were but a passing phase that would end in the establishment of liberty and order. The *Centinel* and the *Chronicle* also defended the Revolution against British attacks, such as that of Edmund Burke.[11] These were popular sentiments. The Massachusetts legislature declared in June 1792 that it viewed

> with peculiar pleasure, the sight of LIBERTY spreading in *Europe*, and from its rapid diffusion, we anticipate the happy period, when the Freedom of all nations will be established on a permanent basis, and the people throughout the World, however differing in language or complexion, enjoy unmolested, the "*Rights of Man.*"

Clearly New Englanders placed great hope in the Revolution, believing that it would bring about profound changes in the world.[12]

The clergy and people of New England continued to support the French as they learned in the autumn of 1792 of Louis being deposed, of the National Assembly declaring France a republic, and of the increasing violence taking place.

When news arrived in January 1793 of the French driving the invading armies from the Republic, celebrations were held in a number of Massachusetts towns. The largest was in Boston, where clergy, judges, and politicians participated in the festivities. At this and other celebrations, toasts were drunk to the hope that French triumphs would lead to the establishment of a free, stable government and the end of all war. Chandler Robbins, Plymouth minister and a friend of Morse, delivered an address in which he alluded to a day, which the French were advancing, "when *light* and *truth, liberty* and *peace,* will descend from the throne above. . . . Then shall private feuds, and national enmities be done away. The sword of war shall sleep in its scabbard."[13]

Still, supporters of the Revolution had to respond to the reports of violence and irreligion. Jeremy Belknap, in October 1792, sounded the claim that Hopkins was to make the next year: he suggested that the millennium would probably be preceded by disaster and suffering. Belknap wondered "what scenes of anarchy and distress may take place" before governments and religion in France became what New Englanders hoped they would. Robbins took a more optimistic position, which much of the clergy adopted. He acknowledged "instances of cruelty and revenge" but asked whether we have "not rather cause of thankfulness to the great Arbiter of the world, that they were restrained from further and greater enormities." In the spring of 1793, when news of Louis's execution reached New England, there was no great outcry of condemnation, though most people there may have wished that his life had been spared. Morse had written his father in October 1792 on hearing a rumor that the king had been killed. He expressed no regret then and remarked only that the "affairs of France wear a more favorable aspect—but doubtless much blood has been shed before this." Though troubled by the bloodshed in France, Congregationalist ministers generally believed it was caused by the people's recent escape from tyranny. They hoped it would not last for long.[14]

The clergy responded in a similar way to the reports of at-

43

tacks on revealed religion and of the spread of infidelity and deism in France. David Tappan, Hollis Professor of Divinity at Harvard, said that "a species of *atheistical philosophy* . . . has of late reared its head in Europe," but he called on Americans not to lose faith in the Revolution. He argued that it was God's method "to extract general good from partial evils, and to make even the wrath and wickedness of men eventually minister to the divine praise." The clergy also suggested that much of the irreligion stemmed from the ignorance imposed upon the French people by the previously established Roman Catholic church. As one minister explained, "When an ignorant people are brought by violent commotions to throw away their superstition, they are very likely to lose the greater part of their religion with it. . . . It will not be strange, if in the progress of these revolutions the grossest infidelity, impiety and vice should spread for a time like an overflowing flood." He was confident, however, that the ensuing misery from these evils would reform the French. In the meantime, as John Lathrop said in the 1793 Dudleian Lecture at Harvard, the New England clergy could behold with pleasure "the successor of those haughty pontiffs, who made the bravest monarchs tremble, and alarmed the nations with the thunders they uttered, now among the smallest of the princes, and using the feeble voice of a suppliant."[15]

The entry in 1793 of Britain into the war against France, which greatly extended the conflict, heightened the millennial hopes of the clergy. They hoped that the millennium might come more rapidly by means of a vast, sudden upheaval than if a mixed monarchy had been easily established in France without war. Even articles in the *Centinel* and the *Chronicle* spoke of the millennium as being close at hand. As Samuel Miller, a New York City Presbyterian minister, asked on Independence Day in 1793, "Can we turn our eyes to the European states and kingdoms—can we behold their convulsive struggles, without considering them as all tending to hasten this heavenly aera?"[16]

Of more immediate consequence, the war between Britain

and France forced hard choices on Washington and on the American people. These choices gave firm shape to the Federalist and Democratic-Republican parties, which until then had differed on the issues of funding, assumption, and the national bank. The war, carried on for most of the next twenty-two years, throughout that period continued to pose the greatest problems the United States would face and to shape its politics until Napoleon's final defeat in 1815. At its outbreak both parties in New England, as the *Centinel* and *Chronicle* indicate, supported American neutrality, while both also believed that Americans owed the French Republic their moral support and prayers. Still, from the beginning there were important differences between the two parties. The Federalists wanted to make a strict neutrality paramount in order to stay out of the conflict. They feared that war with Britain would be disastrous for the United States. The Democratic-Republicans, more confident of the United States's latent strength, wanted to take advantage of the war to force commercial concessions and the return of the western posts from the British.[17]

Early on, the Boston town meeting became the arena in which the two parties battled for public opinion in New England. This was not surprising, for during the struggle for American independence, the town meeting, led by radicals like Samuel Adams, with the crucial support of the Congregational clergy and the country towns like Woodstock, had swung New England to resist the British. Now Federalists and Democratic-Republicans were to contend within the town meeting.

The Federalists opened this new contest in July 1793 when they called a meeting to protest the fitting out of privateers for the French as a violation of American neutrality. The Boston town meeting was followed by others in various New England towns that summer. This drive to secure public support gained impetus as the Federalists became alarmed over the recently formed democratic societies to the south and over France's Ambassador Edmond Genêt and his threatened appeal to the people.[18]

By November 1793 Democratic-Republicans in Boston were engaged in forming a democratic club as an instrument to counter Federalist efforts to shape public opinion. Inspired in part by similar societies in France and especially Britain, the Boston club also drew upon the example of the Sons of Liberty and Committees of Correspondence, which had worked to build up public support for the cause of independence. The proposed society came under immediate attack from the *Centinel,* which since the summer had been censuring the democratic societies. The paper insisted that there was no need for them in the United States, which had a good republican government established by the consent of the people. The societies' only effect would be to "destroy the general harmony which pervades our whole country." The *Centinel* charged that they were the creation of Genêt and some Americans who wanted to divide the people.[19]

Morse shared these fears of the democratic clubs. He referred to the members of the Boston society as "grumbletonians," men who were always ready to speak their distrust of the American government but to praise everything the French did. Morse was still no enemy of the French. While he fretted over the democratic clubs, he continued to be excited by news of recent French victories. "Great events are before us," he wrote his father. "The time will I hope soon arrive when wars shall cease forever. I have great hope that I shall live to see that happy time." Morse considered himself a discerning friend who fully supported the French in their struggle for liberty but who could not approve of their violence and disorder. "The French cause has no enemies here," Morse explained, but "their conduct has many." Morse's great fear was that the democratic clubs might follow the worst example of the French.[20]

By early 1794 the new club, the Massachusetts Constitutional Society, was ready to take its case to the Boston town meeting. Officially dedicated to overseeing the government so that the Constitution was not violated, the society intended to throw its support in the town meeting behind James Madi-

46

son's commercial resolutions. Then before Congress, these resolutions were aimed at Britain and called for treating the commerce of nations with which the United States did not have commercial treaties as those countries treated U.S. commerce. They were opposed by two Federalist representatives from the Boston area, Fisher Ames and Samuel Dexter. Morse had at first supported the resolutions, but the arguments of Ames, Dexter, and other Federalist debaters in the House convinced him that the United States did not have the means to pressure Britain to alter her commercial regulations.[21]

The Democratic-Republicans had the upper hand when they called a town meeting in February 1794. They controlled the meeting and formed a committee which reported back with resolutions supporting Madison's proposals. Better prepared than at the earlier meeting, the Federalists prevailed when it reassembled, as a majority voted in favor of expressing no opinion on Madison's call for commercial discrimination and leaving the matter to the discretion of their representatives.[22]

This outcome greatly relieved Morse. He felt confident that Congress would not adopt Madison's resolutions. Though he had only shortly before supported commercial discrimination, so great was his suspicion of the democratic clubs, he now fully believed that the proposal was designed to provoke a war with Britain. Increasingly both parties were imputing subversive motives to their opponents, and Morse fell easily into this mode of thinking.[23]

Despite his growing suspicion of the political opposition, there was at least the comforting news from France that Robespierre had denounced Genêt as an agent of the Brissotin faction who, without the authorization of the French government, had worked against the interests of both France and the United States. This dispelled any fears that the French might be cooperating with the Democratic-Republicans to undermine the administration and its policies.[24]

Relations with Britain, however, grew worse. By March 1794 even Federalists agreed that the mounting British seizures of American vessels could not be tolerated. They still hoped to maintain peace and called for negotiations. When Washington dispatched John Jay on this mission, Morse placed his hopes for peace on it being successful. Morse was certain that if Jay failed, there would be war, and to him this was a terrible prospect. Like many other Federalists he was so fearful of the opposition that he believed a foreign war would also entail internal convulsion: "Our united prayer is for *Peace*. Thinking men among us fear the introduction of French principles into America."[25]

As troubled as Morse was about "French principles," about violence and disorder, he continued to support the French cause. He wrote Ebeling, a supporter of the Revolution, that "we wish them success in all their virtuous struggles for their *rights*. We *approve* their cause as just and good, but shudder at their enormities in the management of it. On their ultimate success we apprehend depends our security in the enjoyment of our rights & liberties." Morse's belief that French victories were important for the preservation of American freedom was shared by other Congregational ministers and spoken by some of them in orations on Independence Day in 1794. William Emerson declared that if her enemies defeated France, "America, in tears, will behold the triumph. It is even possible she may be called to defend anew her present claim to the joys of independence." Joseph Lathrop warned of the same danger, calling both the Revolutionary War and the war against France British "wars against nature—against the common rights of mankind." The clergy continued to apologize publicly for French excesses, blaming them on the invasion of the combined powers or the prior conditions under which the French had lived. "By recollection and experience," Lathrop assured his audience, "she will soon recover herself, rectify her errors, and settle her government in tranquility and order."[26]

The outbreak of the Whiskey Rebellion in August 1794 tended to convince Morse and others of his outlook that the introduction of "French principles" to the United States was being attempted. Playing on such fears, the *Centinel* and other Federalist newspapers claimed that the Pennsylvania insurrection was the "first *fruits* of the *blessed* harvest sown by *Jacobin Societies.*" The danger was not confined to Pennsylvania, Wherever men uttered the slightest apology for the uprising, wherever they claimed that, wrongful as it was, it was caused by the unjust excise tax, there was proof of "what had for a long time been *suspected* and *denied,* that our country harbours within her bosom vipers who would overturn all order, government and laws, that they might triumph on their ruins." The Whiskey Rebellion was but the most recent attempt, following upon Genêt's activities and the campaign to have Madison's commercial resolutions enacted, to involve the United States in disaster.[27]

Morse fully accepted these claims but thought that the height of the crisis had passed. He believed that the democratic societies were losing their influence because of the Federalist newspaper attack on them but especially because of the Whiskey Rebellion, which "has done more, to bring them into discredit—& I think will effectually convince the people of the pernicious & vicious tendency of such Societies. It is high time they were demolished—our peace among ourselves, & it may be the existence of our present Government depends upon it."[28]

Other Congregational ministers shared Morse's concern over the democratic societies. The first to express publicly has alarm was David Osgood who, in his Thanksgiving Day sermon of November 1794, attacked the democratic societies as "the greatest danger which, at present, threatens the peace and liberties of our country." He urged that Americans learn from the example of France, for

> had the representatives of the nation been left to act their own judgment, uncontrouled by the leaders of faction, they would never have been guilty of those excesses and cruelties which chill all humane minds with horror. But how came those factious leaders by such a controuling power over the convention?

49

Solely by means of those popular societies in which they first gained an influence. These gave to faction its whole force.

As Morse informed Oliver Wolcott, the assistant secretary of the Treasury and Federalist leader who frequently sounded him out on New England clerical opinion, Osgood's were "the sentiments of nine out of ten of the clergy . . . in respect to the 'self-created Societies. . . .' With [only] two or three exceptions, all breathed the same spirit—though their manner was not so particular & pointed as Mr. Osgood."[29]

Osgood's sermon was the first step in the Congregational clergy's involvement in the political controversies of the 1790s. It was not occasioned by the clergy's opposition to France or support of Britain but by their concern over the democratic societies and their determination to do what they could to crush them. Their opposition to the societies grew out of values they had consistently maintained. Now Congregational ministers began sounding warnings based on old deferential politics, revealing an outlook very congenial with that of the Federalist party, an outlook which was, in fact, drawing them within its circle.

As republicans, the clergy maintained the right of citizens to elect their rulers, a right properly exercised in granting power only to pious, virtuous men. Once elected, rulers deserved the people's respect. In 1791 Timothy Dwight had argued that "in the covenant interwoven in the very act of electing, our respect, our attention, and allegiance, are pledged to our rulers." This aspect of free elections—that by their means men pledge their support to their officials—was of as much significance to the clergy as the fact that they allowed the people to choose who would lead them. Government, the clergy contended, had been instituted by God for man's benefit. Those who rebelled against proper authority (the clergy, of course, did not deny the right to cast off unjust rulers) rebelled against God. The good ruler, as Dwight expressed it, "awful in his station, and amiable in his character . . . is justly considered as a fellow-labourer with the Redeemer, in that glorious kingdom of righteousness which he came to establish." Each man had his station in society, some as rulers and others as subjects, and the good of society required that each keep to his own. Holding these views, most Congregational ministers viewed the democratic societies with real concern. By the end of 1794 many of them felt compelled to warn against them.[30]

The Democratic-Republicans were reluctant to confront their clerical detractors. The *Chronicle,* because it did not want to attack the Congregational clergy, did not censure Osgood immediately but instead leveled its criticism at the Boston Episcopalian priest John S. J. Gardiner, who in an unpublished Thanksgiving Day sermon had also denounced the democratic societies. It was a much more dangerous matter to attack a member of the Standing Order, which had done so much to advance American independence. By December 1794, however, with the Federalists printing editions of Osgood's sermon throughout the country, the *Chronicle* was forced to rebuke him.[31]

The newspaper charged Osgood with bringing contempt upon himself by forgetting his ministerial duties and instead fomenting division and party spirit, even becoming "a tool to a 'splendid and PRINCELY' junto." It asked Osgood what was improper about citizens associating to oversee the government, inasmuch as he acknowledged their right to oversee it as individuals. The *Chronicle* also defended the French popular societies and blamed the violence and tumult in France, as had the clergy, on prior conditions and the interference of the allied powers in her affairs. The defense of the French popular societies was undermined, however, by news from France that, since Robespierre's fall in July 1794, they were being suppressed. The *Centinel* gleefully asserted that "the language of the Legislative Authority of France, at the present day, is the language the CENTINEL has held for two years. The Jacobins of *America* will be conquered in France!"[32]

Comforted by this news, in February 1795 the New England

clergy preached their sermons on the national Thanksgiving Day proclaimed by President Washington. The published sermons from that day, like those from the New England Thanksgiving Days in the autumn of 1794, express much praise of the administration for enabling Americans to enjoy liberty, peace, and prosperity. Morse asserted that the United States was the most fortunate nation in the world. It had not been easy, however, maintaining peace in the face of British attacks on our commerce and the "fascinating and dangerous influence" of France on some Americans. This influence, by which he clearly meant the example of the French Jacobin societies, gave rise to a "party, *disorganizing* spirit." Inflamed by the British outrages, this spirit "sprung up and increased, for a short time, with alarming rapidity; and threatened us with all the calamities, first of a foreign, then of an intestine war." Morse was confident though that both the treaty Jay was negotiating with Britain and the new government in France promised to put an end to these difficulties, so that in the future Americans need not expect troublesome proposals like Madison's resolutions or uprisings like the Whiskey Rebellion.[33]

Surveying the situation in France, Morse asserted that the suppression of the Jacobins, "a dangerous conbination of sanguinary men," prepared the way for a better, more orderly administration there. Political and social stability would make for a vast change in the people's religious sentiments. "When peace and a free government shall be established, and the people have liberty and leisure to examine for themselves, we anticipate, by means of the effusions of the Holy Spirit, a glorious revival and prevalence of pure, unadulterated Christianity." This was a common sentiment among the clergy and not just in New England. Two widely circulated tracts, written by middle-state ministers, argued that French infidelity was an instrument in God's hands for destroying the Roman Catholic church. David Austin, a Presbyterian, and William Linn, a Dutch Reformed minister, agreed that "the frenzy cannot last long. Soon as the design for which a wise God hath permitted it, is answered, religion will return in primitive purity and power. The old foundation is demolishing, that a better may be laid."[34]

With their confidence that the Revolution had passed through its most violent, disorderly phase and their assumption that irreligion in France was a painful but necessary step on the way to Protestantism, the clergy continued to wish success to the French. In a sermon on the national Thanksgiving Day, which the *Chronicle* called a "pitiful *recantation* of his former sentiments," Osgood thanked God for French victories over the combined powers. Other ministers once again spoke enthusiastically of the French Revolution ushering in the millennium. Thus even while the Congregational clergy were moving into the Federalist party, decrying the opposition, they had not yet given up on France.[35]

In March 1795, when news of the French capture of Amsterdam was received, the Boston clergy offered prayers of gratitude. To his father, Morse wrote that "the French continue to be wonderfully successful," and Henry Channing, a minister and old classmate from Yale, wrote him, "Laus Deo—France triumphs—and Holland is delivered. The present day is so loaded with momentous events, that my heart exults in having a portion of time at the close of the 18th century." New England Federalists held civic celebrations and, in Boston, even participated in one organized by Democratic-Republicans. The *Centinel* justified Federalist participation, saying that they should celebrate "the emancipation of our Dutch Allies; the successes of the French; and the downfall of Jacobinism in France, and America." In May 1795, in what Morse called an excellent sermon, John Thornton Kirkland sounded the common expectation that the spirit of the French "will probably run and kindle the flames of resistance in every country enslaved, and introduce a new order of things."[36]

Despite the pro-French sentiments expressed on the national Thanksgiving Day and later, the emphasis of the New England clergy's preaching that day had been on the worth of the federal government and Washington's administration of it. The Thanksgiving Day, of course, had been proclaimed so that ministers could rally Americans to support of the national administration, and the Congregational clergy performed that task. Ministers argued that the federal government had clearly demonstrated its value in putting down the Whiskey Rebellion, which otherwise might have spread throughout the nation, throwing Americans into the "wide and wasteful gulf of anarchy and confusion, ruin and wretchedness." The suppression of the rebellion, the clergy suggested, demonstrated two pleasing facts: that the great majority of Americans supported the federal government and that under Washington's leadership it could act with speed, energy, and effectiveness to put down such uprisings.[37]

Some ministers linked the democratic societies to the Whiskey Rebellion. Osgood, for example, claimed that the opposition to the federal government expressed by the societies and newspapers throughout the nation had given the rebels the incorrect impression that the administration was weak and could not take effective action against them. Other ministers contended against the democratic societies' claim that citizens had to keep a close, constant watch over government in order to preserve their rights and liberties. These clergymen said that, while Americans had the right of overseeing government, they also had the responsibility of exercising it wisely. Abiel Holmes warned that distrusting a man of their own choosing, supposing that he would try to harm them simply because he held office, tended "to diminish the energy of the laws—to lessen the attachment of the citizens to the government which they themselves have formed—and to generate a party spirit, destructive of national peace and happiness." Popular societies had done great harm in France, but there at least they could be partially excused because the French had not had a free, established government. Americans, however, should not naïvely believe small groups of men who claimed to exercise the people's right of overseeing the government. These men could easily play upon undue fears to weaken and perhaps destroy the government.[38]

Like Morse, a number of ministers praised Washington's

leadership, especially his decision for negotiations with Britain, which they were confident would be successful. Not surprisingly, the *Centinel* said the Thanksgiving Day sermons constituted "a political Bible—in which might be found the most invincible arguments in favour of good order, peace, and Federalism."[39]

There was only one Congregational minister sharply critical of the administration. Ebenezer Bradford of Rowley, Massachusetts, called the excise tax unjust and said that it had caused the Whiskey Rebellion. He also defended and praised the democratic societies as well as the French popular societies, claiming that the latter were responsible for "the present Liberty of that great and mighty Republic." The *Chronicle* praised Bradford's sermon and one other delivered by Thomas Thacher which contained a much more oblique defense of the societies against the charge of having stirred up the rebellion. These were the only published sermons it could praise.[40]

The newspaper did not attack the great majority of the Congregational clergy for the sentiments they had expressed. Instead, it continued to criticize Osgood and Gardiner, whose "Remarks on the Jacobiniad," a satiric piece about the Massachusetts Constitutional Society, had been printed in another Boston paper. The *Chronicle* also condemned David Tappan because of his published sermon's appendix, which was addressed to Bradford and which argued against the need for democratic societies in the United States, insisting that, indeed, they had been responsible for the Whiskey Rebellion.[41]

Though the *Chronicle* did not censure them, most of the Congregational clergy believed what Tappan argued. Most also hoped that, with the suppression of the Whiskey Rebellion and the public disapproval of the democratic societies, the United States had passed through the crisis. Their hope was shattered in June 1795, when Jay's treaty, then being considered by the Senate, was made public.

Though the treaty provided for the return of the western posts and indemnification for the British seizures of American commerce, it fell far short of what almost all Americans felt their country should have received. They had expected that French victories would force Britain to make concessions to the United States in order to keep peace with it. Under Jay's treaty, however, the American principle of "free ships, free goods" was not recognized, so that American ships carrying products of the French West Indies were liable to seizure by the British. Moreover, they reserved the right to confiscate provisions from American ships bound for France, pledging only to compensate the merchants whose goods were taken. By a small margin, the Senate approved the treaty, but throughout the country Democratic-Republicans began organizing against it, calling on Washington not to give it his approval. In Boston they had an easy time getting the town meeting to pass resolutions that condemned the treaty.[42]

There are no published sermons that reveal what Congregational ministers were preaching during the summer of 1795, but other evidence indicates that they were attempting to resist the tide of popular opposition to the treaty. Most likely, they did not preach in support of it but against the opposition to it, claiming that by denouncing it the people were assuming powers constitutionally delegated to the Senate and president. Because of their stance, the *Chronicle* for the first time criticized the Congregational clergy in general, saying that it was "remarkable that so many of the Clergy appear in favor of the British" and asking whether it was "not time for the Clergy of United America, to renew their former spirit of love and friendship to the *rights of men,* and no more throw their weight into the scale of aristocracy, as many of them have done."[43]

Morse, like many Federalists, was disappointed by the treaty's terms, but he was more alarmed by the opposition to it throughout the nation. He learned from correspondents in New York and Charleston that opposition in those cities was as great as in Boston and that Federalists everywhere had to wait for the public reaction to abate before speaking in behalf of the treaty. They argued, and Morse agreed, that this was the best the United States could do and far better than war with

Britain. He hoped that these views would prevail after an intense, brief period of opposition, but he was not certain they would.[44]

He was extremely alarmed after attending a town meeting in Charlestown, a solidly Democratic-Republican town, on July 21. An associate of his, former Congressman Samuel Dexter, had spoken in behalf of the treaty and argued that it was better than the other two alternatives, which were no redress of any of their grievances or war. War was out of the question because the United States did not have a navy with which to fight Britain. The treaty therefore had to be accepted, though it was not as good as they had hoped it might be, nor as bad as its opponents said it was. This reasoning had not moved the citizens, who had voted by a large majority to condemn the treaty.[45]

Later that day, Morse wrote Wolcott that "the passions of the people had been previously wrought up to a high pitch by designing men & they were determined at all events to 'damn the Treaty.'" He believed the nation to be in its most critical situation since 1775, with the people very liable to be misled by demagogues. If such men rose to power, the United States would experience what France had. There would be "an end of government, of liberty, & every thing but anarchy, despotism, & every *bloody* and *wicked* work. Little do the people who suffer themselves to be led astray by such men think what infinite damage they are doing to the cause of liberty & of Republican[ism]." On the advice of local Federalist leaders, Morse sent one of the Boston papers part of a letter Wolcott had written him expressing reasons for supporting the treaty. Thus Morse did his part to check the opposition, which he believed was led by men who "wish to over turn our government,—for having nothing to lose they have some chance to be gainers in the general scramble."[46]

Despite the public outcry and his own misgivings, Washington approved the Jay treaty in August, and Federalists began organizing public support of his decision. At the height of opposition to the treaty in July, Morse had been encouraged by his understanding that the people outside of the Boston vicinity, meaning most New England farmers, condemned the doings of the town meetings. This impression was confirmed during a trip he took through New England in the late summer, something he did every year and which always included attending commencement exercises at Yale. There he certainly discussed the political situation with clergymen from Connecticut and western Massachusetts. When he returned to Boston, he wrote Wolcott that he had met only one person who opposed the treaty and had discovered that the

> proceedings of Boston and the other towns against the Treaty were generally spoken of with ridicule and contempt & some went so far as to declare that if the Democratic Demagogues in Boston & New York were successful in bringing us into a War, which they seemed to take for granted was their aim, they should be the first object to feel effects of their resentment.[47]

Wolcott warned Morse, however, not to be too optimistic, for the country was still exposed to "considerable danger" from a "general combination" of men who wanted to involve it in trouble: "Though the numbers who are united in this *design* are inconsiderable, yet by their union and the address with which they manage every public discontent, they may possibly prevail." Some disturbances, which took place in Boston in mid-September, convinced Morse of the truth of Wolcott's assertions. For six or seven successive nights, a crowd, composed mostly of boys, had marched through the streets, carrying an effigy of John Jay and cheering Gov. Samuel Adams, a critic of the treaty. The only violence the crowd had committed was breaking some windows in one man's home, and he may have fired on the marchers first. Still, Morse accepted the claims of a *Centinel* writer, who likened the crowd to the Parisian mobs during the Reign of Terror and said that the disturbances had been directed by opponents of the treaty to show that Boston would never accept it and to intimidate its supporters. Echoing Wolcott's earlier charges, Morse now wrote him that the crowd activity proved the existence among the Democratic-Republican opposition of a small, well-organized, and highly effective group of men who were committed to a "general & organized plan, of involving the United States in trouble." He expected that at the next congressional session they would attempt to have the House of Representatives block the treaty.[48]

The *Chronicle* was then urging New Englanders to convene town meetings and approve resolutions calling on the House to prevent the treaty from going into operation. The response to this call was dismal because most New England farmers believed that if the treaty was blocked there would be war with Britain. Only three Massachusetts towns held meetings and approved such resolutions. Significantly, in two of them Congregational ministers supported this course of action. Solomon Aiken and Jonas Clark presented their towns' resolutions to Governor Adams, a gesture meant to show that some of the clergy opposed the treaty.[49]

The great majority of the clergy, however, endorsed the treaty and helped to build up support for it in New England. While the country awaited the battle in the House, published Thanksgiving Day sermons during the autumn of 1795 praised Washington for keeping the nation out of war and warned about the dangers of faction. Such preaching, the *Centinel* claimed, was one reason why New England farmers had "on every late occasion, exhibited the most honorable traits of Federalism."[50]

In December 1795 Morse traveled to Philadelphia, where he met with Wolcott. Along the way and on his return, Morse visited friends and acquaintances in New England, New York, and New Jersey. He regained a measure of confidence as a result of conversations that convinced him that even outside of New England people were coming to a stronger support of the administration. He now felt that the House would not block the operations of the treaty. He was almost jubilant over the celebration of Washington's birthday in Boston and other New England towns. According to Morse, even opponents of the treaty took part in the Boston celebration, leading him to believe that "the storm about the Treaty has almost entirely subsided." This new mood and the recently negotiated treaty with Spain, which was much more favorable to the United States than Jay's, would prove "insuperable obstacles to the disorganizing Spirit which exists in Congress in respect to the Treaty."[51]

Of course, Morse was wrong. In March 1796 Democratic-Republicans in the House managed to carry a vote that Washington submit papers relating to the treaty, which he refused to do. Federalists in Boston responded to this crisis by circulating a petition that called on the House to enact the treaty and warned that peace and even constitutional government were at stake. The Democratic-Republicans, now in a desperate effort to check the Federalists, turned once more to the town meeting. At the meeting on April 25, however, the Federalists greatly outnumbered their opponents, and by a large majority the citizens voted their approval of the petition. Morse had been extremely alarmed about the outcome of the meeting and had attended it. He played some part there for which the *Chronicle* rebuked him, wishing that he "would attend more to the duties of his clerical office, and not attempt to interfere in the proceedings of other towns, and by noisy acclamations disturb the intended order of the meeting."[52]

After the meeting the Federalists formed a six-man committee to circulate the petition to all towns in Massachusetts. The committee issued an address that implored the people to sign the petition because "we must prefer PEACE and PROSPERITY to *War* and *Distress*." Two members of the committee were distinguished Boston clergymen, Jeremy Belknap and Simeon Howard. Throughout the state, ministers passed copies of the petition among their congregations after services on the Sabbath. The petition received great support, many towns voting their approval of it at meetings. These endorsements continued to come in after the treaty had been enacted by a narrow margin in the House.[53]

The *Chronicle* bitterly denounced the Boston committee and

especially the participation on it of Belknap and Howard. The newspaper, in fact, condemned the Congregational ministry as a whole, insisting that they had deceived the people by telling them that rejection of the treaty meant war. "The CLERGY (a few excepted) have taken a conspicuous part in promoting the adoption of the treaty; let them abide the event. When the people feel its operation, they will look to the advisers of the measures."[54]

Entering the political fray to oppose the influence of the democratic societies, the Congregational clergy had gone on to become a principal source of support for the treaty and, in so doing, for the Federalist party. Correctly or not, they believed that rejection of the treaty would lead to a war which would weaken, if not destroy, the government of the United States. Channing spoke the feelings of many ministers when he wrote to Morse of his satisfaction over the treaty's enactment and his fear that, had it been blocked, the government would have been shaken, allowing a tyrant to rise to power. "Had Columbia made shipwreck of the republican faith, I am persuaded that the time would soon come when the creed of Freeman would be expunged from the records of nations, and the hopes of a republican Millennium been blasted forever."[55]

———— * ————

To understand more fully the Congregational clergy's partisan stance, it is necessary to look beyond the political events of the 1790s to the social and religious changes at work in New England society and their effect on ministers. Though they became involved in politics to help preserve peace, the Constitution, and even republicanism, Federalist ministers were also reacting to a range of social conditions they considered abhorrent. Ironically, the American Revolution, which the clergy had fervently supported, had helped to bring about major social changes. Morse said in *The American Geography* that the Revolutionary War had introduced "a flood of corruptions."

The Revolution had severely undermined the old colonial politics of deference to which most Congregational ministers remained loyal. They were alarmed that strongly democratic political aspirations were rising; the democratic societies were one expression of them. Moreover, the position of the Congregational clergy had grown weaker. They were beset by growing religious indifference among their congregations and also by challenges from dissenters who objected to the Standing Order's privileged position. In addition, Congregational ministers found it harder than ever to win the people's acceptance of their moral standards, as practices they considered immoral spread rapidly.[56]

Thus the Congregational clergy faced a host of social conditions that conflicted with their social values, which were conservative with deep roots in New England's Puritan past. This social outlook rested uneasily beside the millennial expectations pervasive among the clergy which made them support American independence and hope that the French Revolution would open an era of universal Protestantism and republicanism. There was a hard edge to their social values, and it was not softened by their happy vision of the future.

In preaching about society the clergy emphasized old themes like the need for order and, of course, religion. They stressed the importance of citizens living peacefully under the rule of their elected officials. This concern was at the bottom of their opposition to the democratic societies with their contention that the people should keep a constant, suspicious watch on their leaders. True happiness in society, ministers contended again and again, grew out of the people's piety and virtue, not their vigilance. A truly pious people would require few laws and little restraint.[57]

The clergy realized that at least until the millennium not all people would be truly pious. Certainly most people who attended public worship in New England did not profess faith and become church members. Ministers believed, however, that some regard for religion short of real piety, especially the fear of a future judgment, served highly salutary social purposes. They argued that those people on whom religion had some hold were capable of exercising a measure of self-restraint, which in turn would enable them to enjoy a corresponding measure of freedom. The more restraint people imposed on themselves, the more freedom they could be safely granted.[58]

Congregational ministers, pointing to their social role in helping to establish conditions that made for a high degree of freedom, defended the laws in Connecticut and Massachusetts that provided for their public support through systems of parish taxes. They insisted that these laws were wise policy because they insured that there would always exist a pious, learned ministry to inculcate morality in the people. The work of the clergy was too socially important to depend on the vagaries of voluntary support. Ministers dismissed complaints about the injustice of Congregationalism being legally established, claiming that the laws did not violate liberty of conscience and were not discriminatory because, by the 1790s, the members of other denominations nominally could have their taxes go to the support of their own ministers.[59]

In keeping with traditional New England values, Congregational ministers assigned responsibility for implanting virtue in the people to the institutions of family and school as well as the church. They considered all three to be of extreme importance in establishing habits of self-control and providing the knowledge to keep the citizens from being imposed upon, by unjust rulers, but especially by demagogues seeking power. This education began in the home, where, under a strict regimen of discipline and religion, the child first learned morality and the essentials of Christianity. It was continued in the schools. A series of essays, printed in the *Centinel,* provided one of the clearest explanations of the desired effects of public schooling. The child,

> from observing numbers, collected from different families, engaged in the same pursuits, and submitting to rules granting no indulgence to individuals must, if not as stupid as a block

catch the idea of a *common* interest, and of a *law* as the mean of its security. These ideas, added to the habit of obedience, and the knowledge of obligation or duty resulting from such habit will render him, suppose him ignorant in other points as you please, a peaceable and tractable, who else would have been a turbulent member of the community.

One minister went so far as to claim that "almost all the vices and evils of life may be traced back either to the want of an education, or an erroneous one," implying that a correct education could eliminate most of life's evils.[60]

Ministers contended that it was essential not only that the people be pious and virtuous but that they elect men of the same character. Religious rulers had the soundest regard for the people, and only they were deserving of that degree of trust which citizens owed those in power. "Under the guidance of such rulers, who consider their subjects as brethren and children, and all their interests of the community as their own," one minister explained, "a people can hardly fail of that happiness of which societies are capable in this degenerate state." The clergy urged that the people let a candidate's "merit be proved by the government of himself, and his subjection to the rules of religion and morality; by making his house the seat of order, and his family a nursery of those virtues which are the basis of a free government; and the town in which he resides, the miniature of a happy republic." Such a man would support education and religion and also punish the immoral, impious members of the community who drank intemperately, used profane language, and broke the Sabbath.[61]

Ministers lamented that these practices were on the rise in New England. They also complained about a great decline in religious instruction and prayer in the home. "Those prayerless and irreligious families are the hives of vice," warned Nathanael Emmons. "And from these, we may expect, will issue swarms of prayerless children, prayerless parents, ungovernable subjects, and prodigies of wickedness, to disturb the peace of society, and to propagate irreligion and immorality from generation to generation." The clergy believed that the increasing irreligion in turn contributed to the sharp growth of intemperate drinking and other vices. One minister said that when he was settled over his Connecticut church in 1796, these conditions existed:

> Intemperance greatly prevailing, and moderate drinkers as they were called, drinking most intemperately. Errorists of every kind, running to and fro, and many, having itching ears, running after them. Some openly avowing their infidelity; while others were proclaiming what they called good news and glad tidings; by which they meant that impenitent sinners, drunkards and all, were sure to go to Heaven.[62]

This statement points to another complaint of the time, the growing open rejection of Congregational orthodoxy. The Congregational clergy believed that "enthusiasm" was spreading among the lower classes and infidelity among the upper ones. Congregational ministers condemned all of the enthusiastic denominations. They berated Baptists as ignorant sectarians; they were even more contemptuous of Methodists and Universalists, who in different ways clearly rejected Calvinism, to which most Congregationalists remained loyal. In addition, from the Congregational point of view, all these denominations divided the people and deprived them of the opportunity to meet as a united community and to obtain the edifying social guidance of the Standing Order.[63]

In the 1790s, however, infidelity was more alarming to the clergy than any sectarian group because they feared that it was spreading faster. In the 1792 Massachusetts election sermon Tappan described what the clergy understood infidelity to be. He called it a "system of ideas," or at least of practical feelings,

> which considers all religious principles, observance and instructors, as the remains of old monkish ignorance, superstition and bigotry, or the antiquated offspring of worldly policy, begotten in the early and ruder stages of society; but which are wholly

unsuitable and useless, if not a heavy tax upon the public, in this more enlightened and mature period of human affairs!

In a Fast Day sermon the next year, Tappan said that skepticism and deism had already tempted—and he feared atheism soon would tempt—"some of the more sprightly and free-thinking geniuses of America; especially as it flatters the mental pride or conceited abilities and learning, gratifies the fashionable taste for extreme liberality of sentiment, and for opposing superstition and priestly tyranny, and at the same time is a very indulgent friend to modish dissipation and vice."[64]

Tappan's depiction of infidelity as appealing to well-educated men who opposed the teachings and traditional prerogatives of the clergy and advocated less exacting standards of personal conduct is illustrated by some events that took place in the 1790s in Windham County and involved the Reverend Eliphalet Lyman of the First Society in Woodstock. The controversy began when an ecclesiastical council, on which Lyman served, refused to settle Oliver Dodge as a colleague pastor over the nearby Pomfret church. The council found substance to charges that Dodge was an intemperate drinker and overly familiar with women church members. Unhappy with this decision, some members of the Pomfret church seceded and formed a new church, over which they settled Dodge. Later, when Dodge accepted an invitation from some Woodstock citizens to preach on a weekday in the town meetinghouse, Lyman rose during the services to express his objections. He explained that, as the town's settled minister, he felt he had to express his disapproval of a man of Dodge's character preaching there.[65]

Soon afterward Lyman came under attack from Zephaniah Swift, the Federalist congressman from the area. In a local newspaper, Swift charged Lyman and the other ministers who had blocked Dodge's settlement with violating those principles in behalf of which Americans had fought the Revolutionary War and for which the French were then contending. Swift called the refusal to settle Dodge an act of ecclesiastical tyranny. He also rejected Lyman's claim that he was a watchman who had the duty of standing guard over what the people of Woodstock heard from the pulpit. "No one truth can be more evident and important than this: that the inhabitants of a society have a right to decide who may preach in the pulpit in their meeting-house, and to assemble there on week days for public worship, at which time their minister has no more concern with them than the pope."[66]

Swift touched upon more than just resentment over the traditional powers of the clergy. He also advised the clergy that they should not preach against "innocent amusements." Following the Revolution, a new kind of lifestyle developed among many men in Windham County. They gambled and drank more than before and attended church less often. Ministers responded by condemning not only intemperate drinking and gambling but dancing and diversions on the Sabbath. Dodge was a different sort of minister than most. He mixed freely with the people and did not hold himself up as a moral steward. This as well as the fact that he did not condemn amusements like dancing made him popular. (His congregation did dismiss him in 1799 when they one day discovered him to be drunk while he was preaching.)[67]

Dodge had also been popular among the people of Pomfret because he had not made use of creeds. At his church the Bible was the sole standard of faith. In his attack on the clergy, Swift urged them to emphasize doctrines less, especially the doctrine of innate depravity, and suggested it would be best if they completely avoided doctrinal issues in their preaching. Instead, they should preach on love and benevolence, the essential elements of Christianity. Swift even went so far as to call New Divinity theology a bundle of absurdities which soured the mind. He insisted that it made no difference what people thought about doctrines, "provided they practice the essential duties of Christianity."[68]

The denial of traditional ministerial powers, hostility to almost any sort of doctrinal Christianity, and the rejection of severe habits of self-discipline badly alarmed the Congregational clergy. These conditions, so completely at odds with their basic values, influenced their reactions to political questions. They linked religious and moral declension to the rise of the political opposition. When Paine's *The Age of Reason* appeared in New England in the autumn of 1794, a time of great concern over the Whiskey Rebellion and the democratic societies, Morse wrote Wolcott that he agreed with him that a " 'mental epidemic . . . is spreading through the world.'" Wolcott had suggested that idea some months before, referring to political unrest, to the Democratic-Republicans in the United States and the Jacobins in France. Morse now gave it a broader meaning, telling Wolcott that "we have too many among us who are deeply affected with the contagious disease both in their politics and religion. And Paine's 'Age of Reason,' and the vile answer to it by Wakefield are, I am afraid helping to spread the disease, this way."[69]

The Congregational clergy were, of course, enormously alarmed by *The Age of Reason,* in which Paine, in promoting deism, bitterly ridiculed Christianity and the very idea of revealed religion. Orthodox ministers, like Morse, considered the reply by Gilbert Wakefield, who had been an Anglican priest, almost as bad. In defending Christianity, Wakefield dismissed as nonsense the doctrines of the Trinity and Jesus' divinity, along with the whole of the Athanasian and Nicene creeds. The orthodox Congregational clergy considered this infidelity, and it was infidelity of this kind rather than deism or atheism that most often confronted them in their parishes. Wakefield's views were similar to those of men like Swift, who considered themselves Christians but cared little about doctrine and who, when they spoke of Jesus, referred to him only as a moral instructor.[70]

Despite the fact that such attitudes were not confined to Democratic-Republicans nor in any sense characterized men of that political persuasion, Morse and other Congregational clergymen saw a connection between the political opposition and hostility to orthodoxy. Morse regarded both as aspects of a "mental epidemic." In their sermons on the Thanksgiving Day in February 1795, many ministers also linked the two together in calling on Americans to support the administration and attend to their religious duty. "Let it not be said of American liberty," John Mellen beseeched his congregation, "that it produces luxury and licentiousness, petulance and party— that it makes infidels, deists, libertines, and knaves." Sadly, it seemed to the clergy that liberty was doing just that. In August 1795, when opposition to the Jay treaty ran high, Morse wrote his father that "we are almost as remarkably *wicked*, as we are *favored*. The increase of infidelity, uncleanness, Sabbath breaking & all that flood of iniquity which springs from these is very alarming." Morse said in *Elements of Geography,* which was published in December 1795, that the number of deists in the United States "is not inconsiderable, and is probably increasing." This assessment was shared by Bradford, the Calvinist defender of the democratic societies. In his reply to *The Age of Reason* Bradford declared that deism had "made great and rapid progress since the glorious revolution in America."[71]

Unlike Bradford, however, most of the Congregational clergy fought the tide of irreligion and immorality by supporting the Federalist party. Their political support of the Federalists of course was made possible because they thought Federalist policies the best, but their identification of Federalism with religion and morality was not logical, as Swift's example should have suggested to them. In a similar example, when the Cambridge Association of ministers addressed the public on the evils of Sabbath breaking, the Federalist *Centinel* printed a reply which asserted that the incomprehensible Calvinist doctrines the clergy preached were the reason people did not attend more to religion: "A few phrases of metaphysical nonsense will easily spoil a discourse otherwise moral, rational and virtuous." Addressing Osgood, a member of the Cambridge Association, the *Chronicle* noted that "if such a publication [as the reply] had been printed in the Chronicle you would have sermoniz'd and anathematiz'd them all 'Thanksgiving Day.'"[72]

The situation was more complicated than just some Federalist laymen rejecting Calvinism and challenging the clergy's authority. Most of the Boston clergy were not Calvinists. John Clarke and Jeremy Belknap, two Boston liberals, wrote replies to *The Age of Reason*, but unlike Bradford, they made no mention of orthodox doctrine, of God sending his coequal, coeternal Son to the world to atone for depraved mankind. (Nor did they deny or ridicule such beliefs, as Wakefield had.) The resurrection of Jesus was the great article of faith for which they contended. Belknap maintained that, by means of the resurrection, God gave credibility to the precepts Jesus taught, showed that, unlike human teachings, those of Jesus had the approval of heaven and marked the path to salvation for all men. This was a view that Swift, who disdained doctrine but spoke of love and benevolence as the essential elements of Christianity, could accept.[73]

Doctrinal differences in the 1790s did not publicly divide the Congregational clergy or engender controversy among them. Early in the decade Morse's attack on James Freeman had threatened to touch off a debate. By 1794, however, when the political contest was under way, he gave this up. Despite their theological differences, the orthodox majority and the liberal minority shared common fears. Both were alarmed by the growth of infidelity, though if forced to state their candid opinion the orthodox would have had to acknowledge that the liberals smacked of it. But they did not have to express such an opinion. Both groups were concerned that many people were rejecting revelation, upon which each defended its own conception of Christianity. Moreover, though the liberals preached a kind of Christianity Swift might have liked, they fully shared with their orthodox colleagues a commitment to the idea that the clergy had a traditional role to play in society. As strongly as the orthodox, liberals condemned the practices of intemperance, profanity, and Sabbath breaking. Nor were they any less concerned about the formation of habits of self-control for the happiness of society.

Despite the complexity of the situation, perhaps because of it, most of the Congregational clergy responded to the unhappy conditions of political unrest, inattention to religion, and immorality by strongly supporting the Federalists. Belknap—speaking before the Massachusetts Congregational clergy at their annual convention in May 1796 at a time when they and especially he were being assailed by Democratic-Republicans for outspoken support of the Jay treaty—defended the clergy's conduct. Their political acts had been made in behalf of religion: "I consider politics as intimately connected with morality, and both with religion. If the political character of a people is bad, their morals are equally bad, and their religion is good for nothing." Fearful and concerned about so many aspects of society, the clergy came to make a commitment that Tappan had warned against in 1793. He had said then that too many people "deified" the Constitution and officers of the government, especially Washington, "expecting these to remove our difficulties, and ensure our safety and prosperity, whether we return to God, and engage his favor and benediction or not." Several alarming years having shown them that the people were not taking to their religious duty, the clergy supported the forces of order where they saw them best expressed, in the policies of Washington. They were seemingly unaware that in making this political commitment they fueled party spirit, one of the evils of the day which they decried.[74]

When Washington's administration ended in March 1797, the clergy's fears were greater than they had been in the spring of 1796 when they had hoped the Jay treaty would put an end to troubles with Britain and not stir up new ones with France. They had believed that order was being established there since the fall of Robespierre. In December 1795 Morse had praised the constitution that gave France an executive directory and a bicameral legislature. In 1796 he still apologized for French irreligion, explaining that the French people's religion was "in a *revolutionary* state; and we hope the time will soon come, when they and all the rest of mankind will embrace and practice the true and blessed religion of JESUS CHRIST."[75]

Federalist hopes that the French would not take offense at the treaty of course proved false. By October 1796 Americans learned of the French policy of treating neutrals as they allowed the British to treat them. Ambassador Pierre Adet announced this to Secretary of State Timothy Pickering in a series of notes, which he also made public in order to help Jefferson win Pennsylvania's electoral votes in the presidential contest. With great alarm Federalists realized that the French were throwing their support behind the Democratic-Republicans. The French, they now said, were helping to push the United States into disaster.[76]

Morse wrote Wolcott, in December 1796, that Adet's correspondence had showed the

> true character of the French nation. . . . Very few of the Clergy in the circle of my acquaintance seem disposed to pray for the success of the French since they have so insidiously & wickedly interfered in the management of our political affairs—& I apprehend the complexion of the thanksgiving sermons throughout New England this year, are very different from those of the last, in respect to this particular.

Morse and the Congregational clergy had supported the French Revolution, believing that it promised to spread liberty and Christianity to all men. They rejected it when they came to feel that French support of the Democratic-Republicans threatened to impose measures upon the United States that would destroy its peace and liberty. In the next several years, as relations between the two nations grew worse, Morse was to make startling charges about the French and the threat they posed to the United States, suggesting that they were working to rob it both of liberty and Christianity.[77]

# Chapter 3

---

# *Morse and the Bavarian Illuminati*

When the crisis of quasi-war with France arose in 1798, no group within American society was more affected by hysteria than the New England Congregational clergy. No group offered stronger support for Federalist calls for a military response to France and for repression at home. These ministers, who had looked toward France just a few years before with immense hope, now became fully convinced that that nation epitomized atheism and anarchy and was working with the aid of American agents to ruin the United States. No Congregational minister labored harder than Morse to propagate this view among the American people. Morse's and his cohorts' extreme fears and their conviction that conspiratorial forces were at work led them to support policies which, once the crisis had passed, proved so unpopular that they cost the Federalists the presidential election of 1800. Thus the crisis with France ended with Federalists losing control of the federal government and much of their viability as a national party. The Congregational clerical opponents of Thomas Jefferson fared a bit better. Though their reputations were badly damaged—none more than Morse's—and though they looked with puzzlement and fear on the coming to power of the new

73

president, they at least survived to address their concerns in different and ultimately far more successful ways.

———— * ————

In the spring of 1798 the Congregational clergy reacted with immense alarm to the news that French officials had refused to negotiate with the three special envoys sent by the American government and even had threatened them, demanding a bribe before talks could begin. The clergy had supported President Adams's decision in 1797 to seek a negotiated settlement. Now on May 8, 1798, the national Fast Day proclaimed by the president, ministers in New England argued that this most recent outrage proved that the French intended to impose their will on the United States. The XYZ affair fit into a long series of French actions, which included the conduct of former ambassadors Genêt, Fauchet, and Adet. All these demonstrated that the French planned to revolutionize the United States, as they had European nations. David Osgood warned that, if successful, they "will sweep away all your liberties, gradually wrest from you your possessions, strip you of your virtue and religion; and after transforming you into French demons, will give you up to be tormented through successive generations under the yoke of a foreign despotism."[1]

The clergy expressed a millennial view different from that of just a few years before. They now believed, as Samuel Hopkins had contended in his tract on the millennium, that its commencement would be preceded by great violence and bloodshed. Nathan Strong explained in April 1798 that he and other ministers had been mistaken in assuming that the French Revolution would soon introduce a golden age of peace and piety. Some "have kept their eyes so fixedly on the promises of a day when the nations shall learn war no more, that they have been ready to hail revolutionary war, as the beginning of millennial peace and good will. They have overlooked the judgments, which we may both naturally and

74

prophetically expect to antecede Christ's universal reign on earth." David Tappan insisted that God was using the French as instruments to punish mankind for the infidelity and wickedness prevailing everywhere. The French inflicted divine judgment on the combined powers, Protestant as well as Catholic, for their "apostacy, oppression, and wickedness." At the same time, they brought suffering upon themselves for their irreligion and violence.[2]

In his Fast Day sermon Morse offered the most detailed account of the threat France posed to Americans. He began by contending that throughout the world, even in the United States, government and religion were under attack. This gave good reason to suspect the existence of a conspiracy, and Morse reported that there was a book that spoke of such a conspiracy. The Scottish professor John Robison's *Proofs of a Conspiracy Against All the Governments and Religions of Europe* revealed the existence of a secret society, the Bavarian Illuminati, a higher order of Masonry founded in 1776 and dedicated, according to Robison, to overthrowing government, religion, and morals throughout the world. He charged that agents of the Illuminati had made their way from Germany into the Jacobin clubs in Paris and were responsible for the anarchic, atheistic direction of the French Revolution. He also claimed that branches of the Illuminati existed in the United States.[3]

In endorsing Robison's book, Morse said that he did not think that Masonic lodges had introduced Illuminism to the United States. Morse suggested that the democratic societies had done that, despite Robison's claim that the Illuminated lodges existed in America by 1786, several years before the societies were formed. Morse also charged that the democratic societies were now working underground to foment dissension and propagate infidelity. It was crucial, he insisted, that Americans ward off these evils by supporting the administration and turning to religion.[4]

Though they did not mention the Illuminati in their Fast Day sermons, many other Congregational ministers issued the same advice, warning their congregations that only religion and the administration's policies of defense measures and resistance to France could save them.[5] They contended that Americans had to unite in support of the federal administration because it was upon their division that the French depended for success in enslaving them. Like Morse, they were sure that their country was vulnerable only because of this internal discord stirred up by agents of the French. Nathanael Emmons said there were those who wanted to overturn the government, but he insisted that "if the friends of our constitution would labor as much to unite the people, as some do to disunite them, we might expect to see, very soon, one political opinion running through all the United States, and bidding defiance to those who wish to divide and destroy them." John Prince concurred that unanimity would make the nation invincible but warned against not being "firmly united among ourselves . . . if we are not well guarded, it [French intrigue] will seize us before we are aware of it."[6]

Feeling that the people had to unite in support of the administration, many Congregational ministers supported the Alien and Sedition Acts, arguing that these were essential for the government to protect itself. Sedition had to be dealt with in a timely manner. Were it not, it would bring on either civil war and anarchy or an ultimate response by authorities that would destroy all liberty. Congregational ministers tended to see little merit in the arguments of those who charged that the Alien and Sedition Acts in themselves were serious infringements of liberty. One minister easily dismissed the criticism of opponents of these measures, claiming that these men "probably, have a hankering for lying and rebellion themselves."[7]

The Congregational clergy in general believed that there were men in the United States conspiring to spread infidelity as well as political unrest. The Convention of Congregational Ministers of Massachusetts, in June 1798, approved an address to President Adams, written by Morse, which decried the atheistic, disorganizing principles that it charged France was trying to extend to other nations. Many Congregational ministers felt their country faced a serious religious threat.

They feared that, to the extent to which America gave in to the forces of corruption, to the extent it became irreligious and immoral, it would come to share in the punishment already being inflicted on Europe.[8]

Certainly no minister was more convinced than Morse of the political and religious dangers to the United States. But in the crisis with France he saw the opportunity for the nation not only to overcome these threats but finally to establish a true national character. For this reason he welcomed the crisis and even looked forward to war. He desired not so much a war against France as one against French influence, against those Americans who did not rally around their government. He wanted to purge American society of this unnatural element. War would make it possible to "distinguish more decidedly between friends & foes among ourselves. I believe there is energy enough in government to silence, & if necessary to *exterminate, its obstinate & dangerous enemies.*"[9]

The American character Morse long had wanted to take shape was essentially a New England character. He had warmly praised the habits and institutions only of that section in his geographical writings. He had hoped that New Englanders' regard for religion and education and their devotion to industry and social order would prevail throughout the entire nation. To these values he attributed New England's support for Washington and its opposition to the Democratic-Republicans. Now in 1798 he felt that New England's institutions were the special targets of conspirators because they were the strongest bulwarks in all the nation against infidelity and opposition to government. The subversion of these underpinnings would "prepare the way among us, for the spread of those disorganizing opinions, and that atheistical philosophy, which are deluging the Old World in misery and blood." The United States stood at a juncture: if New England's institutions fell, all would be lost; but if they prevailed, the country might expect a happy future.[10]

Rising to meet the challenge, Morse and other Congregational ministers tried to replicate the role the clergy had played during the revolutionary struggle. Like ministers of the previous generation, they called on Americans to exercise virtue and unity in the face of a conspiracy that aimed at stripping them of liberty and corrupting their moral and religious sentiments. They sought to stir up that degree of unanimity which had been expressed during the earlier crisis. Certainly Morse remembered the spirit that prevailed in Woodstock as he grew up. He especially liked the Independence Day oration delivered in Boston in 1798, which warned that once again, just as during the Revolution, Americans were threatened by a foreign nation which enjoyed the support of a domestic faction. The oration declared it was owed "to the memories of our forefathers, to those principles, which wrought our Independence, whose truth and value they sealed with their blood, not to tarnish their glories, nor fall behind them in virtue." These words had real meaning for Morse. On a larger stage he emulated the role his father had played as a member of the Committees of Correspondence and inspection, instruments used during the Revolution for imposing unanimity.[11]

Though the Congregational clergy's belief in the existence of the Illuminati in the United States seems astonishing, it was in keeping with the political culture of their day. As Bailyn and others have instructed us, colonial Americans had learned from the British Commonwealth writers of the danger of conspiratorial forces which sought not only to engross political power but to corrupt the people morally as well. American revolutionaries had seen such designs behind the new British imperial policy of the 1760s. The genuine belief that a conspiracy was under way to strip them of their liberty had impelled them to seek independence.[12]

Fear of conspiracy by no means died with the attainment of independence. As an opposition party and perhaps the true heirs of the Commonwealth outlook, the Democratic-Republicans saw in Federalist policies an effort to establish a British-style monarchy in the United States. The Federalists, in turn, charged that the opposition was conspiring to unleash an-

archy. When Congregational ministers warned of conspiratorial forces, therefore, they were speaking in conventional
eighteenth-century terms. Moreover, the idea of a conspiracy
was convincing because it explained everything that troubled
the clergy—not just the course of the French Revolution and
the rise of the Democratic-Republican opposition but the religious and moral conditions that confronted them in their
parishes. The attribution of these disturbing conditions
to the work of a conspiratorial group had the added appeal
of suggesting a simple solution: the elimination of the
conspirators.[13]

While belief in the existence of the Illuminati became widespread among the Congregational clergy, no one was more attached to the belief than Morse. No one took a more vocal
public stand in support of the charge. No doubt Morse's personality—his suspicious nature and tendency to see opponents
attacking him from concealed positions—explains how belief
in the existence of the conspiracy could take such strong hold
of him. Moreover, his reading of Robison's book during that
time of extreme crisis in the spring of 1798 gave it great impact and impelled him to disclose the alleged existence of the
Illuminati in his Fast Day sermon in May.[14]

In November 1798, on the Massachusetts Thanksgiving
Day, Morse again warned of the political and religious dangers facing the United States. Among the latter were vice, infidelity, and atheism, "tares sown among us by an *enemy* . . .
principles which are certain death to morals, freedom, and
happiness." Other Congregational ministers issued the same
warnings on the Thanksgiving Days in New England that autumn. Several argued, as had Timothy Dwight earlier, in an
oration on Independence Day, that the Roman Catholic
church had spawned an infidel conspiracy which, under divine providence, would destroy it. They warned that Americans must stay clear of these infidels and their principles, for
they sought to spread misery throughout the world, to undermine governments and religion no matter how good they
were. There was some uncertainty among the clergy on which

was the greater evil, the fuller manifestation of the Antichrist: the Roman Catholic church or the infidels who were to destroy it. By linking the two together, claiming that infidelity had come out of the Catholic church, the clergy avoided having to make a clear choice.[15]

Thus by November 1798 Morse was joined by a number of other ministers who said it was certain that France had long worked against American interests and now had Illuminated agents in the United States.[16] Still, in the opinion of these men, the United States's situation had improved in the past year. Americans had been awakened to the danger confronting them, and the federal government had severed the alliance with France. The clergy were confident that Americans could now meet the crisis. As one said, "[We were prepared] to raise the standard against *Anarchists* and *Atheists*—collect ourselves in proper force in our respective ranks—unfurl our banners with the emblems of our cause, and *stand fast in the liberty wherewith Christ hath made us free.*" Morse wrote his father that he was encouraged, that "Publick affairs seem to appear with a more smiling aspect."[17]

In his effort to inform public opinion, Morse was emerging as an important Federalist propagandist. His Thanksgiving Day sermon was published with a long appendix based on information supplied by Stephen Higginson, George Cabot, and other members of the Essex Junto. The central charge Morse made, one Federalists had raised before but which he purported to document in great length, was that French intrigue had been directed against America ever since France had extended its aid during the American Revolution and that this intrigue had become worse since the French Revolution.[18]

Morse also reiterated his claim that the democratic societies were the Illuminati in the United States: "The similarity in the movements, the principles, and views of the *Illuminati*, and the *societies* . . . render it highly probable that the latter are the genuine offspring of the former." He repeated his charge that the democratic societies had disseminated atheistic writings, and he also said that they had circulated *The Age of Reason.*[19]

In charging that the democratic societies and, by implication, the leaders of the political opposition were the Illuminati, Morse steered the matter in the direction most Federalists wanted it to go, stigmatizing their political opponents and not the Masons. It was, after all, the Democratic-Republicans who opposed military measures against France and who laid the blame for the trouble with her on the Federalist-supported Jay treaty. At best it seemed pointless to accuse Masonry because such charges alienated Masons, some of them Federalists, who did not like the suggestion that their order was linked to the subversion of government, religion, and morals. One Mason who did not was George Washington. When a minister sought out his opinion of Robison's charges, the general replied that he believed that Masonry was innocent, but he added that he was certain that the democratic societies had sought to undermine the government.[20]

Washington, to whom Morse sent a copy of his Thanksgiving Day sermon, liked the sermon much better than he did Robison's book. He particularly liked the appendix and hoped that it would be widely read, for he was certain that it would have good effects. Other Federalist leaders felt the same and tried to broadcast Morse's charges. Leading party newspapers in Philadelphia and New York printed extracts. Within Massachusetts, Federalist leaders had four hundred copies distributed to the state's clergy by members of the legislature on their return from the winter session in Boston.[21]

Such approval was gratifying to Morse, who, if he could not shape policy, at least wanted to influence public opinion. He wanted badly to be an insider—in 1795 he had written Oliver Wolcott of his belief that it was correct for government officials to keep secrets from the people but had urged that such secrets be confided to him.[22] Morse was also pleased by Federalist commendation because of the issues he genuinely believed were at stake. He said in his New Year sermon in January 1799 that the Antichrist had arisen in the form of infidel France "to punish the nations for their iniquities." He felt his actions helped not only to defend the United States against France and its internal enemies but to protect Christianity.[23]

Morse responded to these threats by doing all he could to warn the public and by attempting to organize the clergy to take an active role against them. His concern led him to make yet another disclosure in his Fast Day sermon in April 1799. He claimed that he now had evidence that proved the existence of Illuminated lodges in the United States. This evidence consisted of some documents of a Masonic lodge in Portsmouth, Virginia, which Wolcott had supplied him. Most of the members of the lodge were French emigrants, which in itself Morse considered suspicious. He claimed that the lodge's documents and some other papers, none of which was in any way incriminating, made it clear that there were at least sixteen Illuminated lodges in this nation. Morse insisted that the members "are regularly instructed and directed by their masters in France, and . . . they are in concert, systematically conducting the plan of revolutionizing this country." He went on to charge that these Illuminati were responsible for Americans' political division, for the dissemination of atheistic writings, and "the apparently systematic endeavours made to destroy not only the influence and support, but the official existence of the Clergy."[24]

In support of the latter charge, Morse cited the *Chronicle*'s condemnation of political preaching and also legislative efforts in Massachusetts to make it easier for dissenters to have their parish taxes go to the churches to which they belonged. He considered both of these to be parts of a larger design to destroy the Congregational clergy. Such beliefs reflect his overwrought state of mind, which impelled him to warn Americans to avoid foreign contagion and "watch the movements, and detect the machinations of their numerous emissaries among us; . . . to reject, as we would the most deadly poison, their atheistical and destructive principles in whatever way or shape they may be insinuated among us; to take heed that we partake not of their sins, that we may not receive of her plagues."[25]

Morse acted impulsively and independently in making the disclosure about the Portsmouth lodge. He had written Wolcott asking his permission to reveal the documents, but he delivered his sermon almost a week before he received a reply. Morse felt compelled to act because of his extreme concern: "I am greatly alarmed at the present state of our country. The foundations of our most precious interests are secretly & formidably assailed, & few seem to be aware of it. I wish we may be awake & wise in season, to defeat the designs of our enemies."[26]

Trying to excite his colleagues in Massachusetts to greater action, Morse worked within the Boston Association of Ministers, seeing to it that this body issued a letter to all the Congregational ministers in the state. This document, which lamented an alleged increase of atheism, irreligion, and immorality, called for a meeting of delegates from the various local associations to address these problems. The meeting never took place, probably because the Massachusetts associations were so weak that they could not take this action. Instead, Morse and some associates managed to win the Convention of Congregational Ministers's approval of an address that bewailed inattention to religion.[27]

Morse did not limit his efforts to Massachusetts. He distributed the address of the Boston Association in other New England states. He also sent copies of the convention's address to Wolcott for him to distribute among the Philadelphia clergy: "You will see by these things that the Clergy are not asleep this way. They ought everywhere indeed to be awake."[28] In May 1799 Morse even traveled to Philadelphia to consult Federalist officials and to encourage ministers he visited along the way to meet the threat to religion. In Hartford he heard Cyprian Strong deliver the Connecticut election sermon in which he warned of the Illuminati. Morse wrote his wife with satisfaction that the secret order "is generally believed here to exist in our country." He found opinion more divided in the middle states, where some Presbyterian and Dutch Reformed ministers believed in the existence of the Illuminati, but others did not. Still, in clergymen like John Abeel, a New York Dutch Reformed minister, and Ashbel Green, a Philadelphia Presbyterian, he found men who shared both his fear and his determination to fight infidelity. Morse's visit, in fact, gave rise to discussions about the need to establish periodicals in Philadelphia and New York City to "diffuse just principles in morals, politics and literature," though nothing came of this talk.[29]

While in Philadelphia, Morse met with Wolcott and Secretary of State Timothy Pickering, discussing the political situation and his efforts with them. On returning to Charlestown, he received a book from Wolcott which intensified his dedication to exposing the Illuminati. This was Abbé Augustin Barruel, *Memoirs, Illustrating the History of Jacobinism,* which, like Robison's book, was concerned with the Illuminati but made the conspiracy even more extensive, tracing its origins to the early eighteenth century with the work of Voltaire and D'Alembert. After reading it, Morse wrote to Wolcott that he was "convinced that the *Jacobins,* like their father, the first *Disorganizer,* can transform themselves into any shape, even into that of an angel of light, in order to accomplish their purposes, prejudices, vices—in a word, all that is wrong in human nature, against all good."[30]

Morse's concern was shared by other Congregational ministers who throughout 1799 and 1800 continued to insist that Americans had to defend themselves against intrigue by supporting the government and attending to religion.[31] Like Morse, these men believed that the clergy had a special role to play. Acting out New England tradition, they and rulers were to aid "each other in the great and godlike design of making an happy nation."[32]

Although belief in the Illuminati was common among the clergy, Morse exposed himself to attack because he asserted their existence more publicly than most. He was in the forefront, the one claiming to have evidence which proved the existence of Illuminated lodges in the United States. By the summer of 1799 his assertions led to a counterattack against

84

him in which the Reverend William Bentley of Salem played a major role.

———— * ————

Ever since Morse had made his first charges in May 1798, Bentley had spoken and written against him. Besides being a religious liberal and a Democratic-Republican, Bentley was a Mason. Like other Masons, those in Massachusetts resented Robison's charges. In June 1798 the state's grand lodge sent an address to President Adams, pledging their support to the government and complaining about the unjustified attack upon them by Robison and those who accepted his claims. This led Morse to deliver an oration before a Masonic lodge that month to show that he did not believe that American Masonry was suspect. This gesture did not entirely satisfy the Masons. The Massachusetts grand master, Dr. Josiah Bartlett, a member of Morse's church, wrote in a Boston newspaper that Robison was an enthused man who exaggerated the scope of the Illuminati. Bentley went even further and completely rejected Robison's charges. He was not content merely to argue that the Illuminati did not exist in the United States or, if they did, that they were not related to the Masons. Robison's accusations, Bentley said before a Masonic lodge in June 1798, were ridiculous and false. He also supplied the Boston newspapers with articles from the British press denouncing Robison.[33]

Morse responded to these hostile British reviews by sending other ones which praised Robison's book to the Boston newspapers.[34] Feeling that these were not sufficient, in August he began issuing a series of letters in the *Massachusetts Mercury* defending Robison and himself. Morse struck a characteristic defensive posture, insisting that he had been attacked unjustly and without provocation. He claimed that he was merely vindicating himself against the charges of some Masons, with whose order he had no controversy. Unaware that Bentley was supplying most, perhaps all, of the documents against

Robison, Morse mistakenly assumed he faced broader opposition.[35]

This effort to justify himself did nothing to ease his mind or abate his feeling that he was being persecuted. He concluded his series by insisting that he had undertaken this defense because of the actions of the Masons, the "intemperate and indiscriminate opposition" to Robison, and also attacks on himself. "Had I not been personally, repeatedly and unjustly attacked, I surely should not have felt the necessity of vindicating myself in the manner I have done." Morse had become so upset by Bentley that he even repeated the accusation made by Dwight in his oration on July 4 that the mock communion, a rite of the Illuminati, was celebrated in some American Masonic lodges. This, of course, was impolitic (as his charges about the Portsmouth lodge in April 1799 would be) because it placed the stigma on Masonry, not the political opposition, while it also undermined his claims that he believed American Masonry to be innocent.[36]

As annoying as was Bentley's opposition in 1798, it was far less damaging than his later actions. These were made possible because both Bentley and Morse were correspondents of the German geographer, Christoph Ebeling, who like Bentley was a liberal both in politics and religion. In March 1799 Ebeling wrote both men, informing them that the Bavarian Illuminati had existed some years before, having been established to oppose the Jesuits, who, he said, conspired to take control of the German universities. Ebeling explained that the now-defunct order had sought only liberalization in church and state. He denied that the members had had the atheistic, anarchistic aims Robison imputed to them. Ebeling ridiculed *Proofs of Conspiracy* for its many erroneous statements about the men whom it described, and he even charged that it was written as propaganda at the behest of officials in the British government.[37]

Morse's serious troubles began in July 1799 when he was reading Ebeling's letter to a fellow minister who was a Mason and perhaps skeptical of Robison's accusations. Samuel Huntington, an old Yale classmate, stopped by Morse's home that afternoon and heard part of the letter being read. Morse did not know that Huntington was a Mason and a Democratic-Republican. But in August Morse learned from the Congregational minister in Norwich, Connecticut, where Huntington lived, of a rumor circulating there that Ebeling had written to Morse denying Robison's charges. It was also being said that Ebeling had claimed that Robison was insane, had been forced to flee Britain because he had committed forgery, and that he had written the book in order to be readmitted. (Ebeling had said none of these things.)[38]

Morse replied to the Norwich minister that, though Ebeling indeed had ridiculed and rejected both Robison's and Barruel's representations of the Illuminati, his letter actually supported their charges. Ebeling had said that the Illuminati did exist. He rejected Robison's interpretation of their principles because, though a good man, he was in favor of French principles. As Morse explained to another man, Ebeling "is evidently of the *New divinity modern Socinianism*—which is very little different from Illuminism & in politics a modern French Republican. No wonder then he should dislike Robison & Barruel." Considering Ebeling's views, "what he says against Robison's work, so far from discrediting it—confirms its general authenticity, & importance." At the very least, this shows Morse's tendency to distort facts to serve his purposes.[39]

By September 1799 rumors about Ebeling's letter to Morse were spreading beyond Norwich. The Hartford *American Mercury*, a Democratic-Republican paper, charged that Morse had received a letter from Ebeling which rejected Robison's claims and which accused the Scottish professor of being insane and a criminal. Morse wrote to the paper's editor denying this report and demanding to know the source of it. The editor insisted that he would supply the identity of the informant only if Morse first supplied the letter and proved the account to be false. Morse refused to do this because, he said, he did not have Ebeling's permission to make his letter public and he did not want to embarrass him. Morse was undoubtedly aware that most readers would not make the same allowance for Ebeling's views that he did. Rather than concluding, as he did, that Ebeling's adamant denial proved the existence and operation of the Illuminati, they would accept the latter's assertions. So instead of Ebeling's letter, Morse offered to submit a certificate from two associates of his, Harvard professors David Tappan and Ebenezer Pearson, vouching for his interpretation; but the editor insisted on the letter itself.[40]

With the publication of the alleged abstract of Ebeling's letter to Morse in the *American Mercury,* Bentley realized that he had an opportunity to embarrass Morse. In October, Bentley sent the Worcester *Massachusetts Spy* a copy of Ebeling's letter to him. It was printed as a letter from a gentleman in Germany to a correspondent in Massachusetts, which invited the public to assume that it was the letter written to Morse. In November the *New London Bee* reprinted it and said that it was Ebeling's letter to Morse. Later in 1799 it was printed as such in the Philadelphia *Aurora,* the most widely circulated Democratic-Republican paper in the nation. There was no great misrepresentation on Bentley's part in this affair; the letter *was* written by a man in Germany to a correspondent in Massachusetts. When it was assumed that this was the one written to Morse, Bentley did not come to his aid by declaring that it actually had been written to *him.* If Morse wanted to prove that it was not the one written to him, he would have to produce the real one, which Bentley knew contained the same charges about the absurdity of Robison's claims and the same specifics about the book's inaccuracies.[41]

Morse was in a difficult position. He wrote the editor of the *New London Bee* and denied that the published letter was the one sent to him, but as he would not produce the actual letter as evidence, his claim meant little. He wrote his father that "the circumstances attending this attack are extremely aggravating."[42] There was good reason for his discomfort. Ever since he had made his first charges about the Illuminati in May 1798, he had been under severe attack from the *Chronicle* in Boston. With the publication of Ebeling's letter to Bentley in the *Aurora*, he became a national object of ridicule. He was even attacked as a member of the "New England Illuminati," an order of Federalist Congregational clergy who played on the people's fears in order to establish monarchy and a religious establishment.[43] Under such attack and unable to publish Ebeling's letter to vindicate himself, Morse decided to bide his time and collect supporting evidence from Europe which he could later submit to the public with the corroborating statement by Tappan and Pearson.[44]

———— * ————

The political situation by the end of 1799 by no means compensated for Morse's personal distress. Having worked to rally public support in behalf of the administration, he was greatly upset by Adams's decision to seek a new negotiation with France, which brought division to the Federalist party. In June 1799, a few months after the president had indicated his willingness to dispatch a new mission, Morse had written Wolcott of his concern that France was setting a trap for the United States and that prospects of a settlement with her would open the way for more intrigue, which could easily undo that national character which had taken shape since the rupture with her: "I am infinitely more afraid of their principles than their *arms* & peace wd. open a wide door to the former which have already done us incalculable injury." Morse hoped that the mission would not be sent, but when the envoys departed for France in November he wrote Wolcott that he and his friends did not know how to respond: "*Dissent* is painful—even *opposition* to the measure might be impolitic, & dangerous—*silence* is hardly to be expected from Republicans with our habits,—& *approbation,* I candidly confess for myself cannot be given with present information, but at the expence of *honesty* & *truth*." The work of forging an American character was being abandoned. Morse feared "a temporary reign of *American* Jacobinism," which would be brought about by the

Jeffersonians throwing their support to Adams and his accepting it. "This should it happen, would in truth be hoisting ag$^n$. the flood gates ag$^t$. French principles & influence, whh had, with so much labour & difficulty been shut down, & exposing us afresh to a ruinous inundation." Washington's death in December heightened Morse's fears. Like other ministers, he warned that this might be the first in a series of judgments inflicted on America for its sins.[45]

By March 1800 Morse reversed his position on the new negotiations with France. His change of attitude was caused by the new French (Napoleonic) constitution which gave greater power to the executive. "Nothing short of it in energy could in my opinion controul that disorganized and disorganizing nation." Less afraid of peace with France, he hoped that the envoys would be able to attain it. In supporting the mission, Morse concurred with New England clerical opinion as it was expressed in Thanksgiving Day sermons at the end of 1799. The published sermons suggest that the clergy did not share the outlook of the High Federalists who so strongly opposed Adams's policy.[46]

Though he now hoped for peace with France, Morse was not optimistic about the political situation in the United States nor about the larger struggle taking place in the world in terms of which he viewed American politics. As he said in his Thanksgiving Day sermon in November 1799, he saw a great battle shaping up between atheism and evangelical Protestantism. Atheism, which had opened a war against Catholicism, was going on to a contest against all Christianity. Referring to the nascent evangelical movement in Britain and the first stirrings of the Second Great Awakening in New England, he claimed that the forces of irreligion had stimulated an "amazing accession of zeal and activity to the cause of pure Christianity." Morse and his Congregational associates were confident that Christianity would ultimately win out in this battle, but they were not certain that the United States would ally itself with that side. Even if it did, as Morse wrote to a friend, there would be much suffering in the whole before the conflict was resolved. "'The Man of Sin' . . . must rise to his acme & be destroyed—the Jews be collected to their own country, & the Gentile nations be brought to the knowledge & acknowledgment of the truth—& then the world will enjoy universal peace & rest."[47]

To Morse, the political signs in the spring of 1800 indicated that the United States was not allying itself with the cause of evangelical Christianity. As a result of the mission to France, the Federalists were badly divided. Morse felt that they were also listless compared to the opposition. Federalist inactivity depressed him, and the opposition's industry, he wrote Wolcott, "[has], I confess, almost extinguished my hopes of better times." He wrote to another correspondent that he feared "at least a temporary reign of Jacobinism in this country." He became even gloomier in May after Secretary of State Pickering was dismissed by Adams and the Democratic-Republicans carried the New York legislature. This last event, it was realized, would throw that state's electoral votes to Jefferson. Immensely disturbed about the now-open division among Federalists, Morse wrote Adams, assuring him of his support.[48]

Despite his own fears, Morse was astounded that some thought that Jefferson would actually be elected president by the American people. He wrote Moses Fisk, an emigrant New Englander in Tennessee, of his disbelief that Christians in that state and Kentucky would vote for Jefferson and Burr, "two professed Deists, & opposers of Christianity." Morse argued against the opinion expressed earlier by Fisk, who rejected his claims about the Illuminati conspiracy, that both political parties sought the welfare of the nation. Though most Democratic-Republicans were friends to their country and Christianity, Morse insisted that "*some of* the *leaders* of the Jacobins, are hostile to our present Constitution, & would sincerely rejoyce at the extirpation of Christianity and its institutions."[49]

These extreme fears led many Congregational ministers to preach against Jefferson's election, making much of his alleged infidelity. Their arguments followed those of the most widely circulated anti-Jefferson tract, *Serious Considerations on the Election of a President,* published anonymously but the work of William Linn, a New York City Dutch Reformed minister and a friend of Morse. Linn based his attack on *Notes on Virginia,* arguing that some of Jefferson's remarks showed that he rejected the biblical account of the flood and the common origin of mankind. Jefferson thus shared the principles of the Illuminati, so his election would injure Christianity. His influence alone would be damaging to Christianity, and he might even actively try to undermine it.[50]

The New England Congregational clergy tended not to publish the sermons in which they expressed their warnings about Jefferson. An unpublished sermon Morse delivered just before the Massachusetts gubernatorial election in 1799 does, however, suggest the manner of their preaching. Like Linn, Morse found damning evidence in *Notes.* He cited a passage in which Jefferson contended that in the past some Christian authorities had persecuted innocent people as proof that Jefferson was tainted by modern philosophism. Morse concluded the sermon by calling on his congregation to protect their religion from infidels who wanted to rob them of it: "From all known infidels then let us withdraw our confidence & support. We are highly criminal if we knowingly contribute in any way to increase their influence or power for in so doing we contribute to our own & our country's ruin." Such preaching during the presidential campaign led Democratic-Republican newspaper writers to charge that the clergy were working in league with the Essex Junto to defame Jefferson.[51]

In the autumn of 1800 during the election campaign, Morse was finally able to shake off that depression which he had suffered since the previous autumn. His depression had partly been caused by the political situation: the division among the Federalists and the signs of growing Democratic-Republican strength. But it was also caused by the difficulties in which his allegations about the Illuminati had involved him. He wrote to one correspondent in April 1800 that he was attacked on all sides, but he did not back off from his charges. That same day he wrote a letter to Josiah Parker, a Virginia Federalist congressman who had informed him that the lodge in Portsmouth, which Morse had claimed was Illuminated, was harmless. Morse lectured him to the effect that good men should be careful in sanctioning the conduct of "*secret* societies of foreigners among us. In doing this, they expose themselves to censure, whenever the safety of our country renders it necessary publicly to denounce such Societies." In May he provided the Hartford *Connecticut Courant,* a Federalist paper, with the certificate by Tappan and Pearson, vouching for his interpretation of Ebeling's letter. That month Morse also received a letter purportedly from the Illuminati. With hieroglyphic symbols, the letter warned that he could expect punishment for his writings against the order. Alarmed and certain that this was not a prank, Morse wrote Pickering asking for his and Wolcott's advice on the matter: "Should this faction gain the ascendancy we may from this know what their opposers are to expect."[52]

Two things brought Morse out of his depressed mood. He was sustained by his religious faith, his belief that God in his providence controlled all events. He wrote Wolcott that he was so depressed about the political (and he might have added his personal) situation that "nothing but a firm belief of a wise overruling Providence can yield me any solid consolation." The same thought was expressed in other of his letters in the spring of 1800. Believing that all things occurred as God willed, Morse was able to consign the fate of the nation and himself to providence.[53]

The other thing that changed his mood was a new project to which he could devote himself and which enabled him to put at some distance that depression which was never far away, even in his most sanguine moods. This project was a new Federalist newspaper, the *New England Palladium,* which was conceived along the lines of the papers Morse had discussed with Green and Abeel during his visit to the middle states in the spring of 1799. The *Palladium*'s prospectus said that the paper was dedicated to preserving "the government, morals, religion, & state of Society in New England. To defend these on the one hand, & on the other to expose *Jacobinism* in every form both of *principle* & *practice,* both of *philosophism* & *licentiousness,* will be the supreme object of this publication."[54]

Morse worked out plans for the *Palladium* with Dwight. In particular, they hoped that the paper would help to unite the Federalist party and heal the effects of the mission to France and Alexander Hamilton's attack on Adams. Morse's spirits were so roused by these plans that he was now even confident that Adams would be reelected, an outcome that he had doubted in the spring and that the *Palladium* could not at all further because it was not to appear until January 1801. Dwight, through his brother Theodore, was able to line up the support of Federalist leaders in Connecticut; but High Federalists like Wolcott were, at best, skeptical about the possibility of uniting the party, and some would not even consider aiding Adams's effort at reelection. Still, Morse was confident despite Wolcott's misgivings that the *Palladium* would succeed. He did fear, however, that "if this project fails of success . . . we are destined by divine Providence as a punishment for our sins, to experience the awful calamities necessarily consequent on a prevalence of Jacobinism."[55]

Morse also intended to use the *Palladium* to vindicate himself and his charges about Illuminism. He had been denied access to some Federalist newspapers, including Boston's *Columbian Centinel,* because their editors were Masons. At last with the *Palladium* he would have a journal in which he could mount a vigorous defense. By December 1800 he was consulting Theodore Dwight and others on the strategy with which he should proceed in this matter and the materials he should submit.[56]

Morse's plans for the *Palladium* were upset, however, even before the first issue appeared. By the end of December news arrived that all of South Carolina's electoral votes had gone to Jefferson and Burr, giving them the election. In his shock, Morse found solace in his belief that the Democratic-Republican victory was part of God's providential scheme: "It becomes us to submit—& even to rejoyce that God reigns. The wrath of man shall surely praise him, the remainder he will restrain." Within a few days, Morse, like many other Federalists, became intrigued with the possibility of throwing the election in the House of Representatives to Aaron Burr. Burr was, aftar all, the son of Aaron Burr, Sr. and the grandson of Jonathan Edwards, both eminent Calvinist ministers. As Morse explained to his father, though Burr's "present character & principles are no better than they ought to be, yet who knows, but that, as he is the *Son of many prayers,* he may turn about & become a good man. He has eminent talents & great energy."[57]

While the choice of president was being resolved in Washington during the early months of 1801, Morse was forced to make a defense of himself against further charges arising out of the Illuminati controversy. He had to because of an attack upon him that appeared in the new organ of the Democratic-Republicans, the Washington *National Intelligencer.* This piece almost certainly was written by Bentley, for the author was familiar with Ebeling's correspondence. He charged that Ebeling had informed a number of ministers in New England that the accusations made by Robison and Barruel were false. The author also cited a letter Ebeling had written to an unnamed American in which he acknowledged having written the letter that had been printed in the *New London Bee* as his letter to Morse. Thus it was clear that the New England Congregational clergy had viciously attacked the Democratic-Republicans even after receiving ample refutation of Robison and Barruel from Ebeling.[58]

Morse made his defense not in the *Palladium* but in the *Chronicle,* which had reprinted the piece from the *National Intelligencer.* He explained that Samuel Miller, a New York City Presbyterian minister, was the person to whom Ebeling acknowledged that he had written the letter that had appeared in the New London paper but that he also made it clear that it had not been written to Morse. The *Chronicle* in turn printed a letter Miller had sent to a New York City paper stating these facts. Unfortunately for Morse, Miller added that he did not believe Robison and Barruel and that he thought Morse had "endeavoured to promote the currency of their publications, with an indiscreet and excessive zeal." Morse continued his defense by arguing that the man who had sent the letter to the *Massachusetts Spy,* the one which soon after had appeared in the *New London Bee* and the Philadelphia *Aurora* as Ebeling's letter to him, had tried to impose on the public and make them think that this was so. Morse subsequently learned and reported that the man was Bentley. Tacitly admitting that Ebeling's letter to him contained the same charges as the published one to Bentley, Morse professed that he was innocent of having identified the political opposition with attempts to destroy Christianity, morality, and government, though clearly he had. He insisted that he and some other Congregational ministers had simply sought to present the truth, which they still felt lay with Robison and Barruel. Morse repeated his claim that Ebeling, though a good man, was not impartial, so that the clergy need not accept his interpretation of the religious and political designs of the Illuminati.[59]

As he wrote to some correspondents who rejected his claims about the Illuminati, Morse could not abandon his conviction that the order existed and was active in the United States. Though perhaps not everything in Robison and Barruel was to be accepted, there was too much going on in the world not to believe that there was a design behind it:

> That there have been & still exist extraordinary efforts, & formidable combinations, to subvert established principles in government, religion & even morals, there can, I think, be no doubt. Such wonderful & alarming effects which are visible all over the world, must have adequate causes,—& those assigned by Robison & Barruel appear to me as probable as any which have come to my knowledge.

Though its operations were difficult to describe, the effects of the conspiracy could easily be seen. "It is operating like a *can-*

*cer* on the stamina of our civil & religious Institutions—&
many good people seem determined not to believe the danger, till the destruction of the foundations of all that is dear to
us, is accomplished."[60] Morse even wrote to Ebeling in March
1801, telling him that he still accepted Robison's account but
asking for any information that could prove that Robison was
wrong:

> If Robison & Barruel have misstated their *principles* & de-
> signs,—it is desireable to know explicitly what they were. His
> mistakes as to the names, professions & characters of some in-
> dividuals do not affect his main points. Any observations whh
> you may send me for publication on this subject, I will readily
> communicate for I wish for nothing but truth.[61]

Both Morse and Timothy Dwight still wanted the *Palladium*
to take up the subject of Illuminism. Dwight suggested to
Morse that the editor, Warren Dutton, a recent graduate of
Yale, should devote a section of the paper just to that, because
"nothing would excite more interest in the public mind, or do
more good just at this time." After May 1801, however, Illuminism disappeared as a topic in the *Palladium*, probably because
it was not nearly the subject of interest that Morse and Dwight
thought it was and because there was nothing to do with it but
rehash the charges of Robison and Barruel. Still, Morse encouraged Seth Payson, a New Hampshire minister, to prepare
an abstract of Barruel's and Robison's books with a defense of
them. Morse, Harvard professors Tappan and Pearson, and
perhaps Timothy Dwight helped to revise the book, which appeared in 1802. It caused no great stir. Payson did not expect
it to because, as he wrote Morse, the public was no longer interested in the Illuminati. As late as 1806, however, Morse was
still concerned. A young man who had studied theology with
Morse reported to him from Edinburgh, Robison's home,
during a visit there that he could discover nothing about
Illuminism.[62]

The *Palladium*, which was founded to preserve New England's institutions and to expose philosophism, came under

heavy attack by Democratic-Republicans in the spring of 1801 because free copies of it were being sent to the clergy throughout New England with an address which warned that a party hostile to religion, government, and property had assumed control of the federal government.[63] Democratic-Republican writers contended that by means of the paper and its free distribution the Essex Junto was attempting to win the clergy over to its cause of overturning the Union and establishing monarchy and a religious hierarchy. The high point of this attack came in December 1801 when Att. Gen. Levi Lincoln, writing as "The Farmer" in the Worcester *National Aegis*, condemned the *Palladium* for sending free copies to the clergy and especially for the address, which proved that the *Palladium* set itself against the will of the people and the government they supported. He warned that the people would not pay their parish taxes for the support of clergymen who opposed the federal government. Merely receiving the newspaper, he said, was proof of such opposition.[64]

Federalists argued that Lincoln's essay demonstrated that the Democratic-Republicans sought to persecute the clergy. Morse, of course, had warned that the settled ministry was among the New England institutions that the Illuminati especially wanted to destroy. He had helped to establish the *Palladium* because he felt these institutions had to be preserved by energy and activity on the part of the Federalists. In 1802 he wrote to his father that it was "necessary . . . for all good men to be vigilant & active in opposing their [the opposition's] nefarious designs against their [New Englanders'] happy & wise Institutions both civil & religious." The alternative was the fall of the Constitution and the dissolution of the Union.[65]

The dominant group of the orthodox Congregational clergy staked all on the preservation of these institutions. The outlook expressed in century sermons some of these ministers delivered in January 1801, just a few weeks after the victory of Jefferson and Burr, was the same one Morse had set out in his Thanksgiving Day sermon of November 1799. In these last times when Christianity contended against infidelity, it was crucial that New England cling to its institutions. Doing so, the region would both save the nation and aid the Christian cause, helping to forward the commencement of the millennium.[66] In an artillery election sermon in 1803, Morse urged New Englanders to continue their traditions of education, piety, and cooperation between rulers and clergy in promoting religion. These were to be maintained by rejecting innovation and by electing pious men, not those who attacked the clergy and ignored religion.[67]

These were familiar themes which the clergy had preached under Washington and Adams and continued to preach under Jefferson. Ministers regularly emphasized the importance of education and religion for establishing habits that made social life pleasant.[68] They defended social deference and subordination.[69] They cautioned their people to avoid innovation and to remain loyal to their old habits.[70] In making these points, however, the clergy now were calling just for the preservation of New England traditions, no longer for support of the federal administration, which had been a main point of their preaching the decade before. Some ministers even warned that the people had to be cautious of the men in power. The "Farmer's" writings, they argued, exposed the designs of these men. Their enmity to the clergy demonstrated that the Democratic-Republicans opposed the institutions that had long preserved New England in happiness.[71] Ministers implored the people not to vote for irreligious men, warning that the consequences of raising such men to power would be the loss of their liberty and religion.[72]

New Englanders did not respond warmly to the Federalist clergy's admonitions. The *Palladium* failed to receive adequate support from Federalists and came under new management in March 1803. Of far greater consequence, the political opposition grew in New England. Jefferson even carried Massachusetts and New Hampshire in the 1804 presidential contest.

During Jefferson's first term, Morse complained that he only courted popularity by reducing taxes and the size of the army and navy, measures taken at the expense of national character and strength. Morse felt that the Democratic-Republicans exerted energy and zeal in carrying elections but that Jefferson displayed neither quality in his administration of government, which was without direction and real purpose. One reason Morse had preferred Burr over Jefferson was because Burr had a reputation for will and great drive, not for being a dreamy innovator. Like other Federalists, Morse was intrigued with the possibility of going to war against Spain in 1803 when it closed off the Mississippi. He wondered whether that would not "tend to increase Federalism, and unite the country." Instead, in Morse's view, Jefferson timidly bought time from France by purchasing Louisiana.[73]

On certain occasions, however, Morse's deeply suspicious nature asserted itself, and he entertained the thought that there was a sinister design behind the few really controversial measures Jefferson supported during his first term. In February 1802, just after the judiciary law was repealed, Morse wrote Massachusetts senator Dwight Foster that he considered this act proof that the Democratic-Republicans intended to undo the work of Washington's and Adams's administrations and to place the country "in a worse situation than we were in in 1786." This fear made him wonder whether New England should not secede from the Union: "Ought we suffer ourselves to be forced into the vortex of certain destruction, & to sacrifice all that is dearest to our hearts, at the shrine of the A[theis]t & D[emocra]t?" He again raised the question of secession to New Hampshire senator William Plumer in 1803 after the Senate approved the treaty providing for the Louisiana Purchase. He argued that the Purchase and the Twelfth Amendment (which the Democratic-Republicans supported and which provided for electors to cast separate ballots for president and vice-president so that there would not be a repeat of the situation of 1800) was made to strengthen the opposition's control over the federal government so that they could ultimately "avow their intentions" and introduce Jacobinism to the United States. Though Jacobinism here would not be as terrible as in France, New Englanders should not submit to it. If they remained in the Union, Morse feared that they would "be by degrees, drawn into a vortex, in whh our religious, political & literary Institutions, & all the principles & habits, whh are their fruits, & whh are our glory & happiness, will be ingulphed and lost."[74]

Morse expressed these extreme fears only sporadically, immediately upon hearing news that distressed him. These episodes are further illustrations of his tendency to exaggerate the impact of actions of which he disapproved and to see sinister motives behind them. These fears did not represent his general outlook in the first years of the nineteenth century. In these years, while Morse and much of the orthodox Congregational clergy were concerned with preserving New England's institutions and habits, they became involved in the work of the Second Great Awakening. The Awakening helped to preserve and even to extend much of what was involved in these institutions, habits, and principles, while in the process it also transformed and adapted them to nineteenth-century American society.

# Chapter 4

---

# *Revivals and Benevolent Societies*

With the defeat of the Federalist party in 1800, Morse and many of his orthodox colleagues increasingly concentrated on nonpolitical means of addressing the religious and moral conditions that alarmed them. They had made some such efforts on a limited scale before the onset of the Second Great Awakening in 1798, and as this movement gained momentum, they worked especially through it to achieve their goals.

Much of the character of the Awakening in New England obviously derived from the revivals which swept across the region, but it was also shaped by the work of benevolent societies that began to appear about the same time as the revivals. Sustaining each other, revivals and benevolent societies operated together to make the Second Great Awakening different in some very important respects from the first Great Awakening. In New England it was marked by extreme order and the absence of most of the destructive elements which had attended the Great Awakening.

Morse played a major role in establishing and administering a number of benevolent societies. He was also prominent in the one really divisive aspect of the Second Great Awakening in New England: the struggle among Massachusetts Congregationalists which brought on their formal division into orthodox and Unitarian camps. Morse did more than anyone else to hasten the separation, which the revivals and rise of the benevolence movement would have forced, perhaps slightly later, without his efforts. This story may be found in the next chapter; here the subject is revivalism and the benevolence movement in New England.

———— * ————

The revivals began in 1798 at a time when most of the New England Congregational clergy felt the nation's politics were going badly, and of course Thomas Jefferson, their archenemy, was elected president in 1800. Because of the revivals and the beginnings of work of the missionary societies, however, the orthodox clergy expressed a surprisingly confident outlook in the century sermons some of them delivered in January 1801. These ministers were confident even though they reiterated the point they had made before in the past two years: that these were the last times when the Antichrist contended violently against Christianity. Infidels, spawned by the Roman Catholic church during the the eighteenth century, were trying to destroy not only it, which the clergy believed they would do, but all forms of Christianity. Ministers, however, pointed to biblical prophecies which, they said, declared that Christianity would triumph and that the number of Christians would be immensely enlarged by revivals and the activities of missionary societies. Revivals and support of the benevolent societies in the United States encouraged the clergy to believe that their country would not fall a casualty in the great battle like the nations of Europe, and these happy signs strengthened their resolve to see that it did not.[1]

The orthodox clergy were not only extremely pleased but rather surprised by the revivals that had begun in Connecticut in 1798 and soon spread to towns in Massachusetts. The Great Awakening had left unpleasant memories because of the division it engendered—the loss of people to the Separates, Baptists, and even Episcopalians. Almost none of the Congregational clergy had ultimately been pleased by the disorder, antinomianism, and lay itineracy of the Great Awakening, much of it, after all, expressing hostility to the educated, settled ministry. Then, too, the Awakening had occasioned debates among the orthodox and liberal clergy of the period, which was also considered bad both for the position of the clergy and the cause of religion.

So it was with some uncertainty that, by 1790, Congregational ministers began making more vigorous efforts to counter irreligion and promote revivals. They acted more out of fear than hope, especially out of their overriding concern with irreligion and immorality, which seemed to them to have been spreading rapidly ever since the American Revolution. This concern bred a new commitment among Morse and many other ministers to catechize the children in their parishes in the hope that this would prevent them from being corrupted by deism. Ministers also began holding meetings to pray for revivals. By the mid-1790s many churches observed a quarterly concert of prayer and met the first Monday every third month to pray for revivals around the world. This idea was not new. Jonathan Edwards had proposed it in 1747, but David Austin, a New Jersey Presbyterian, revived it and labored hard to have the concert accepted by churches throughout the United States. It won the support of the Presbyterian Synod of New York and New Jersey and was observed by two-thirds of the Connecticut Congregational churches. In other New England states, orthodox ministers like Morse introduced it in their churches.[2]

These efforts showed no immediate results, though one suspects that the new intensive religious instruction of children laid a basis for later religious experience. In 1798 religious interest, so long dormant, sprang to life. No doubt the unsettled conditions of the time enhanced the efficacy of ministerial labors. These conditions included the underlying forces of mobility and economic development transforming American life. Moreover, the real possibility of foreign and even civil war as well as the imaginary but powerful fear of conspiratorial forces within American society perhaps served as even more potent catalysts.

The orthodox Congregational clergy were quick to endorse the revivals. In April 1799, within a year of the revivals' first appearance, Morse declared that by their means God "hath *made bare his holy arm*—displayed his wondrous power, for the conversion & salvation of sinners—& many . . . have been emboldened to renounce their allegiance to Satan, to join themselves to the Ch^n. Chh. and there is evidence to believe that this good & animating work of God is still progressing." Several months later he said that the revivals were leading to the "universal establishment" of Christianity.[3]

There was good reason for the clergy to be so enthusiastic. For the first time in many years, large numbers of people were joining the churches. Morse had said in his New Year sermon in 1799 that his church had lost members in the last two years. This was not unusual. Nathan Perkins, in giving an account of the revival in his Connecticut parish, said that only five people had joined his church in the previous four years. Other ministers reported similarly dismal conditions before the revivals.[4]

The fact that these revivals were extremely orderly also greatly encouraged orthodox ministers. There were no outbursts, no lay itineracy, no challenges to the authority of the ministry. Ministers stressed these points in the narratives in which they described the revivals in their parishes. As Deacon Morse wrote concerning a revival in Woodstock, "the work seems to be carry^d. on; not with firy zeal; or an earthquake or a mighty rushing wind, but with a still small voice." A Connecticut minister noted that, during the revival in his town,

the silence observable among those who were going to or returning from these meetings, was very impressive, and frequently noticed with surprize and pleasure. Little or no tumult or noise, and the appearance of most, much as if they had been going to, or were returning from the funeral of some near relative or friend. And while in the house, nothing was said but by the minister; for so little disposed were people to take an active part in any religious exercise, except singing, that it was difficult to get one publicly to propose or ask a question. Many were swift to hear, but all slow to speak.

Others ministers attested to the same kind of behavior on the part of their congregations.[5]

The clergy were largely responsible for the orderliness of the revivals, though the fact that the Methodists and Baptists now existed to attract the more turbulent spirits or those seeking a different religious outlook also helps to explain the orderliness of the Second Awakening. Ministers were quick to step forward when an unusual concern for religion appeared among their people. They organized religious conferences or began supervising those their people had initiated. At these meetings they presented readings and guided discussion. They also held frequent lectures in which they clearly and calmly delineated orthodox doctrine. Mindful of the disorders of the Great Awakening, they did not try to excite outward expressions of emotion and did not call on the converted to relate publicly their conversion experiences. Frequently preachers from neighboring towns assisted during a revival, offering some freshness of style without any of the risks of the itineracy of the earlier awakening. Often during revivals there were either lectures or conference meetings every day of the week. When the minister was unable to attend a conference, the people read sermons or religious magazines, which were of course prepared by ministers. In these ways the clergy exercised a close watch over the religious experiences of their people and kept them within proper bounds.[6]

It was no wonder, then, that the clergy happily endorsed the New England revivals. They were far more reluctant, however, about endorsing those to the south, which broke out in 1800 in Kentucky and Tennessee, where large crowds gathered and where many of those attending fell to the ground groaning, seemingly paralyzed by a conviction of their sinfulness. The New England orthodox clergy generally endorsed the southern revivals after receiving assurances from Presbyterian ministers, whom they respected, that such behavior arose from a genuine sense of sin and that those subjected to such attacks proved to be truly religious. Morse stated his candid opinion about the southern revivals in a letter to a British evangelical leader: "We know not what to make of the *fallings* &c in Kentucky, which have attended the remarkable revival of religion in that quarter. We wait to know the permanent effects. We dare not say that there is not a good work going on there, but it is mixed with uncommon evil, and gives great occasion to the adversary." Morse's statement refers to the fact that the excesses of the southern revivals gave ammunition to those who were, at best, skeptical about revivals; and these critics included the liberal Congregational clergy. Orthodox ministers publicly praised the southern revivals for rescuing souls from infidelity, but they never would have permitted such behavior in their parishes and were happy that they were not confronted by it.[7]

The orthodox embraced the revivals in their parishes so warmly because it finally seemed that the infidel threat was being turned back. The revivals certainly checked the long-lamented drift away from religious orthodoxy, and many ministers even claimed that Calvinism was reasserted as a result of the Second Awakening. In truth, however, certain aspects of that religious system were weakened by revivalism. To be sure, the Calvinist notion of human depravity prevailed, but use of the revival led to the tacit acceptance of human ability at the expense of the doctrines of election and predestination. Like many other orthodox ministers, Morse would always include these doctrines as part of orthodox faith, but he largely ignored them in his preaching. They were to be accepted but not to be taken so seriously as to be an obstacle to those undergoing a conversion experience.

Lyman Beecher expressed the outlook of much of the orthodox clergy in one of the most widely read sermons of the Second Great Awakening, *The Government of God Desireable*. In it, Beecher defended the idea of God controlling the world, but he insisted that man was free and concluded with a call for immediate repentance, which he claimed was within everyone's power. The emphasis of orthodox preaching was on the notion that men are sinful and in need of a divine Savior and on the likelihood of finding acceptance if they turn to him. For this reason the orthodoxy of the Second Great Awakening, very much a product of the revival, might best be described as evangelical Protestantism rather than rigorous Calvinism.[8]

The revivals encouraged the orthodox clergy to intensify their efforts to move out of what they now regarded as an unhappy middle ground between cold morality and destructive fanaticism that they had occupied since the collapse of the Great Awakening. They were able to channel energies released by the revivals into other religious enterprises, which in turn helped to promote further revivals. The earliest and most important of these were missionary societies.

To some extent the American missionary societies developed out of earlier, more limited efforts begun in the 1780s. In Massachusetts in 1787 the Society for Propagating the Gospel Among Indians and Others in North America was formed, largely out of embarrassment after a Scottish society appointed a board of commissioners in Boston to administer the funds it contributed to evangelizing some American Indians. As its name suggests, the Massachusetts society pledged itself to aiding Indians, but it was more seriously committed to aiding settlers in the District of Maine, to preserving among them those educational and religious institutions considered essential for law, order, and civility. Morse was elected a member of the society in 1792 and its assistant secretary in 1795. The society could do little in these years because it had little money to spend. It was unable to send out missionaries and could only have some Bibles and books distributed.[9]

The Connecticut General Association was able to do more. In one of the earliest efforts to counter irreligion, it began in the 1780s sending missionaries to the settlers of New Hampshire, Vermont, and New York. Like the Massachusetts society, the General Association saw itself helping to keep alive New Englanders' traditional allegiance to churches, schools, and a settled ministry. In its operations the General Association set the basic pattern missionary societies were to follow: it raised money by contributions to send out ministers who took leaves of absence from their churches. These missionaries traveled about the new settlements, where they preached, administered the sacraments, and called upon the people to attend to their religious duty. They also distributed Bibles and tracts during their tours.[10]

Some more specialized missionary organizations would probably have been developed because of the scale of migration to new settlements and an increasing concern during the 1790s, occasioned by the heated politics of the time, over the character of those settlements. More than ever, it seemed crucial to see that the expanding nation developed sound religious institutions. As it were, English societies, formed that decade as a result of the British evangelical movement, provided a useful example of organization, a new vocabulary, and a broader outlook. Citing the work of the British, American clergymen began forming missionary societies in imitation of them.[11] The first so formed was the New York Missionary Society in 1796. Two years later the Connecticut General Association established the Missionary Society of Connecticut to carry on its work. This was followed in New England in the next several years by the formation of the Massachusetts Missionary Society, the Hampshire (Massachusetts) Missionary Society, and the New Hampshire Missionary Society.

These societies described their work differently from the Connecticut General Association earlier in the decade. The association had spoken only of the need to preserve those institutions essential for religious and social order. It had not referred to a contest against foreign-based infidelity or even to the idea of converting the world and advancing the millennium. Like the British clergy involved in the benevolence movement, however, American clergymen began saying that Christ had come to save all men, that all were in need of Christianity, and that it was the duty of Christians to see that all received the Gospel. With Paine's *The Age of Reason* in mind, the clergy also began to speak of the need to contend against an aggressive infidel threat. Imitating infields who leagued together to destroy Christianity, Christians must join together to spread the Gospel throughout the world. Other ministers believed, as did Morse, that "the singular & combined efforts whh have been made within the last half century to corrupt & extirpate Christianity seem to have called for the corresponding, extraordinary efforts to preserve its purity, strengthen its foundations, & extend its influence."[12]

All of the American missionary societies spoke of the goal of converting the world to Christianity and stressed their commitment to send the Gospel to the heathen, specifically the American Indian. The New England societies, however, concentrated on white settlers, as had the General Association of Connecticut. They applied their rhetoric about the conversion of the heathen to this work on the frontier, where they labored among a people who were not heathens but whom the societies feared might be reduced to such were missionaries not sent them. As Abiel Holmes said before the Massachusetts Missionary Society,

> God forbid, that we should permit our heathen neighbours to perish; especially, that we should *hide ourselves from our own flesh,* and suffer our *brethren and kinsmen,* already Christianized, to relapse into heathenism, for the want of Christian instruction! If, my brethren, ye have any love to your country, ye will assist us in imparting to its destitute inhabitants, that *knowledge,* which, by making them good citizens, will essentially contribute to the *stability of our times.*

In the new settlements missionaries called people to meet for prayer on the Sabbath and worked to organize churches and establish schools, preparing the way for the settlement of regular ministers.[13] Morse performed a mission in the summer of 1800 which was typical of hundreds performed under the patronage of the societies. In August he traveled to the Isle of Shoals off the coast of Maine, where he preached, baptized and catechized children, and distributed religious tracts outlining the religious duties of Christians. Under the auspices of the Society for Propagating Christianity Among Indians and Others, Morse raised money to have a building erected to serve as both meetinghouse and schoolhouse. In November he returned to preach the dedication sermon at the meetinghouse. The next year the society provided a minister who preached on Sundays and taught school during the week.[14]

The great goal toward which the missionaries worked was the settlement of educated ministers. In many sermons delivered before the societies, clergymen insisted that the settled ministry was essential for establishing religious and social order. Solomon Williams said that without a regular clergy the inhabitants of the new settlements will

> soon lose the virtues and neglect the duties of our religion. Their minds uncultivated, their hearts hardened—their families neglected, in a very short time they will live without God, without Christ, without the Spirit, without the Lord's day and fall into heathenism, and become a generation of evil doers: ungospellized they will be uncivilized.

Clergymen often argued that the ministry was the prime means of bringing men to the Gospel and of preserving Christianity in its purity. They often likened themselves to the apostles of the primitive church. When Bible societies began to be formed, the Missionary Society of Connecticut declared that they should be auxiliaries to the missionary societies. Ministers in these years often sounded the theme that the ministry and not the Bible was the prime means by which Christ established and sustained his church.[15]

For years the clergy had been concerned about their position in society. It was one of the reasons so many of them had fallen into anti-Jacobinism and so strongly opposed Jefferson's election. His election had heightened those fears. Moreover, Congregationalists in Connecticut and Massachusetts were alarmed by efforts to dismantle the establishments in those states. In the clergy's statements before missionary societies about the role of the ministry, their defensiveness is obvious.

At the same time, in the work of the societies and the outburst of revivals, the clergy were working toward securing their position on a different basis. Even while they clung to establishments in Connecticut and Massachusetts, they were refining the instruments of a voluntaristic, competitive system. The legalistic basis of the Standing Order was giving way to the voluntaristic basis of the nineteenth-century evangelical ministry.

In the new settlements where the New England societies worked to establish the settled ministry and those other institutions they considered essential for religious and social order, they were confronted by two kinds of people who were obnoxious to them and to whom they were equally so. One group were people, sometimes called "infidels" in the missionary societies' report, who were uninterested in religion. Not deists or atheists—"Nothingarians," as they were sometimes called—they simply were not concerned with religion. They felt no need to follow the appeals of the missionaries to gather on the Sabbath for public worship, much less to support someday a minister who would pry into their lives.

The other general group were sectarians of various persuasions, and these gave the missionaries much more trouble. One minister confronted by them said that they were often "more injurious to the maintenance and propagation of the turth, than direct opposers." There were various groups, some of them very small. Not the largest but the most objectionable to orthodox Congregationalists were the Universalists, who differed so sharply in their religious outlook. Far larger were the Baptists and Methodists. These two denominations were most often mentioned in the reports of Congregational missionaries, and with good reason, for they grew vastly, especially in the southern states, during the Second Great Awakening. Baptists increased from 100,000 in 1800 to more than 313,000 in 1830; the Methodists, from 64,000 to 476,000. Their growth far outran that of Congregationalists, who grew from 75,000 to 140,000, and Presbyterians, who increased from 40,000 to 173,000.[16]

Most of the Congregational clergy, when not in immediate

confrontation with Methodists and Baptists, would agree with Morse's description of them in the 1789 edition of his *Geography*: "They are generally a moral, well-meaning set of people. They exhibit much zeal in their worship, which appears to be composed of the mingled effusions of piety, enthusiasm, and superstition." As he wrote in 1804, he liked to consider both denominations

> as *pioneers* to clear the way for the regular and permanent establishment of the institutions of religion. Their clergy have access to, and influence over a class of people, who perhaps would not profit by the labours of more learned and regular divines. The Lord of the harvest selects labourers, fitted to cultivate every species of plants in his vineyard.

Morse was able to take this rather detached view because he lived in eastern Massachusetts and was not challenged by these sects. Baptist ministers in that part of the state were, despite their lower social status, not very different from the orthodox Congregationalists; increasingly they were educated, they of course supported revivals, and they were involved in benevolent societies of their own. Already established, they posed no great threat to the Congregational clergy in eastern Massachusetts. Morse was even willing to demonstrate his approval of them as sound Calvinists in protesting against the liberal Congregationalists, whom he considered the real threat in the Boston area.[17]

Ministers in western Massachusetts and even more so missionaries in settlements from the District of Maine to Ohio could not be so detached. In gathering Congregational churches and preparing the way for settlement of regular ministers, they had to struggle against Methodists and Baptists. Congregationalists were much more contemptuous of the Methodists than the Baptists. They considered the Baptists sound, though often ignorant, Calvinists who differed from them mainly in being too restrictive in their practices, as in their rejection of infant baptism. On the other hand, the

Methodists were frankly Arminian and outspokenly anti-Calvinistic. Congregational polemicists charged them with rejecting the scheme of grace and with preachng a false gospel.[18]

The most disturbing thing about both sects was not their doctrines or practices but the zeal with which they labored to build up their ranks and opposed the establishment of Congregationalism in the new settlements. Congregationalists had long complained that sectarian itinerants traveled about, trying to lead people astray. In 1791, for example, a convention of Congregational ministers in New Hampshire warned against strangers who, "putting on a feigned show of zeal for God, are going about to deceive and mislead mankind." Three years later, Noah Worcester, a New Hampshire minister, accused the Baptists of coming into towns when Congregational religious societies were divided or when there were troubles with the settled minister and using these misfortunes to enlarge their sect. Both Baptists and Methodists profited from the farmers' discomfort and dislike of the rather aristocratic bearing of the Congregational clergy. Both played to the democratic sentiments of the common man, insisting that a call from God was all the training a preacher needed. They attacked the institution of the paid ministry and often charged that the college-trained Congregational clergy preached only for their salaries. Itinerants often spoke of their concern for the spiritual state of the people under such ministers and defended their proselytizing in towns that had a settled Congregational minister. As one Methodist preacher said, "Those towns or societies, which have settled ministers who (r-e-a-d) preach either speculative truth, or dry morality, in a soft easy way, and wish to keep out all others who differ from them, are in a worse predicament than others who have no ministers."[19]

It was this kind of sectarian intrusion and the divisiveness their mere presence created that most disturbed the Congregational missionaries and ministers. With a good deal of exaggeration, one minister charged that itinerants divided existing churches and forced their dissolution. He claimed that the new churches then often disappeared, leaving none. With their largely anticlerical religious outlook and their appeals for a warmer kind of religious experience, the sectarians did stymy the efforts of the missionary societies to establish the settled clergy in the new settlements as directors of social order who could work to unite the community around the old New England ideal of the village church and school. For this reason, some Congregational ministers attacked sectarians in Fast and Thanksgiving Day sermons. They accused them of creating division and spreading heresy and error, which, intentionally or not, worked to the advantage of infidelity. Somewhat more obliquely, a few Congregational ministers censured them for their support of the Democratic-Republican party, and one minister even accused them of uniting with the Antichrist in his war on the Christian church. Many members of the Standing Order would have agreed with Walter King, who wrote Morse that the Baptist leaders seemed "to be governed only by selfishness, & democracy."[20] Despite the difficulties created by the settlers' different backgrounds and the efforts of sectarians to divide them further, the Congregational societies pledged themselves to meet the task. They often spoke of the settlers' endangered position in order to stimulate greater support.[21]

Conversely, another point stressed in raising support for these missions was the success of the missionaries. Despite the many complaints about infidels and sectarians, the work of the societies went very well. Many of the settlers were Congregationalists or Presbyterians, happy to listen to the preaching of the missionaries and eager to form churches over which they could settle ministers. One missionary wrote Morse that during his tour through part of upstate New York, the people expressed a strong desire for settled ministers and schoolteachers. They even donated $300, enough to print forty thousand small tracts. The reports of the missionary societies spoke of sectarian errors being checked and of Congregational churches being formed. A missionary happily reported to the Hampshire Missionary Society that in one

New York town there were "both baptist and methodist preachers; and one universalist teacher in the county of St. Lawrence; but the body of the people are steady, regular, and moral." By 1807 missionary societies were formed in Vermont and the District of Maine, areas that had been missionary grounds but were by then sufficiently evangelized to join in the work with the older societies.[22]

Besides building up Congregationalism on the frontier, the missionary societies enjoyed increasing support at home. The annual contributions steadily increased until later in the decade when the embargo and nonintercourse began to take their toll. By then, however, the societies had been able to adopt the policy of settling ministers over more restricted areas, largely limiting them to one church with some additional duties in the immediate vicinity. This was thought to be a more effective way of preparing people for the time when they would settle and support a minister of their own.[23]

During the first decade of the nineteenth century, new, more specialized benevolent societies were established. In fact, by 1810, the basic structure of the antebellum benevolent empire was set. Morse contributed much to this development. He introduced the tract society, first developed by British evangelicals, to the United States. As early as 1795 Morse knew of Hannah More's tracts in Britain, and he later corresponded with George Burder, secretary of the Religious Tract Society formed in London in 1799. In 1802 Morse had more than thirty-two thousand tracts printed and sent to clergymen in the District of Maine, Tennessee, and Kentucky for distribution in those places. The next year a large bequest enabled Morse to organize the Massachusetts Society for Promoting Christian Knowledge, the first tract society in the United States. It concentrated on distributing tracts in eastern Massachusetts and the District of Maine but also cooperated with a western Massachusetts missionary society, printing tracts for it to distribute on the western frontier. Morse's society soon led to the formation of tract societies in other states by Congregationalists and other denominations.[24]

In establishing his tract society, Morse looked to the British to show him the way. He wrote Burder asking for a copy of the Religious Tract Society's constitution, for information on its manner of distribution, and for some copies of tracts that could be reprinted in the United States.[25] Morse, however, did not regard himself as passively copying the British example. He saw himself confronting infidels who, he believed, had distributed antireligious writings like *The Age of Reason* on the frontier. Ebenezer Pearson, one of Morse's colleagues in the society, said that it was formed to meet the exertions of the Illuminati, atheistic Jacobins, and American infidels who were circulating their writings in the United States: "An antidote was necessary to counteract this moral poison. By books of almost every description had this poison; variously prepared, been circulated through the community. Books therefore appeared the proper vehicle for conveying the only remedy, *the truth, as it is in Jesus.*"[26]

Morse believed the tract was a weapon of infidelity which must be turned to the benefit of Christianity. He argued that tracts represented an easy, effective, cheap way of reaching a mass audience. They had to be evangelical, referring to salvation through the atonement and grace of Christ, without lapsing into sectarian points. Helpful as it was to evangelical Protestantism, the tract was detrimental to Calvinism. Because it was brief and had to be hard hitting, there was no place for the doctrines of election or predestination in the tract. As one minister noted in praising Morse's society, it produced tracts that set out orthodox doctrine without downplaying "moral agency in man"; that is, without arguing, as did New Divinity ministers, that the unconverted could do little, or nothing, to affect their state. The society's tracts were in keeping with the outlook of the Old Calvinist party, to which Morse was attached. In fact, it printed tracts by leaders of that group which urged people to use Christian means. This society was a bridge between eighteenth-century Old Calvinism and nineteenth-century evangelical Protestantism, confirming Mead's observations about the relationship between the two.[27]

The Bible society, another type of benevolent society, also

appeared during the first decade of the nineteenth century. Like the tract societies, the American Bible societies were directly inspired by the British and Foreign Bible Society established in London in 1805. The first American one was formed in Philadelphia in 1808. It was followed in the next several years by others in Connecticut, Massachusetts, New York, and other places. While Morse was in the southern states, spending the winter of 1809/1810 on a retreat from his difficulties with Boston liberals, he helped to organize the Georgia Bible Society in Savannah and the Charleston and Beaufort Bible societies in South Carolina.

Morse was a friend and correspondent of Robert Ralston, a leader of the Philadelphia society, the most important in the nation. Morse and Ralston worked out an agreement between the Massachusetts and Philadelphia societies, the two joining to obtain from Britain plates neither could have afforded individually but which permitted them to print Bibles more cheaply than they could by any other method. Morse envisioned even closer cooperation. He tried to persuade the Philadelphia Bible Society to take the lead in forming a national society, which would be able to print Bibles more cheaply and collect accurate information on the needs of all parts of the nation. The Philadelphia society declined, however, arguing that a national society would not receive as much support as a number of local ones.[28]

In addition to his work with Bible and tract societies, Morse acted in other ways to promote and extend the benevolence movement. In 1805 he began publishing the *Panoplist*, a religious magazine whose title suggests something of Morse's personality. The *Panoplist* grew out of Morse's appreciation of the value of communications to the evangelical cause. The first successful magazine was the *Connecticut Evangelical Magazine*, which the Missionary Society of Connecticut began publishing in 1800 and which pointed the way for the *Panoplist*. In short order, Morse applied his editorial and promotional skills to make his the most widely read religious magazine in New England.

The magazines printed several kinds of articles. One of the most effective was biographies and deathbed accounts of the departing faithful. These were more popular than articles on orthodox doctrine. As one person wrote the *Connecticut Evangelical Magazine,* the personal accounts were "more powerfully felt by many, who are difficulted to follow metaphysical discussions." In this way these articles were like tracts. They outlined orthodox doctrine and drove it home with an emotional appeal. But they also simplified orthodox doctrine, playing up the need to turn to God, playing down the notion of election.[29]

The magazines' accounts of revivals also served important purposes. Before the appearance of the magazines it was common for a revival to be stimulated by news of one taking place in a neighboring town. The magazines managed to arouse revivals with reports of very distant ones. These accounts were often read at religious conferences. Deacon Morse wrote his son that "our Evangelical Magazine seems to be a great means & help to carry on the good work; as some parts of them are read in the weekly conferences." Moreover, the magazines worked not only to stir up revivals but to keep them orderly by describing what was a true revival and what was not.[30]

By reporting on the spread of Christianity and work of missionary societies around the world, the magazines also provided their readers with the sense of being involved in the great task of evangelizing the world. By organizing and contributing to local auxiliary societies, Christians could feel that they were advancing the millennium. The benevolence movement, Morse observed as early as 1799, "had the double effect of propagating Christianity at home and abroad."[31]

In effect, benevolence movement leaders used the societies and magazines to harness and direct energy aroused during revivals. By means of these tools, they maintained the piety awakened in revivals, channeled support into activities which brought forth new churches on the frontier, and they tended to prevent religious excitement from resulting in division and strife. The calm, orderly, and managed character of the Second Great Awakening gave it continuity so that it did not burn out in several years as the Great Awakening had.

Two groups of people were especially important in the benevolent societies and revivals of the Second Great Awakening. One of these was women. Women had long represented the majority of communicant members in the New England Congregational churches. Narratives of revivals indicate that they usually represented two-thirds of those converted during the Second Great Awakening.[32] In addition, revivals often began among them.[33] Women also supported the benevolent societies, contributing money to them and forming auxiliary societies. Between 1804 and 1811, for example, the Female Charitable Association of the Hampshire Missionary Society never contributed less than 19 percent of the funds raised within the county, and women contributed money to the society in other ways. The first female cent society, whose members donated one cent per week, was formed in Boston in 1802 as an auxiliary to the Massachusetts Missionary Society. After ten years the society had received $4,500 from female cent societies. Throughout New England all kinds of auxiliary societies were formed. The American Board of Commissioners for Foreign Missions reported in 1817 that of its auxiliary societies, 81 were composed of men but 173 of women. By 1816, women's support of benevolent enterprises was so accepted that a girls' school in Boston established a charity society in order *"to initiate the Young Ladies into the routine of Society business,* and qualify them to become useful hereafter in the formation and direction of other societies."[34]

Women's support of the benevolence cause was significant in several ways. Their support contributed immensely to its success, and that was important in defining a new position for the clergy in the nineteenth century. Despite the debacle of the Congregational clergy's anti-Democratic-Republican political campaign and the move toward disestablishment, they led the way in establishing the clergy in general as moral and religious stewards over American society. The respect and support they received from women at a time when they complained of a general disrespect for the ministry were important in accomplishing this.

In turn, female support of the benevolence movement helped to win women a new social role in the nineteenth century. Ministers said that it was proper for women not only to support religious causes but to assist the clergy as stewards by administering relief to the poor through charity societies. As early as 1810, Timothy Dwight contended that women were better equipped than men to aid the poor because of a more sensitive nature, which they could apply to problems in an efficient manner. The experience women gained working in benevolent societies, as well as the idea that women should put their elevated moral and religious nature to the task of uplifting society, later provided a basis for their involvement in reform movements like abolitionism and eventually the women's rights movement.[35]

The other group important for the success of the benevolence cause was young men. Like women, young people were the most frequent subjects of conversion, and revivals often had their origins among them. The narratives of revivals do not spell out precisely the sex of these young converts or their ages. Some narratives describe people between the ages of fifteen and forty as young converts, and some mention converts as young as eight.[36] A minister in Vermont did provide a detailed description of those converted during a revival in his parish: 40 were between the ages of eight and fourteen, 50 between the ages of fourteen and twenty-two, and 57 or 58 older than twenty-two.[37] Whatever the general proportion of young people to other converts and of young men to young women converts, the clergy was extremely excited by the prospects for the church from the conversion of young men.

Ministers were needed for the church. They were needed for the new settlements to combat other denominations and in eastern Massachusetts to counter the liberals. As the *Panoplist* expressed it, only a learned clergy could contend against Unitarians and sectarians: "A judicious learned, and pious ministry, will be the great instrument in the hands of Divine Providence, by which error will be refuted, enthusiasm repressed, and a guilty world renovated, delivered from the power of sin, and filled with the knowledge and glory of God." The clergy agreed with Andover professor Ebenezer Porter that an adequate number of future ministers could only be raised up by revivals. The problem remained of how to prepare these young men for the ministry, because most of them could not afford the training which was essential. The solution was education societies that provided financial support for poor ministerial students in colleges and seminaries. The first of these was probably one formed in Vermont in 1804. By 1812 a number of local education societies existed throughout New England. The *Panoplist* appealed to the rich for the support of poor students, but as with the other societies, the support of women was crucial for the success of this cause. This manner of providing ministers illustrates how smoothly revivals and benevolent societies operated together during the Second Great Awakening. Young men, whose piety was aroused in revivals, were prepared for work in the new settlements, where in time they could introduce the familiar benevolent institutions.[38]

The establishment of theological seminaries like Andover, which was founded in 1808, was also important for providing ministers for the church. At the colleges and then at the seminaries they attended, pious young men met and formed schemes for evangelizing the United States and the world. Such people were responsible for the creation of the first foreign missionary society in the United States. In 1810, five Andover students, who had begun making their plans while students at Williams College, offered their services as foreign missionaries to the General Association of Massachusetts. In response, the association formed the American Board of Commissioners for Foreign Missions (ABCFM). The *Panoplist* began promoting the cause of foreign missions, printing British writings, like those of Claudius Buchanan and Melville

Horne, which had excited among the students an interest in missions to the Far East. The magazine became the unofficial organ of the ABCFM, pledging all its profits to its missions.[39]

Despite the financial distress of the times, the New England public responded warmly to the ABCFM's call for support. Morse helped to prepare an address which declared that, with the world in chaos, the biblical prophecies were being fulfilled. The Roman church and the Islamic religion were about to collapse, and now was the time to send the Gospel to all mankind. In December 1811 the first auxiliary society to the ABCFM was formed in Boston, and by June 1812 auxiliaries existed in the principal New England towns.[40]

By the time war was declared against Great Britain, most of the pieces of the later, more developed benevolence program existed: Bible, tract, education, and foreign and domestic missionary societies. The war increased the clergy's commitment to press on with their work. This was already their response to the Republican programs of embargo and nonintercourse, which, in disrupting New England's commerce, reduced the contributions they received.

In responding to these policies and finally to the war, a large number of the orthodox clergy adopted the millennial scheme of British Bishop Stanley Faber, who argued that the most complete and final manifestation of the Antichrist was France. France, unlike the Roman Catholic church, was atheistic. Infidel philosophers of the eighteenth century, including the Illuminati, had prepared the way for the Jacobins to establish atheism in France. Despite their fall, the rise of Napoleon, and his reestablishment of the Catholic church, France was still atheistic. Reestablishment was a sham, a hollow gesture made to delude the ignorant. The pope, as one admirer of Faber's scheme explained, was a "mere puppet in the hands of the mighty Napoleon." The world was divided into two camps: France the Antichrist opposed Britain, who countered French arms while supporting the spread of the Gospel around the world.[41]

Faber's views were endorsed by the *Panoplist* in 1808. In

1811 Ethan Smith, a New Hampshire minister, summarized and embellished Faber's arguments for an American audience. Smith's book bore the recommendations of both Old Calvinist and New Divinity leaders. Smith repeated Faber's claim that France was the Antichrist and added that the French had agents working in the United States to swing us into alliance with them and into war with Britain.[42]

Many of New England's orthodox clergy made the same claims, insisting that France was the true Antichrist which—with the Roman church, which it controlled, and the Islamic religion, which it would come to control—would be destroyed at the battle of Armageddon to introduce the millennium. Ignoring British attacks on American commerce, they argued that Britain, in standing up to Napoleon and defending its commerical rights, fought for the preservation of liberty in the world. They lavished praise on her for her support of benevolent causes. Smith called the formation of the London Missionary Society "a second *Pentecost.*" Ministers often made similarly exaggerated claims about the British and Foreign Bible Society.[43]

While they reiterated the need for piety and the support of religious and educational institutions, decried the prevalence of vice, and condemned party spirit,[44] many of the orthodox clergy flamed with opposition to the embargo and nonintercourse. These policies, as one minister wrote Morse, were punishments inflicted on Americans for their many sins, which included the election of the infidels Jefferson and Madison: "As long as we are a sinful people, it looks to me, a righteous God, will scourge us. This *demon* of democracy, will twist into every shape—come up in new dresses, & corrupt our country till we are *ruined.*" The embargo and nonintercourse worked to the detriment of Britain and to the advantage of France, who was as opposed to commerce as to religion. They showed that the United States was moving toward alliance with Antichristian France and war with Britain. Allied with France, the United States would fall with her: "RUIN will ensue; AMERICA will be given, into the power of anti-christ, and the destroying Angel, as he flies through heaven will cry wo, wo, wo, to the once happy land."[45]

Not all the Congregational clergy shared these views. Liberals, while also denouncing Republican policy as unwise, biased toward France, and disastrous to New England, did not accept or preach the millennial outlook set out by the orthodox clergy. The liberal literary publication *Monthly Anthology* said that it liked the political sentiments in a Fast Day sermon delivered by a New York Presbyterian minister—his criticism of the election of immoral, irreligious men—but took exception to his millennial views, which the magazine mistakenly attributed to Faber.[46] There were even a few Democratic-Republican Congregational ministers, both orthodox and liberals. In their published sermons most of these called for moderation and defended the embargo. But one of them, Solomon Aiken, accused his Federalist brethren of itching for an established national church.[47]

Most of the orthodox clergy believed, however, that there were two sides in the world, that of atheism and France and that of Christianity and Britain. They were alarmed by the movement of the United States toward war with Britain, which to them meant alliance with France and the stark possibility of sharing in the punishment to be meted out to all who supported the Antichrist. Still, they believed and insisted that Christianity would prevail. In a sermon before the ABCFM in 1810, Morse said that Christianity's progress could be seen in the sending of missionaries around the world. As Samuel Taggart, a Federalist congressman and Congregational minister, wrote to Morse, the growth of the church "is a pledge that altho the present state of things may operate severely by way of correction it will not issue in our destruction." When war was declared in June 1812, the *Panoplist* called on its readers not to despair but to support benevolent causes. It said that many people were already looking to God for relief, realizing that "from national reformation alone can any confident anticipations of national prosperity be made." Many believed that efforts had to be made to suppress vice because they felt that

the morals of a nation and its chastisement were directly related. Despite their fears, the orthodox clergy moved on to extend the work of the existing societies and even to institute
moral reform, to address themselves finally to evils they had
condemned for decades.[48]

By June 1812 one of the other major aspects of the Second
Great Awakening in New England, the division between orthodox and liberal Congregational ministers, was well advanced and checked only by common Federalist fears. But as
both groups braced for war, the issue of liberal apostasy within Massachusetts Congregationalism, long a concern of Morse,
was about to be inflamed by him.

# Chapter 5

---

# *The Struggle against Liberalism*

Despite Morse's inattention and apparent indifference to the ways in which the Second Great Awakening eroded Calvinism, he did commit himself to certain theological issues. At the outset of his ministry he committed himself to defend the doctrines of the Trinity, the divinity of Jesus, and human depravity. These were the essentials of his faith. He believed that man could obtain salvation only through recognition of his sinful nature and acceptance of Jesus as a divine mediator.

Morse's orthodoxy stood in contrast to the theological opinions of the liberals within Massachusetts Congregationalism. When he was settled in Charlestown, liberalism consisted mainly of Arminian views about human nature. The orthodox position on human depravity seemed too extreme to liberals. They maintained that man was not completely depraved, that he had the capacity for doing good as well as evil. Acting on this ability, he could win God's approval to some degree through his own efforts.

There were also some liberals who privately questioned the orthodox position on the divinity of Jesus. The great majority of these were Arians. They rejected the concept of the Trinity, of three persons in one God. Instead they believed that Jesus was divine without being the Deity but that his death played some role in restoring man in God's sight. The most radical and the smallest group among liberals were Socinians. They believed that Jesus was human. They essentially regarded him as a moral instructor, not a mediator, who pointed the way to salvation to all men. Though there were significant differences between Arminianism, Arianism, and Socinianism, all these views, in the opinion of Morse and other orthodox ministers, were erroneous and dangerous. In the eyes of the orthodox, each tended, to a lesser or greater degree, to prevent man from recognizing his sinful condition and utter need of a mediator.

There was more to Morse's dedication to orthodoxy than theological convictions. In part, it was also a way of countering his father's complaints about the time he devoted to his geographical writings. Unwilling to give up that work, Morse was apologetic in the face of his father's criticism: "I hope I shan't over do matters. I know 'of making books there is no end'—& I must confess I have a greater itch for publishing books now than I ever had—but I intend to be prudent & not proceed too fast." In the same letter, he reported his preaching in behalf of the doctrine of the Trinity and his commitment to defend it if liberals attacked it. This commitment was a way of proving to his father and perhaps himself that he was not ignoring his most important ministerial concerns.[1]

There was also a tactical dimension to Morse's opposition to liberalism. From the outset of his ministry Morse dreamed of a vigorous, inclusive American church, of an informal orthodox union that would embrace New England Congregationalism and the prestigious Calvinistic denominations to the south: Presbyterians, Associate Presbyterians, and Dutch Reformed. Such a union, Morse and his friends in these denominations believed, would strengthen Christianity and enable it to keep pace with the development of the United States. Morse was very aware, however, that the orthodox outside New England looked with distaste on the liberal element within Massachusetts Congregationalism and did not seek alliance with it. Morse was prepared to combat liberalism and did undertake his limited efforts in the early 1790s so that his hope for an orthodox union might be realized.[2]

By the mid-1790s, however, Morse's efforts to oppose liberalism were halted by the political struggle, inasmuch as almost all the Congregational clergy, including the liberals, supported the administration and the Federalist party. Religious controversy was suppressed for the sake of political unity. Still, it could not be completely prevented. The Federalist clergy's claim that they defended the cause of religion against France and her American abettors led some of the orthodox to wonder about the worth of that faith professed by some liberal ministers. This concern led David Tappan, Harvard professor of divinity, to warn the Massachusetts Convention of Congregational Ministers in 1797 that the clergy should not accommodate themselves to the "perverted reason and liberality of an unbelieving age," that they should not make Christianity a matter of merely practicing virtue and of regarding "God or . . . Jesus Christ merely as an useful instrument of morality." They must remain true to their calling by preaching on human depravity and the need of a mediator.[3]

William Wilberforce, the principal lay leader of the British evangelical movement, made similar arguments the same year in *A Practical View of the Prevailing System of Professed Christians.* He insisted that the orthodox positions on human depravity, Christ's atonement, and the influence of the Holy Spirit were the basic teachings of Christianity. An edition of his book was published in Boston in 1799 as part of a campaign by Morse, Tappan, and other orthodox ministers to press Wilberforce's views on the public. In April 1799 the *Massachusetts Mercury* printed a sermon which had been delivered on the Fast Day that month. The unacknowledged preacher recommended Wilberforce's book and cautioned against those in New England who, though they might abhor French infidelity, partook of it themselves by accepting only Jesus' moral teachings: "in those other parts of the same scriptures which teach the fall and depravity of man, the necessity of regeneration by the Spirit of God, and of redemption through the blood of his Son, they have no more faith than avowed deists."[4]

Other orthodox ministers also expressed this view. One of them, Eli Forbes, in his sermon before the Massachusetts Convention of Congregational Ministers in May 1799, urged that the clergy emphasize doctrine in their preaching, not "the commandments of men, or the refinements of philosophy, or empty speculations." There were enough concerned orthodox ministers in attendance at the convention for it to approve a letter to all their brethren in the state which asked whether a "mistaken catholicism" had not "substituted exterior decorum in the room of inward holiness, and afforded protection and support to a spirit of indifference to the leading principles and duties of religion."[5]

These actions by orthodox ministers touched off a minor religious debate among Federalist allies. Soon after the anonymous sermon appeared in the *Massachusetts Mercury,* someone wrote to protest the claim that orthodox Christians were more moral than liberals. That he denied, and he pointed to President Adams, who, he claimed, was a Socinian. The Democratic-Republican *Chronicle* seized on this and feigned surprise that Federalist orthodox ministers denounced some men as Socinians and deists while "holding up their patrons and heroes of the same principles as deserving not only the esteem, but even the adoration of the multitude." This forced a Federalist to warn in the *Mercury* that the paper had been imprudent in printing the article that called Adams a Socinian because this tended to divide his supporters. The Federalist asserted that, expediency aside, Adams was not unorthodox and cited one of his Fast Day proclamations which referred to Jesus as a redeemer and mediator.[6]

Both liberal and orthodox Federalists learned a lesson from this newspaper exchange. In the summer of 1799 Boston liberals printed an English reply to Wilberforce: Thomas Cogan's *Letters to William Wilberforce.* Cogan argued against Wilberforce's views on human depravity, insisting that man has impulses for good as well as evil and the power to act on them. Morse's associates David Tappan and David Osgood replied for the orthodox in the Boston newspapers, but they and their opponents made no gaffes like the one earlier that year and managed to keep politics out of their articles.[7]

This debate subsided by the end of the year, and religious differences were once more forced into the background because both the orthodox and liberals wanted to avoid controversy. Still, the orthodox cautioned that Christians must cling to the leading articles of their faith. Timothy Dwight, for example, in his century sermon, warned against explaining away certain doctrines in order to make Christianity palatable to more people, for that was the path to infidelity. Joseph Strong said in a Connecticut election sermon that liberals whose "professed object is to display its [the Gospel's] harmony and extend its popularity . . . in fact do more than the avowed infidel to disorganize its parts and enfeeble its energies." Similar remarks were expressed in Thanksgiving and Fast Day sermons, most of which were directed against Jacobin innovation and implored New Englanders to cleave to the habits of their forefathers.[8]

By October 1804 Morse believed that orthodox opposition and especially the revivals of the past few years had checked the growth liberalism had sustained in eastern Massachusetts since the American Revolution. He expressed this opinion to an English correspondent and without any hostility described the liberals as "a few elderly ministers, reputable for their understanding and character, who are Arminians . . . and a considerable body of younger men of good abilities & character, who may be denominated Arians." There were also some Socinians but no more than ten and only half of them "*avowedly*" so.[9]

As Morse was soon to learn, he had miscalculated the situation. He discovered this as liberals acted to have one of their party appointed professor of divinity at Harvard. The professorship had been vacant since August 1803 when Tappan, Morse's friend, had died. It remained so for more than a year because Joseph Willard, the college's president, and Eliphalet Pearson, professor of Hebrew and a member of the Harvard Corporation, resisted the appointment of a liberal. When Willard died in September 1804, the majority of the corporation was prepared to press its choice over Pearson's objections that only a man of Calvinist principles fit the terms of the professorship, which had been established in the eighteenth century by Thomas Hollis, an English Baptist.[10] Liberals began sending to the Boston newpapers a number of articles which argued that, after a year, it was time to act on the divinity professorship.[11]

Taken by surprise, the orthodox finally responded, arguing that due speed was to be desired but that some members of both the corporation and board of overseers wanted to elect a Unitarian to the office. That would violate the intentions of the Puritan forefathers in founding the college as well as the terms of Hollis's bequest. Liberals replied that it was most important to elect a man who loved and pursued the truth, not a dogmatist. The Puritans, after all, had been dissenters, and Hollis had not prescribed adherence to a particular scheme of theology. The *Columbian Centinel,* the major Federalist paper, tried to close off debate, announcing that it would publish nothing more on the controversy, for it divided Christians at a time when it was important that they be united. The *New England Palladium,* Boston's other important Federalist paper, also wanted to stop printing articles on the subject. Despite the desire of both papers, both groups pressed them to continue printing their articles.[12]

Morse became greatly alarmed in December 1804, upon realizing that the liberals were active and not dormant as he had thought. There was a clear threat that Arminians might assume both the college's presidency and the professorship. To Morse this represented a revolution, one he feared "more than a political revolution." By the end of the month his fears had grown, and he now believed that a Unitarian campaign was underway to seize control of Harvard. He felt that this had to be resisted, even though opposition would "seriously affect the usefulness of the University, & the peace of the State." Morse decided that it was more important to resist liberal control of Harvard than to remain silent for the sake of Federalist unity. He was able to make this decision in December 1804 because Jefferson's election in 1800 had not had the disastrous consequences he feared it would and because, in any case, Jefferson had just been reelected. Morse of course did not like Jefferson's policies, but in his opinion, liberal control of the college meant the rejection there of religious orthodoxy. He and other orthodox ministers believed that orthodoxy lay at the core of New England's institutions and traditions, which they saw themselves defending against the Democratic-Republicans.[13]

For this reason, Morse pledged himself to oppose the election of Henry Ware, the candidate of the liberals within the Harvard Board of Overseers, on which he sat as the settled minister from Charlestown, one of several towns whose Congregational clergy composed the board along with a number of state political officials. In February 1805 the corporation overrode Pearson's objections and sent Ware's nomination on to the board, where Morse expected that it would be approved. At the board's meeting on February 14 he outlined the grounds of his opposition, which had already been expressed within the corporation by Pearson: that Hollis had been a Calvinist and had stipulated that only such a man was to be elected; that the corporation had refused to examine Ware but that a published catechism he had prepared proved that he was unorthodox in his views on human nature and the character of Jesus. As Morse expected, Ware was approved anyhow.[14]

Morse thought the matter of such importance that he should present the public the reasons for his opposition to Ware's appointment, which he did in March 1805 in the pamphlet *The True Reasons On Which the Election of a Hollis Professor of Divinity in Harvard College, Was Opposed at the Board of Overseers.* This was the first step in his campaign to arouse and unite the orthodox forces in the state. His immediate goal was to prevent the liberals from going on to elect one of their numbers to the vacant Harvard presidency now that they had prevailed in the contest over the professorship.

*The True Reasons* received a hostile review from a new liberal literary publication in Boston, the *Monthly Anthology*. The reviewer charged that Morse misrepresented the situation, that Hollis had not restricted the choice of future professors to Calvinists, just to Christians considered orthodox in their own time. Morse was disturbed by this review. He sent a reply to the *Anthology* and not only defended the claims he had made in his pamphlet but accused the magazine of using anonymity to attack him. Always inclined to consider opposition to himself as the work of a silent, well-organized cabal, he responded in this way to the *Anthology* review. He was certain that the magazine was a tool of the liberals in a campaign to seize control of Harvard and to propagate surreptitiously their religious views among the people of New England.[15]

The Anthology Society, formed later that year to take charge the magazine, was indeed composed largely of liberals. Its members soon included liberal ministers William Emerson, William E. Channing, John T. Kirkland, Joseph S. Buckminster, Joseph Tuckerman, and Samuel C. Thacher. But its president was the Episcopalian clergyman John S. J. Gardiner, so it was not a liberal organization in the sense of being anti-Trinitarian. Gardiner's and the other members' devotion, however, to Arminianism and to the Federalist party made for hostility to Morse's campaign to organize the state's orthodoxy against the college government.

Morse became convinced that the orthodox required a magazine of their own, one that could unite them and focus their energy. Morse hoped that his new magazine, the *Panoplist,* which appeared in June 1805, would win the support of the two factions within Massachusetts orthodoxy, the Old Calvinists and the New Divinity party. He believed that union among the orthodox was essential before there could be a separation between them and the liberals. As early as 1805 he contemplated separation, feeling that Unitarianism was the "*de-*

*mocracy* of Christianity. It dissolves all the bonds of Christian union, & deprives religion of all its efficacy & influence upon Society."[16]

Uniting the two orthodox factions proved to be a difficult task. New Divinity men, to be sure, were as opposed to liberalism as Old Calvinists like Morse. In a sermon before the Convention of Congregational Ministers in 1804, Nathanael Emmons, the leading New Divinity theologian, rejected the liberals' appeal for fellowship among those who differed on basic doctrine. Samuel Spring, another leader, decried Ware's election as a "total revolution of the theology of the University from the doctrine of God's incarnation to the degrading system of Unitarians."[17]

Still, there were important theological differences between the two orthodox factions, and these were reflected in conflicts over the issues of baptism, communion, and church discipline. From the beginning of his ministry, Morse, as an Old Calvinist, had observed the Half-Way Covenant and baptized the children of noncommunicant members of the congregation. He also had invited the baptized, noncommunicant members to come forward to take the Lord's Supper, almost treating it as a converting ordinance. Although he had not published anything on these issues, in the 1790s he had helped to circulate pamphlets written by Joseph Lathrop, Moses Hemmenway, and others. These ministers had defended the Half-Way Covenant and had set extremely low standards for admission to communion, calling only for moral behavior and some glimmer of faith.[18]

Emmons had led the New Divinity response, rejecting the right of noncommunicant members to have their children baptized and insisting that those who sought admission to communion should present some evidence of their faith. He had accused the Old Calvinists of attempting to replace piety with morality as the major concern of the church by telling noncommunicants that moral behavior was evidence of their fitness for the sacrament. New Divinity ministers, primarily concerned with the piety and purity of the church, warned such people of the sinfulness of taking communion if they were unsanctified.[19]

Old Calvinists believed there were no sure signs of sanctification and so argued that it was better for men to act on their hope than to refrain because of their uncertainty. In addition, they supported a strengthening of church discipline, believeing that the church must serve as an agent of morality in society by watching over its members and educating their children. It could not fulfill that function if it frightened off all but those who were confident of their piety. In their view, New Divinity principles and practices undermined the social side of the church's role in pursuing a purity of faith that could not even be determined by men.[20]

Given these differences, Morse found it difficult to win New Divinity support for the *Panoplist*. It did become a success, largely because of Morse's experience in promoting his geographical writings and his acquaintance with ministers throughout New England. Still, the most important object was to unite with the *Massachusetts Missionary Magazine,* the publication of the Massachusetts Missionary Society, which New Divinity men dominated. Tortuous negotiations began in 1806, but New Divinity leaders so mistrusted the Old Calvinists that they did not agree to the union of the two magazines until 1808. But once this agreement was reached, the *Panoplist* worked to promote union and cooperation between the two orthodox factions on the broad basis of evangelicalism and to prepare the way for separation from the liberals.[21]

In a further act of harmony, the two orthodox groups agreed to unite in establishing a theological seminary. In 1806, when a liberal was elected president of Harvard, Morse had given up on his hopes of recapturing the college by having an orthodox man chosen. Morse resigned his seat on the board of overseers and began making plans for a seminary at Andover.[22] Morse soon learned that a group of New Divinity ministers was laying plans to establish its own seminary, and this possibility alarmed him. He believed that the two camps either had to unite in one seminary or waste their strength in division and jealousy. Negotiations began in April 1807 and proceeded very slowly, at times driving Morse into periods of depression. Spring, the New Divinity leader whose support was crucial, was most hesitant about uniting with those "who will not give up the half-way convenant, and are forever pleading for the duty which pertains to the BEST actions of sinners." In February 1808 the New Divinity leaders and their patrons finally agreed to unite when a compromise was reached giving them the protection they desired against the future appointment of professors they might consider unsound. With this guarantee and a creed for the seminary to their liking, the New Divinity ministers were willing to attempt a union with the Old Calvinists at Andover.[23]

Timothy Dwight, a friend of the project who had helped to win over the New Divinity men, preached the dedication sermon in September 1808. He pointed out that the new seminary meant a change in the way ministers were to be instructed. No longer were they to study separately under different ministers, often becoming disciples of their instructors. Now they would study together under several professors, receiving a common education. Such an education, as an article in the *Panoplist* had argued, would tend to heal the kind of division that was fostered by their studying under and forming loyalties to different teachers. The seminary did, in fact, work to produce a new kind of minister in the nineteenth century, the evangelical. Andover trained men who could cooperate and who were adept in helping the church to keep pace with national development because of their ability to conduct the work of the benevolent societies, which were becoming so important in American religious life.[21]

The price of this new spirit of cooperation and harmony was the loss of that theological rigor and even the concern for precise theology that had been so important in the eighteenth century and that, though it had divided the clergy into different camps, had made for rigorous works of theology like

139

those of Jonathan Edwards. In this way, despite the concessions made to the New Divinity party in establishing the seminary, the kind of education provided there tended to
undermine that sect, to which precise theology was so important. Andover produced ministers who tended to be eager
and energetic defenders and promoters of orthodoxy rather
than perspicacious theological thinkers—men more like Jedidiah Morse than Nathanael Emmons.

United now at Andover, the orthodox forces began to lay
plans to carry the battle to Boston, the center of liberalism. In
a gesture that was intended to show that they considered
themselves members of a national orthodox community, they
chose Edward Dorr Griffin, a New Jersey Presbyterian, to be
one of the seminary's professors. One of the most effective
revivalist preachers in the nation, Griffin was also to be associate pastor of a new orthodox church in Boston. Morse and
the other ministers who conceived of this scheme hoped that
Griffin's preaching would put liberalism into decline. Nothing
came of this hope. Park Street Church was dedicated in 1810,
but because an installed minister could not be attracted,
Griffin had to give up the Andover professorship and devote
all his energies to the church, which badly needed a settled
minister just to sell its pews and meet its debts. Griffin's settlement did little to revive the church, and in 1815 he left it to
return to his old New Jersey congregation.[25]

The orthodox offensive movement centered on Park Street
Church was not openly declared. It could not be for several
reasons, one of which was political. With the imposition of the
embargo in 1807, Federalists of both liberal and orthodox
religious persuasions once more felt the need to close ranks as
Democratic-Republican commercial policy began to take its
toll on the New England economy. Politics checked religious
debate, though it could not dispel the hostility between liberals
and orthodox. Daniel Chaplin, an orthodox minister, in his
sermon before the Convention of Congregational Ministers in
1808, inveighed against those who left orthodox doctrines out
of their preaching: "'How many pervert and corrupt the pre-

cept of the law and the doctrine of the covenant, by their partial, superficial, and erroneous instruction; and cause men to
stumble, by their wicked examples!'" Having made this point,
he caught himself and called for a spirit of conciliation among
ministers who differed on doctrinal issues. They had to avoid
the bitter spirit that prevailed in politics. It was essential that
they present a united front against the forces of infidelity. In a
sermon in 1809, John Foster, a liberal, urged that the clergy,
instead of fighting among themselves, "stand in our lot with
firmness, and direct our united energies to the improvement
and salvation of our beloved country." Their Federalism and
extreme fears once again inflamed, both liberals and orthodox
were alarmed that the Democratic-Republicans, if unopposed,
would bring ruin to the United States.[26]

Another reason there was not an open campaign was because many, maybe even most, of the Congregational clergy in
Massachusetts dreaded controversy and its potential effects.
Liberals were committed to avoiding debate, and many orthodox ministers believed that neither religious faction would
benefit from it. It would only lower public esteem for the clergy and weaken regard for religious institutions. Many Congregational ministers felt that the sectarians stood to gain the
most from it. Controversy might even lead to disestablishment, and support of the parish laws was still one thing upon
which almost all the clergy agreed. Then too, the eighteenth-
century ideal of ministerial fellowship between all the members of the Standing Order in an area still held a good deal of
power for ministers who enjoyed friendly meetings in their associations. Morse even continued until 1811 to attend meetings of the Boston Association of Minsters, though almost all
members were liberals. Even after then, he continued to exchange pulpits with John Lathrop, who was unorthodox but
with whom he had been in fellowship since 1789. Other ministers, less committed to the public defense or orthodoxy than
Morse, also tended to ignore religious differences for the sake
of friendship.[27]

For these reasons, public religious debate did not advance

far, though that did not prevent growing distrust and suspicion between the two factions. The two sides did not do much more than express positions they had stated during the controversy about Ware's election in the winter of 1804/1805. Liberals did not preach against orthodox doctrine; they simply left it out of their preaching. Instead they preached what Ware called the "clear doctrines and plain duties" of the Gospel, especially emphasizing morality. Liberal ministers also spoke of the need for toleration and forbearance and warned against the introduction of creeds and confessions of faith to the Massachusetts churches.[28]

Orthodox spokesmen continued to condemn the liberal practice of excluding orthodox doctrines from their preaching. Morals, they argued, should be preached in connection with doctrine. Samuel Worcester contended that "the moral and social virtues are to be represented as genuine in the sight of Heaven, only when they spring from a heart renewed by divine grace, and purified by the faith of the gospel." The orthodox also rejected the liberal conception of toleration, claiming that it meant ignoring religious opinions believed erroneous and even disastrous for Christianity. Some defended the use of creeds at Andover seminary and within the recently formed General Association of Massachusetts, contending that they were useful as concise expressions of the meaning of Scripture, which provided a clear basis for union among Christians.[29]

Despite this limited debate, the Congregational clergy were careful to make a public show of solidarity. In 1808, after the orthodox won the struggle to have Joshua Huntington chosen the colleague pastor at Boston's Old South Church, three liberal ministers participated in his ordination, at which Morse delivered the sermon. The same year, William E. Channing, one of those liberals, preached the ordination sermon for John Codman, an outspoken Calvinist, at the Second Church in Dorchester. Orthodox and liberals also participated in Horace Holley's ordination at Boston's Hollis Street Church in 1809. Joseph Eckley, an orthodox minister, called on Holley to strive in his preaching at establishing a *"radical change of heart"* among his congregation, not just "external morality." John Lathrop, in delivering the charge to Holley, spoke of the need to keep peace with his fellow ministers.[30]

Concern for maintaining peace among the clergy was not limited just to the Boston area. It won the *Christian Monitor* broad support among the Massachusetts clergy. The *Monitor* was established by a group of liberal ministers in the Boston area in an effort to counteract the *Panoplist*'s attempt to organize the orthodox. It was a liberal publication in the sense that it left controversial questions out of its pages and sought to smooth over doctrinal differences among the clergy. "If we agree in the *experience* of religion," the *Monitor* asked in its preface, "is it so essential, as some think, that we unite in the belief of the same doctrines and observance of the same exterior rites?" This magazine enjoyed support among more than just the liberal clergy. More than 150 Massachusetts clergymen aided it in getting subscriptions. One of them was Joseph Lathrop, minister in West Springfield, who was a leader of the Old Calvinist party and who had been offered the Yale professorship of divinity in 1793. In July 1805 Lathrop had written Morse that he feared controversy between the *Panoplist* and the *Monitor*; "they might soon become merely polemical & operate to excite disaffection in the clergy toward one another & prejudices in the minds of the people against that order of men." It would be best, he thought, if the two united "in supporting the common cause against the common adversary; & . . . would contend earnestly for the faith delivered to the saints."[31]

Lathrop was not indifferent to liberalism. In a sermon of 1808 he called it a "damnable" heresy to deny redemption through Christ and to represent salvation as a reward for practicing morality. He also thought that something should be done to prevent unorthodox men from being licensed to preach. Still, like many other orthodox ministers, he was restrained from acting because he feared damaging the position of both the clergy and religion.[32]

Despite these powerful reasons for curtailing controversy, the differences between the two factions were so deep that they prodded some into actions and accusations that embittered relations between liberals and orthodox. Relatively small groups on both sides pressed the issue. Among the orthodox there were Morse and the other men involved with the *Panoplist* and the General Association of Massachusetts, and among the liberals there were the young ministers associated with the *Anthology* and later *The General Repository*. Each group saw, in the writings and actions of the other, justifications for its own acts.

Liberals were most upset by the formation of the General Association in 1802 and the efforts of its supporters to extend its power and influence in the state. Morse was one of its most active supporters. Ever since his settlement in Charlestown, he had been concerned with reforming and strengthening Massachusetts's ecclesiastical structure. Morse was familiar with and admired both the Connecticut associational and the Presbyterian systems. He thought both of them superior to the ecclesiastical forms in Massachusetts, where the local associations were not united in a statewide association and did little but bring the clergy together for social meetings. He complained that as a result there was no order or harmony among the churches and that they differed greatly in practice and doctrine. Morse tried to work for reform in the Convention of Congregational Ministers but accomplished nothing. In 1792 and 1794 he conceived plans, not acted upon, for those ministers who favored reform to establish their own organization.[33]

Morse wanted to introduce the Connecticut system of a general association and consociations to Massachusetts. He believed that a stronger ecclesiastical structure would make possible the implementation of Old Calvinist practices and make for a broad, inclusive church, loosely affiliated with other denominations in the United States. These reforms were not directed solely at liberals, nor were they acceptable to a large segment of Massachusetts's orthodoxy who, as Congregationalists, disliked Presbyterianism and its close approximation in Connecticut.[34]

Morse did believe that part of reform should consist of establishing uniformity of doctrine, and this became a greater concern as his fear of liberalism grew. He wanted the revived associations to pay closer attention to the sentiments of the candidates they licensed to preach and the ministers they ordained. They should refuse to license or ordain the unorthodox. In addition, the introduction of consociationism to Massachusetts would enable the ministers in a local association to meet and rule on matters involving the churches within the association. Morse approved of a consociation trying an unorthodox minister and dismissing him from his pulpit, even if the great majority of his members and congregation supported him.[35]

Morse could do little to promote ecclesiastical reform in the 1790s with attention focused on politics. In 1803, encouraged by the revival of consociationism in Connecticut and especially by the formation of the General Association of Massachusetts by five associations in the western part of the state the previous year, he decided it was time to act. He was willing to go slowly and was not then particularly concerned about liberalism because he believed that its growth had been checked. He worked out a plan for the Convention of Congregational Ministers at its meeting in May 1804 to create a committee composed of Arminian, Old Calvinist, and New Divinity ministers. (Before his fears about an aggressive Unitarian threat were excited, he correctly regarded these as the three main groups within Massachusetts Congregationalism.) Morse hoped that the committee members would realize the need for change and in a spirit of compromise would agree on reforms that would include the participation of all the local associations in the General Association. The convention, however, appointed a committee that was limited in its duties to sounding out the local associations and reporting back on its findings. Only fifteen of the twenty-four associations bothered to respond, and only seven of those fifteen favored participation in the General Association. Consequently, nothing came out of the convention at its next meeting in May 1805. By that time, Morse was immensely alarmed by Ware's election and enter-

tained wild plans, which were not acted upon, for the orthodox to impose the General Association on the convention and
force the liberals to secede if they would not go along.[36]

Morse had to be content with building up the General Association, which he now regarded as a means of checking liberal
growth, without the support of the convention. He promoted
this cause in the *Panoplist,* which carried a series of articles that
called for the orthodox clergy's participation in the association. Union among the orthodox was essential to stay the influence of unorthodox clergy as well as to correct the lapse in
church discipline and the want of attention to the baptism and
education of children.[37]

There was no rush by orthodox ministers to join the General Association. Both Nathanael Emmons and Joseph Lathrop
opposed it. Emmons opposed any infringement on the congregational liberties of the churches, and Lathrop believed that
the association would be inclined toward heavy-handed methods and would create division without aiding orthodoxy.[38]

Still, the association gradually won increasing support, and
by 1811, eleven associations participated in it. One of these
was the Union Association, formed that year by Morse and
other orthodox ministers who had belonged to largely liberal
associations in four eastern Massachusetts counties. They
formed the new association so that they could join the General
Association. Morse had considered this action but delayed taking it for three years, hoping that the convention would finally
support the association and spare him the necessity of breaking off from the Boston Association. Though Morse had spoken of the need for separation since 1805, especially when he
was particularly alarmed by the liberals, he also had a linger-
ing hope that satisfactory reforms could be achieved without
creating a schism in Massachusetts Congregationalism.[39]

Liberals regarded the General Association as part of an
orthodox campaign, which included the *Panoplist,* Andover
seminary, and Park Street Church, to introduce an orthodox
creed to the Massachusetts churches and to brand as heretics
those who would not accept it. Two episodes in Connecticut,

where liberalism was almost nonexistent but where the orthodox used consociations to stamp it out altogether, greatly influenced the liberal view.[40]

In 1804 a local association in Connecticut voted to break off fellowship with John Sherman of Mansfield when it learned that he had rejected the doctrine of the Trinity. As a result of the association's act, some of Sherman's church members called on it to convene as a consociation and try him. Realizing then that he could not retain his pulpit, Sherman and his supporters in the parish invited nine ministers, seven of them from Massachusetts, to hear his case. Five of these men served on the ex parte council. It voted for Sherman's dismissal because of the division in the church but recommended him as a preacher to other churches. It also urged the Mansfield church to resist the spirit of contention which it said the association had provoked.[41]

A similar but much more widely publicized case occurred in 1811 when some members of Abiel Abbot's church in Coventry, Connecticut, appealed to the local association to try their minister for heresy. Abbot and the majority of the parish were willing to call a mutual council, but they objected to trial by the consociation because neither the church nor Abbot had ever recognized its authority. Still, on rather dubious evidence of the church being under its authority, the consociation tried and dismissed Abbot. Refusing to honor this decision, Abbot and the society called an ex parte council of ten Massachusetts ministers, seven of whom served on the council in June 1811 and voted his dismission, but only because of the division in the church. It refused to rule on Abbot's opinions, contending that no ecclesiastical body had that right. The council called on Christians not to attempt to impose creeds on their brethren and urged that they make belief in the Gospel the only basis of fellowship.[42]

Massachusetts liberals took the extraordinary step of intervening in the ecclesiastical concerns of Connecticut because they agreed with Abbot that a movement was in progress in all New England to introduce creeds and consociations. It was being attempted in the name of their Puritan ancestors but in violation of the principles of those reformers who had asserted the primacy of scriptures and had committed themselves to the search for greater truth. Consociationism was ecclesiastical tyranny. Instead of "a pope in one man," Abbot said of Connecticut, "we have a pope in many."[43]

By 1810, concerned orthodox ministers, however, were convinced of a liberal campaign to spread their influence. That year the *Panoplist* warned that liberals were trying to propagate Socinianism, the most extreme of Unitarian views, in New England. It argued this after Eliphalet Porter preached a sermon before the convention in which he contended that Christianity consisted in faith in one God and in Jesus as the Christ and in acceptance of his moral precepts. Opinions about the doctrines of original sin, total depravity, moral inability, the Trinity, Christ's nature, or the workings of the Holy Spirit would neither gain one salvation nor bar one from it. In reviewing this sermon, the *Panoplist* insisted that it was related to other efforts in the past several years to promote Socinianism. It pointed to the preparation by the Brattle Street Church in 1808 of a hymnal that left out orthodox doctrine, as did a collection of psalms assembled the next year by William Emerson of the First Church. The magazine also charged that two recently published editions of the Old and New Testaments, which were sponsored by liberals, were part of this plan. Both, the *Panoplist* contended, contained erroneous, unorthoox refrences to Jesus. It went on to charge that a conspiracy was taking place: the "dagger is concealed, until the object of assault appears unarmed and unsuspecting, or it is drawn only as pressing danger imperiously demands it." The magazine challenged the liberals to declare their full, unreserved beliefs.[44]

That would have been difficult for the liberals to do. By 1812, both orthodox and Unitarian church historians agree, most of the Boston clergy were Arians. They did not believe in the doctrine of the Trinity, but unlike Socinians, they still believed that Jesus was a divine person whose death played a role in the pardon of sin. Above all, their opinions were unsettled, and they were unprepared to engage in a debate in which they would have to defend them. Most were content to omit or treat vaguely doctrines about which they had grown unsure.[45]

There was, however, a small group of young ministers involved with the *Anthology* who pursued a more aggressive course. In 1808 Joseph S. Buckminster began promoting liberal versions of the Bible, and Samuel C. Thacher led the attack on the orthodox for seeking ecclesiastical domination. These efforts convinced many of the orthodox that liberals were conducting a surreptitious attack on them while pleading for toleration and trying to evade an open statement of their religious beliefs. Then too, the often-snide tone of the *Anthology*, its carping over the literary style of orthodox publications, angered the orthodox.

John S. J. Gardiner, the Episcopalian president of the Anthology Society, came to agree with the orthodox. He resigned his membership in the society in 1810, perhaps because of the magazine's endorsement of Griesbach's Greek Testament and the Improved Version of the New Testament. On Christmas he preached a sermon in defense of the Trinity, and in June 1811 he warned that Unitarians were tying to spread their beliefs in the state by ridiculing Trinitarians and by claiming that all men of learning shared their sentiments. Their professions of candor and charity, he insisted, were hollow: "The candour of an Unitarian resembles the humanity of a revolutionary Frenchman. It is entirely confined to words."[46]

In May 1812 Morse preached the sermon before the convention of Congregational Ministers and argued that Christian charity and fellowship rested on belief in orthodox doctrine, clearly implying that it would be legitimate for the orthodox to break off from the liberals. Morse, however, did not pursue that point, did not call for separation and the end of fellowship between the two broad factions. Certainly the theological differences and the bitter feelings between the two were by now sufficient to bring about separation, but the political situation and the approaching war still prevented Morse from pressing for this drastic action.[47]

The limited struggle between liberals and orthodox continued during the war. Some of the orthodox in their Fast and Thanksgiving Day sermons even alluded to Unitarianism as one of the sins for which the nation was being punished with war. Samuel Taggart warned in July 1812 that infidelity was changing its outward form:

> If the crude, absurd, and vulgar blasphemies of Thomas Paine will not pass current, it can assume a milder form, and insinuate as much of its poison as possible, under the name of liberal, rational and catholic christianity; liberal to every class of opinion only to the truth as it is in Jesus. And whoever impartially examines some of the popular opinions in vogue, under the name of christian doctrines, will find little else in them than infidelity in disguise.

In the opening address to its ninth volume in June 1813, the *Panoplist* said that liberal doctrines had to be resisted, that they were being "zealously propagated from the press and the pulpit," leading some "in the downward road to perdition."[48]

By this time the *Anthology* no longer existed. The Anthology Society stopped publishing the magazine in June 1811 because it lacked the funds to employ an editor and had lost a number of members, some like Buckminster, to death. The *Anthology's* place was filled in January 1812 by another liberal publication, *The General Repository,* which was edited by Andrews Norton. Now it defended the liberals, contending that the charges in the *Panoplist* were part of an effort to spread the dominion of "Andoverian Calvinists" throughout the state.[49]

The *Repository* proved, however, not to be a satisfactory instrument for the liberals' defense. Its articles tended to be too academic, too harsh in language, and as the *Panoplist* suggested, too Socinian in religious outlook for most members of the liberal party. In July 1812, for example, the magazine contained an article that denied the deity of Jesus. The majority of liberals were at most Arians and did not want to be identified with the more extreme Unitarian view that Jesus was merely human. The *Repository* continued through October

1813, but in May 1813 *The Christian Disciple,* a new liberal publication, appeared in Boston.[50]

Some liberal ministers, fearful that the orthodox planned to introduce creeds and consociations to Massachusetts, decided that their cause required a more popular publication than the *Repository.* The main purpose of *The Christian Disciple,* William E. Channing explained, was to contend for Christian liberty and the independence of the churches: "Our great desire is to preserve our fellow-Christians from the systematic and unwearied efforts which are making to impose on them a *human creed* and to infuse into them angry and bitter feelings towards those who differ from them."[51]

*The Christian Disciple* differed greatly in tone and content from the *Repository.* Though it vigorously insisted on the primacy of Scriptures and argued against creeds, it did not attack or ridicule orthodox doctrine. Nor did it print pieces stressing liberal views. In many ways it was similar to orthodox religious magazines, carrying articles on the importance of family religion and other practical topics. This magazine and the effort to preserve peace and fellowship among the liberals and orthodox could do nothing, however, to change the basic differences between the two factions, which were kept unexpressed only by the pressures of wartime.

By 1814, not even the war prevented Morse from calling for separation. He made this call when he published *An Appeal to the Public.* In it he disclosed his controversy with Hannah Adams, which he insisted liberals had stirred up in order to destroy his reputation and effectiveness because of his opposition to Ware's Harvard professorship in 1805. This controversy, like the earlier painful episode caused by Christoph Ebeling's letter about the Illuminati, reveals a good deal about Morse's personality.

The publication in 1804 of *A Compendious History of New England,* which Morse wrote with Elijah Parish, minister in Byfield, Massachusetts, gave rise to the controversy. The book's appearance alarmed Adams, who had published a longer, more expensive history of New England in 1799. An unmarried woman who earned her living from her writings, she feared that the new history would undermine the sales of her published work and prevent the success of an abridged edition she planned to write. She spoke to Morse shortly after his book was published, but, a timid person, she did not speak openly of her concern and did not ask for redress. Instead, she reminded him of her previous work in the field, said that she planned to prepare a shorter version, and asked if he minded. Morse did not sense her hidden meaning and told her that he had no objections to her publishing an abridged edition. A few weeks later, however, he conveyed to her Parish's concern that her new history might interfere with their book's sales and Parish's threat that they might have to issue a shorter, cheaper edition. Adams wrote to Parish, explained to him that her only income consisted of her books' sales and in turn received a cordial reply in which Parish said that he had not understood her circumstances and retracted his threat.[52]

In December 1804, after disposing of the copies of the first edition of their book, Morse and Parish made arrangements for a second, somewhat shorter edition to be printed the next year. When Adams learned of this in July 1805, as she prepared to have her abridgment published, she became alarmed that they meant to block the sales of her book and complained to her friends, who included influential religious liberals. One of them, Stephen Higginson, Jr., a member of one of Massachusetts's leading Federalist families, became her spokesman. He approached Morse and persuaded him not to publish the new edition in 1805. Morse, however, did not agree that he owed Adams anything, and in 1808 he and Parish made arrangements for the printing of the second edition the next year.[53]

This caused rumors of Morse's cruelty to Adams, which had been started in 1805, to be repeated. In October 1805 the *Monthly Anthology* had reviewed both *A Compendious History* and Adams's abridged history and said hers was the superior book. William Emerson, the anonymous reviewer, also accused Morse and Parish of having tried to supplant Adams's abridgment. They replied in the *Anthology* that they had not tried to do so, that they had not even known that she planned to write one until their book had been published. Again writing anonymously, Emerson said that Morse, with his many abridged editions, should have assumed that she too planned one and that, in any case, he and Parish had tried to dissuade her from publishing it when they did learn of her plans. If they were concerned about their reputations, he advised them to give her the profits from *A Compendious History,* along with the copyright.[54]

Because of the recurrence of such charges, Morse asked Higginson in December 1808 to submit the matter to a body of referees. Morse supplied a list of men, all Federalists and mostly liberals, from which Higginson picked the three referees. He selected liberals. Both Parish and Dwight advised Morse against submitting to a tribunal of liberals, fearing that they would be prejudiced. Morse explained that he had chosen liberals because he thought their decision clearing him would carry greater weight. Perhaps Morse believed that common Federalism would prevail over religious animosities. Maybe he was exposing himself to a decision which he could call unfair and label an instance of liberal persecution.[55]

The referees heard the two sides in April 1809. Higginson's attorney said that the publication of the new edition of *A Compendious History* was the execution of the threat Parish had made in 1804, and he urged the referees to rule that the profits should go to Adams. Morse contended that he had erred only in forwarding Parish's sentiments to her in 1804 instead of writing to him and resolving the problem as she subsequently did. He and Parish, however, had never promised not to publish future editions of their work, and they did not owe her that favor in 1808 after she had allowed herself to be used by their enemies, who spread insulting charges about them.[56]

The referees ruled that Morse and Parish, as everyone agreed, had violated no legal right of Hannah Adams. Still, because of her preoccupation with the subject and her financial situation, she had deserved consideration from anyone planning a similar book liable to diminish her profits. The referees called for Morse and Parish to hold back their book from sale until they made "reasonable offers of compromise" to her.[57]

Morse refused to end the matter by making Adams an offer of compensation and saying that he had intended no injury. Instead he pursued a course of action which exposed him to more just criticism than the original charges, which had turned on the moot question of whether he should have anticipated that Adams would prepare an abridged edition and what regard that entitled her to. He chose to ignore the obvious meaning of the award, informing Adams of his willingness to meet with her to make offer of compromise but that these would not include pecuniary compensation. She refused to meet with him, and he considered the matter at an end, contending that he had fulfilled the terms of the award.[58]

Morse probably reacted this way because he could not easily admit mistakes, even unintentional ones, and the liberal attack to which he had been exposed certainly did not dispose him to do so. It also was in keeping with his character to distort the meaning of the award to justify himself, just as he had distorted the meaning of Ebeling's letter to him in 1799.

Morse's response to the award did not ease his anxiety. He remained extremely upset by the charges against him, so distraught that he traveled to South Carolina, where he spent the winter of 1809/1810. In 1812 he complained that the rumors still circulated. He considered making a public statement on the controversy and charging liberals with persecuting him, but his friends persuaded him to hold off. The next year, two allusions, which did not mention his name, to his "ungenerous and dishonorable" treatment of Hannah Adams appeared in *The General Repository,* and these severely disturbed him. His friends insisted that he exaggerated the problem. Moses Stuart, a professor at Andover, wrote him that "the evil apprehended from it is magnified in your imagination a thousand fold at least. It deserves no more of distress—of anxiety—or attention." Stuart's assurances that the matter was little known is confirmed by the fact that William Bentley, who detested Morse and had friends in Boston, knew nothing of the controversy until Morse made it public.[59]

It was part of Morse's nature to exaggerate opposition to himself and to imagine that he was confronted by foes who meant to destroy him and his cause. He had reacted this way during the Illuminati controversy, and the reaction had bolstered his refusal to back off from his accusations. So he reacted again, refusing to accept the referees' judgment but not letting the matter end there. He pressed for vindication, writing the referees in March 1813 for their opinion on whether he had fulfilled the award. They replied that they had meant in the award that Adams deserved compensation. Not satisfied with this, Morse wrote them again in August, asking them to state how much he owed her and for what act on his part. The referees made a final, curt reply in October, repeating what they had said in the award. When he received this letter, he was trying to persuade Adams to submit the matter to a new arbitration, if they were unable to agree on the meaning of the award, as it was certain they could not. She refused.[60]

Morse decided to present his case to the public, first with a letter in the *Centinel* in March 1814 and then with his *Appeal* in May. He set out all the evidence in the nearly two hundred–page book and insisted that, despite the referees' explanation of the award, he had fulfilled it. He charged that liberals had used Adams's groundless charges to injure him because of his opposition to their taking control of Harvard. The effects of the liberal revolution there could be seen in the support which men associated with the college had given to the *Monthly Anthology, The General Repository,* and the Improved Version of the New Testament. A silent campaign was being conducted against orthodoxy, of which his persecution was but one part. Morse argued that not all liberals were bad men or aware of the conspiracy, just as he had argued that not all Democratic-Republicans were infidels and anarchists. He insisted, however, that most liberals were being misled by men who conspired to lead them gradually to Socinianism, just as he had insisted that the political opposition had been duped by a small band of leaders. Morse concluded his *Appeal* by urging the orthodox to separate from the liberals and insisting that they had to stop the spread of liberalism in order to preserve both true religion and the New England character which rested on it.[61]

Hannah Adams and John Lowell published replies to the *Appeal,* both of which made much of Morse's evasion of the spirit of the award. Lowell, who had been Timothy Pickering's lieutenant in calling for opposition to the war and whose father, as a member of the Essex Junto, had supplied Morse with material for his Thanksgiving Day sermon of November 1798, now likened him to a Democratic-Republican demagogue trying to whip up the lower classes with his accusations that Unitarians were a small, wealthy group engaged in a religious conspiracy. Sidney Morse, recently graduated from Yale, responded for his father. He argued that the existence of a liberal conspiracy was as certain as that of French influence over the national administration, something Lowell had argued in his antiwar pamphlets, though in neither case could specific evidence be cited. Lowell, he charged, had practiced the duplicity of a Jacobin, "a true Jacobin, according to the strict definition of the term, and we may add too, that the Unitarianism which he advocates is the genuine Jacobinism of Christianity." Thus Sidney Morse, who had published a tract calling on New Englanders to unite in opposition to the federal administration, attacked his fellow Federalist pamphleteer as a Jacobin, demonstrating that Federalist party unity was being stretched to the breaking point as religious differences rose to the fore.[62]

Morse received expressions of support from orthodox ministers throughout New England who agreed with him that he had been subjected to liberal persecution. Still, orthodox leaders would not go as far as Morse wanted and opposed his proposal that the *Panoplist* review the Hannah Adams controversy. They did not want to attach the orthodox cause too closely to Morse, no matter how genuinely they sympathized with him. In addition, the orthodox were not yet ready to call for separation. In the summer of 1814 the *Panoplist* did no more than report on a controversy that had taken place several years earlier at the Second Parish in Dorchester, where liberals in the congregation had opposed the refusal of John Codman, their minister, to exchange pulpits with liberal members of the Boston Association. Morse had cited that in the *Appeal* as another instance of liberal persecution.[63]

Peace finally allowed Morse to press for separation. In April 1815 he had a chapter printed from a British book, Thomas Belsham's *Memoir of the Life of Theophilus Lindsey.* Belsham and Lindsey were prominent British Unitarians who held far more radical theological opinions than the Massachusetts liberals. Most significantly, this chapter, which appeared as the pamphlet entitled *American Unitarianism,* contained a letter from William Wells to Belsham. Wells was a Boston bookseller and a member of the Anthology Society. In his letter, which was written in 1812, he said that liberal ministers did not preach openly but described liberalism "making a silent but rapid and irresistible progress" in the Boston area. Belsham mentioned the publication of the Improved Version and Griesbach's Greek Testament and also the *Anthology* and the *Repository* and claimed that all these aided liberalism's growth.[64]

In June 1815 Jeremiah Evarts, who had assumed editorship of the *Panoplist* in 1810, charged in the magazine that this pamphlet proved that liberals were engaged in a conspiracy. He insisted, as Morse had in his *Appeal,* that a small band of conspirators was attempting to lead the people to Socinianism by stealth. Evarts urged the orthodox to separate: "It is the reproach and sin of Massachusetts, that while all the orthodox, from Connecticut to Georgia, are unanimus in withholding communion from Unitarians, she is lagging behind and dallying with this awful and responsible subject. [65]

Liberal ministers, as Arians and not Socinians, were offended by these charges. William E. Channing responded for them in a pamphlet, and this led to a debate between him and Samuel Worcester. Morse hoped that this debate would persuade the orthodox of the need for separation. In his pamphlets Channing denied that the liberals were Unitarians in Belsham's sense of the term: Socinians who regarded Christ simply as a man who serves as a moral instructor to mankind. Nor had the liberals been guilty of hypocrisy or of anything to warrant attacks as heretics and demands for their excommunication. They preached what they read in the Bible, leaving aside difficult and abstruse "metaphysical" questions, like the Trinity, which were not central to the message of the Gospel. They looked to actions for indications of true Christianity rather than to the dogma professed.[66]

Worcester argued that liberals did not preach the real Gospel because they ignored Christ as the divine savior who made atonement for sinful men. This was the essence of Christianity. The orthodox must separate, lest they offend God and impair their own faith by maintaining fellowship with ministers who rejected these doctrines. Worcester fared better in this part of the debate simply because he expressed his own orthodox views and made much of the fact that Channing, aside from denying that his were the same as the religious sentiments of Joseph Priestley and Belsham, would not clearly state his position on the doctrines of the Trinity and the atonement.[67]

Channing was probably reluctant to state his views more openly because, as Wells had written Belsham in 1812, the liberals had little faith in the people: "It must be assumed as an axiom, that a persevering controversy upon this question, would render the multitude bigoted and persecuting Calvinists." Politics had convinced the liberals that the people would not choose wisely: "I have seen the contest between truth and falsehood, *before the multitude*; between every thing which is respectable and every thing which is detestable, so unequal in politics, that I dread the event in matters of religion." The liberals' best issue, Wells had also written, was their opposition to creeds, which some of the orthodox wanted to introduce to check the growth of liberalism, but which cost them the support of other orthodox ministers who feared and opposed such measures.[68]

While Channing and Worcester exchanged arguments, the General Association considered the question of introducing consociations to Massachusetts. In June 1814 it had created a committee, on which Morse served, which reported the next year in favor of consociations. Consociationism was to have been the capstone of the orthodox movement, following up on the success of the *Panoplist,* Andover seminary, and the benevolent societies. It was intended to facilitate separation by establishing clear lines between the two factions. The consociations were thereafter to check the future growth of liberalism. The General Association delayed deciding on the matter until June 1816, when it refused to endorse the plan because so many orthodox ministers opposed it.[69]

The effort to establish consociationism afforded Channing an opportunity to take the offensive, which he did in his final pamphlet. He argued that consociations were ecclesiastical courts which would rob the people of their congregational rights. Lowell made even stronger use of the issue by contending in two pamphlets, one of them entitled *Are You a Christian Or a Calvinist?* that the orthodox clergy was pushing forward a scheme of ecclesiastical tyranny. To such charges, Worcester replied unconvincingly that consociationism was not inconsistent with the Cambridge Platform, that it would even help "to revive congregationalism in its purity."[70]

By alarming some orthodox ministers, the attempt to establish consociationism may have slowed separation. Nonetheless, as the *Panoplist* said in reviewing the debate between Channing and Worcester, lasting attention had been directed to the question of which religious system a minister maintained. The debate gradually drew the liberals out to express what they did believe, not just what they did not. Channing's sermon in 1819 at the ordination of Jared Sparks in Baltimore is often called the first clear expression of American Unitarian beliefs. This sermon led to a second major debate, this time between Henry Ware, Jr. and Leonard Woods. It continued to spell out the differences between Unitarianism and orthodoxy. In this way the effects of the debate of 1815/1816 were gradual. Separation did not occur immediately, and it could not, because, given Massachusetts's ecclesiastical structure, separation was a matter of ministers acting individually to bring their ministerial exchanges and fellowship into conformity with their doctrinal beliefs. The process was so gradual that no precise date can be given for the separation between Massachusetts's orthodox and Unitarians, but clearly Morse had set it in motion. In time, separation did not take place, limiting Unitarianism to where it existed in eastern Massachusetts. Morse's campaign against liberalism was one phase of his work during the war. He was involved in many other activities less controversial but just as important for the shape of nineteenth-century evangelical Protestantism.[71]

# Chapter 6

## *Toward an Evangelical Union*

When war was declared against Britain in 1812, the great majority of Congregational ministers, orthodox and liberal, reacted with alarm. Many of them spoke out against it in special Fast Day sermons during the summer of 1812 and continued to condemn it until peace was finally attained. The orthodox clergy also responded to the conflict by pledging to extend the work of their benevolent societies. They committed themselves, too, to take action against behavior which ministers in New England had long condemned as sinful. In the long run, the clergy's work in the benevolent societies and the newly formed moral societies proved of greater significance than their opposition to the war. After the war, in the calm of the Era of Good Feelings, these efforts brought into existence a number of national societies and the full development of the antebellum benevolence empire.

Without breaking with the Federalist party, orthodox Congregationalists increasingly looked beyond it for support during the war. In the 1790s, Federalists had been their constituency, men who shared a common political outlook but who differed among themselves on religious issues. By 1812, because of the Second Great Awakening and growing orthodox concern about liberalism, these differences had grown

161

clearer and were regarded as more important than before. Moreover, the Awakening with its revivals and benevolent societies had helped to bring into being a distinct religious public among whom the orthodox clergy had labored after 1798. To this public—which included women as well as men, adolescents as well as adults—orthodox ministers appealed for continued support of the benevolence movement and for the new venture of moral reform. These ministers also became more and more aware that this religious public was confined neither to the Federalist party nor to New England but was national in scope. This perception influenced their activities during the war and induced them afterward to join with other denominations in national benevolent societies. Unlike the Federalist party, which had dug its political grave with its response to the War of 1812, orthodox Congregationalists were prepared in 1815 to ally themselves with other evangelicals in establishing their common religious and moral values in American society.

———— * ————

Almost all the Congregational ministers who preached Fast Day sermons during the summer of 1812 denounced the war. Very few of the many published sermons—no more than six —supported the war.[1] All the clergy believed that the conflict was a punishment for the nation's sins, but the antiwar ministers maintained that much of the required expiation should consist in opposition to the war, which they declared unjust and unnecessary. Most of the clergy concurred with the charges Morse made in his Fast Day sermon. He insisted that the war was unjust because it was not warranted by British conduct; it was offensive, not defensive in character. It also promised to cost the lives of many Americans and to impair even further the morals, already bad, of the rest. Morse and other ministers complained that it was especially wrong to make war on Britain, a nation that was doing more than any other to defend and propagate Christianity throughout the world. Most distressing of all, the war served only French interests and threatened to drive the United States into an alliance with France, which would have disastrous consequences. William E. Channing, a liberal, did not call France the Antichrist, as did some orthodox ministers; but he agreed with them that alliance with her would be "the worst of evils, threatening at once our morals, our liberty, and our religion."[2]

Most of the Congregational clergy were firm but restrained in calling for opposition to the war. They recommended that their congregations petition and speak against it, as they had the constitutional right to do. In tacit support of DeWitt Clinton, ministers also called on their people to elect new, more religious men who would put an end to the war. During the summer of 1812, New England was flooded with published antiwar sermons that served to promote Clinton's presidential candidacy.[3]

James Madison of course was reelected. Still, many ministers continued to preach against the war and its supporters,[4] often invoking the prospect of the United States going down to ruin with Antichristian France.[5] Clerical opposition to the war undoubtedly helped to win support for the calling of the Hartford Convention. As Nathanael Emmons declared in November 1813, several months before the convention was proposed in the Massachusetts legislature,

> the people have no occasion to disobey or rebel. Let them only say . . . that their countrymen shall not be slain, that war shall cease, that peace shall be restored, that commerce shall be encouraged and protected, and that every State in the Union shall be justly and impartially governed, and these desirable and most important events will speedily be brought about.[6]

Two young men, who helped Morse prepare the 1812 edition of *The American Universal Geography*, wrote antiwar essays which also built up support for the convention. These were his son Sidney Morse and Sereno Dwight, one of Timothy Dwight's sons. In their pamphlets, which originally were printed in newspapers in Massachusetts and Connecticut, the two argued that the war was but one of many measures hostile to northern interests which had been forced on the nation by the unfair power the South held in Congress. This power rested on slave representation and the admission of new slave states populated by relatively few free citizens. The admission of the new slave states had disrupted the sectional balance of power established in 1789, when the South was granted slave representation because the North had more states and as a result more senators. Northerners, threatening to leave the Union if balance were not restored, must demand either an end to slave representation or the consolidation of the slave states admitted since 1789.[7]

These concerns were reflected in the circular letter of January 1814, issued by a meeting of citizens in Northampton, Massachusetts, which called for a convention of the northern states. Many of the same problems were eventually addressed in some of the constitutional amendments recommended by the Hartford Convention in December 1814.[8] Morse had hoped that the fall of Napoleon would make possible a general peace, but the defeat of the French in 1814, an event celebrated in New England, was followed in the autumn by British naval attacks on New England coastal towns. As early as January 1814 Morse had tried to persuade some members of the state legislature of the need for the convention, feeling that if Massachusetts took "'bold & lofty ground; the other states will follow us.'" When the legislature approved the plan in October with no end of the war in sight and New England under attack, Morse wrote his father that the convention "is, under Providence, the source of my hope of salvation to our country. I hope all the N. Eng$^d$. states will unite in sending Delegates & that wisdom, firmness & energy will mark all their deliberations."[9]

New England, however, was not united. The legislatures in Connecticut, Massachusetts, and Rhode Island sent delegates, but those in New Hampshire and Vermont did not. Even within Massachusetts, a vocal Republican minority objected to the convention. Though the convention lacked the degree of support Morse hoped it would attract, he still looked forward to it. But he was not sure what action it should take and wrote his father in November that he hoped God would "guide this important body into right measures." Certainly Morse concurred with the delegates in the long list of grievances they issued. He probably also agreed with the minister who wrote him that, besides the convention's firmness, he liked its moderation, its not threatening secession, which would "disappoint the Kentuckians & other madmen." The convention vented frustrations, but it roused no hopes for an end to the war.[10]

When news of peace reached New England in February 1815, most of the Congregational clergy saw it as the work of God, as a gracious reprieve from deserved punishment, not as the result of American arms or New England's protest. William Wilberforce wrote in reply to a letter from Morse that he was particularly struck by his sense of God's providential workings in the "political World." Morse prayed that peace would "be improved by us so as that it may be a blessing indeed for us." In this prayer he joined with many other ministers who called on Americans to put aside sin and party spirit.[11]

A good beginning in a battle against sin had already been made during the war. In sermons delivered in the summer of 1812, many ministers insisted that the conflict had been brought about by American sins, especially intemperate drinking, Sabbath-breaking, profane swearing, and the election of irreligious men. This description of the moral condition of the nation was familiar, but the war gave it a new urgency, for the conflict threatened finally to align the United States with Antichristian France. That was a prospect the Federalist clergy had long feared and which to them promised the certain destruction of their country along with the other enemies of religion. Ministers argued that the dire situation of the nation called for reformation. In July 1812 the *Panoplist* insisted that "from national reformation alone can any confident expectations of national prosperity be made." Sermon after sermon proclaimed that only repentance and continued support of the missionary cause, the cause of Christ and his Church, could save the nation.[12]

The clergy acted not only on extreme fears but on the great hope, clearly expressed by Morse in a sermon before Boston's auxiliary society of the ABCFM and uttered by many other ministers during the war, that this war and the others of the past twenty years prepared the way for the millennial era of peace and universal Christianity. This too was a familiar point, one that had been made in the century sermons of 1801, and it too was lent new force by the War of 1812. As Deacon Morse wrote his son after reading an oration which had been delivered in July 1814, he was convinced that "the reign of democratic tyranny and delusion will speedily come to an end. A new era is commencing; a golden age of peace, & light and liberty is dawning upon the globe; and in spite of human policy; in spite of Satanic guile; the kingdoms of this world, are about to become the kingdoms of our Lord & Saviour."[13]

An important part of the clergy's efforts to reform Americans' behavior and so preserve the nation consisted of a crusade against intemperance, an evil ministers had long condemned but which they did not really act against until 1810. Intemperance by then was perceived to be a growing problem. It was increasing, and public authorities were doing little to stem the tide. As the *Panoplist* argued in February 1813, it

> has within the last twenty or thirty years swollen to a mighty flood . . . spreading over the face of the whole country, threatening to sweep away, in its course the strongest bulwarks of religion and government, together with the sentinels that should guard, and the arms that should defend them; and bearing on its fiery surges, a huge and frightful mass of wreck and desolation.

In addition, as Jeremiah Evarts had argued in the *Panoplist* in 1810, intemperance drained away large sums of money that could much better be spent in supporting religious and educational institutions, a claim given special force by the economic conditions of the times, which pressed hard on the benevolent societies.[14]

Several years before the war, the general associations of Connecticut and Massachusetts, in consultation with other ecclesiastical bodies in New England and the Presbyterian General Assembly, took up the problem. Connecticut's General Association in June 1812 made recommendations which the New England Congregational churches endorsed: Christians should give up the use of whiskey and rum, the only forms of alcohol with which reformers were concerned at that time; intemperance should be a subject of ministerial reproof and church discipline; and local societies should be formed to pressure officials to enforce the existing laws concerning the sale of alcohol. Besides insisting that intemperance involved the waste of much money, the *Panoplist's* articles and most sermons on the subject contended that the excessive drinking of spirits entailed the certainty of ultimate physical and moral ruin without serving any possible good. Reformers had little hope of reclaiming the intemperate, but they thought it crucial that the public be aroused and the laws enforced to curtail the evil.[15]

Moral socieities began to be formed throughout New England to combat intemperance. Such societies had existed in England at the close of the seventeenth century, and more recently they had been revived as part of the British evangelical movement led by men like Wilberforce, with whom many American ministers corresponded. In the United States Nathanael Emmons in 1790 and Lyman Beecher in 1803 had established moral societies in their parishes. These were the only ones, until alarm over the great increase of intemperance and war-bred concern over sin spurred the orthodox to emulate the well-known example of their fellow evangelicals in Britain.[16]

In 1813, two statewide moral organizations were formed, the Massachusetts Society for the Suppression of Intemperance and the Connecticut Society for the Promotion of Good Morals. The most significant thing about these societies was that the Federalist Congregational ministers, who organized them, tried and succeeded in getting Democratic-Republicans and people of other denominations to support them. In part, they made this effort to reach beyond their party and their churches because of disenchantment with the Federalist party. Such disenchantment is not surprising in Massachusetts, where liberals comprised much of the Federalist leadership; it is perhaps more surprising that there was not outright rejection of such leaders. But unease and even disillusionment with the party existed among Congregational ministers in Connecticut, where orthodoxy was supreme. In 1811, when Federalist leaders refused to support the ministerial choice for the governorship—a man who was a firm friend to the ministers' religious and moral causes—because he might fare poorly with voters not in sympathy with those causes, the clergy felt shocked and betrayed. In their opinion, Federalist leaders, in their concern with winning elections, were acting almost as shamefully as Democratic-Republican politicians.[17]

The Congregational clergy's disappointment with their party was compensated, however, by their realization that a large part of the public endorsed their moral and some of their religious causes. In 1811 Beecher was almost amazed to discover that Democratic-Republicans and non-Congregationalists were providing ample support to the Connecticut Bible Society. Neither this perception nor their disatisfaction with the Federalist party brought on a revolution among the Congregational clergy. They continued to look with condescension on Democratic-Republicans and continued to believe Federalist principles the best, though they felt their party was not living up to them. Nor did support from Baptists and Methodists induce them to abandon their commitment to Congregational establishments. Still, during the war, Congregational ministers moved beyond their traditional base of support to enlist the general religious public in the campaign to impose evangelical moral standards in New England.[18]

Arch-Federalist that he was, Morse was even able to organize a local auxiliary to the Massachusetts society which included Democratic-Republicans and non-Congregationalists. No wonder, then, the confidence he expressed in addressing its members as he contended that, threatening as the specter of immorality was, such associations of citizens could shape public opinion and impress on elected officials their duty to enforce the laws rigorously.[19]

In the view of orthodox Congregationalists, moral societies were allied to benevolent associations in establishing order and countering the forces of irreligion. The two kinds of associations worked together "in one vast and flowing tide of influence to sweep away every thing, that may oppose evangelical morality and evangelical principles, and to fill the land with peace and righteousness." Claiming that intemperance had received a blow from which "there is reason to hope it will never recover," the *Panoplist* in January 1814 called for similar efforts in another cause: preventing the profanation of the Sabbath.[20]

Within Massachusetts both the General Association and the Convention of Congregational Ministers appealed to the state legislature on the matter, and this body in turn issued an address to the people on the importance of the Sabbath. The Christian public responded warmly to these calls. Throughout New England, county conventions of local moral societies were held to concert measures for enforcing the laws concerning the Sabbath. In an address before the moral society in Andover, Ebenezer Porter told the citizens that in two years they had prevented traveling on the Sabbath: "You said, the evil *shall cease*—and it *ceased*."[21]

Such success was possible because, at the urging of moral societies, officials in a number of towns prevented citizens of other counties from crossing through on the Sabbath, and they prosecuted offenders the same day, making punishment swift and sure. The Massachusetts Supreme Court declared these practices illegal in October 1814, which exasperated the moral reformers but did not end their work. William Bentley, who was not in sympathy with them, expressed great anger in his diary over a meeting of delegates from moral societies in Essex County in December 1814. He did not mention the Hartford Convention, which was meeting at the same time. That is perhaps surprising but appropriate, for the causes of the moral societies, unlike the proposals of the convention, had a long future ahead of them in nineteenth-century America in the form of the sabbatarian and temperance movements. If these causes did not have their precise origins in these New England societies, they certainly received a great impetus from them.[22]

The Christian public also provided the existing missionary soieties cordial support during the war. Contributions to the Misionary Society of Connecticut in 1814 exceeded those of 1812 by $700 despite the hardships of the war. With this money and other resources, the society spent $5,227 on missionaries in 1814, whereas it had spent only $2,560 in 1811. Similarly, both the Hampshire Missionary Society and the Massachusetts Missionary Society were spending significantly larger sums of money toward the end of the war than at the beginning. The ABCFM, which sent its first missionaries abroad during the war, enjoyed even greater support. Its contributions rose from $4,000 in 1812 to $10,000 in 1815.[23]

Most important, these societies' directors, ardent Federalists like Morse, conceived of their work in national terms. They clearly opted during the War of 1812 to convert the rest of the nation, not to lead away New England in secession. The national-minded character of the New England benevolent societies is best illustrated by their support of and response to the tours to the western and southern frontiers by John Schermerhorn and Samuel J. Mills in 1812/1813 and by Mills and Daniel Smith in 1814/1815. The first tour, which Morse helped organize, had been conceived before the outbreak of the war, as the societies prepared to extend their operations and braced themselves for the expected crisis.[24]

Schermerhorn's and Mills's report, published in 1814, described the deplorable western conditions: lack of educated ministers and much religious ignorance. The frontier areas contained some religious people who deserved assistance but many more immoral, irreligious people who ought to be converted and reformed. The report of the second tour, in calling for the sending of missionaries, Bibles, and tracts to the frontier, spoke of the unformed character of the people there and of the need for "Presbyterians" (in which Smith and Mills included Congregationalists) to unite in establishing a religious character among them. They could not leave the task to Baptists and Methodists, many of whose preachers, the authors said, were "exceedingly illiterate." "Christian America," the report concluded, must arise and act.[25]

These recommendations were bound to strike a responsive chord in Morse, who since the 1780s had been concerned about the formation of a national character and who for some time had hoped to see broader, truly national benevolent societies established. In 1814 the education society at Yale College issued an address, written by Beecher, Morse, and Evarts, that stressed the lack of settled, educated ministers in the United States, especially west of the Alleghenies, where, according to Schermerhorn and Mills, there were two million people and only 130 qualified ministers. The address called for a vast effort:

> The nation, all the pious and well-disposed part of the nation, must unite and engage sytematically and vigorously in this work of self-preservation. The evangelizing of the nation must not be a secondary object to any one. It must stand forth in all its magnitude, as the prominent object upon which all eyes are fixed; for which all hearts beat, and in which all hands are employed. A Bible for every family, a school for every district, and a pastor for every 1000 souls, must be the motto upon the standard, round which the millions who enjoy these blessings must rally for the purpose of extending them to those who do not.

Perhaps speaking out of experience with the Federalist party, the address asserted that only religion, no political party or program, could correct the national ills and establish peace

and happiness throughout the nation. Christianity was essential to make democracy safe, for, as the address stated, the
right of suffrage exercised by a man who does not feel the
restaints of the Gospel "will be a sword in the hand of a mani-
ac, to make desolate around him, and finally destroy himself."
Only a common ministry and common religious and educational institutions would make for a lasting union, "would produce a sameness of views, and feelings, and interests, which
would lay the foundation of our empire upon a rock. Religion
is the central attraction which must supply the deficiency of
political affinity and interest."[26]

These concerns, not abated by the war's end, led in October
1815 to the formation of the American Education Society,
nominally the first national benevolent society but really a regional society of New England Congregationalism. In the addresses delivered before the society in its early years, its
supporters explained that the frontier regions suffered either
from no religion or from defective sectarian preaching. The
American Education Society, pulling together the existing
local education societies as auxiliaries and calling on the Christian public to form others, sought to train educated ministers
for those areas, to prevent, as one minister said, the Mississippi from becoming as shrouded in ignorance as the
Ganges.[27]

It was to be some time before the American Education Society could provide ministers for the distant frontier. The New
England missionary societies, however, turned with increased
vigor to building up Congregationalism in New England, New
York, and Ohio, where they had long worked. The Missionary
Society of Connecticut did more in the southern and far western frontiers than any of the other societies, but even it concentrated a far greater proportion of its resources on the
older areas.

After the war, Congregational fear of infidelity was finally
receding. The missionary societies now regarded themselves
as competing with other denominations and no longer contending against infidels. Even in the West, the General Associ-

ation of Massachusetts reported in 1817, because of the work of their Presbyterian allies, "an open opposer of Christianity can now hardly be found." Clearly the battle was now to be waged against Baptists and Methodists. Forming churches and then benevolent societies in the older areas, the New England societies created a broad base from Maine to Ohio, which they hoped to enlist in evangelizing areas farther to the west and south.[28]

The postwar growth of the benevolence movement was aided by revivals taking place throughout the nation, bringing unprecedented numbers into the churches. In 1816 a minister in Connecticut reported that, though the people in his area had conceived of 1798/1799 as one of the grand eras of the church, now "it is believed, that in no single period of their history have they been visited with so many, so extensive, and so powerful revivals of religion, as they have witnessed during the year past."[29]

In trying to consolidate the benevolence movement where it existed and to extend it farther to the west, its organizers developed new methods to complement the familiar ones. The entire nation had to be reached, and this required new means of action. Acting as a religious entrepreneur, Morse did much to build up the evangelicals' arsenal. In 1814, before the war ended, he had established the New England Tract Society. It did not concern itself with distributing tracts; that, it left to local tract and other benevolent societies. Instead this society concentrated on producing mass quantities of tracts and establishing depositories where they could easily be obtained for distribution. Clearly, efficiency and organization were finding places within the benevolence movement.[30]

Morse also displayed his openness to innovation in his support of sabbath schools. These had long existed to the south of New England, especially in Pennsylvania. New Englanders, however, had been resistant, feeling that the home was the proper place for basic religious instruction of children, though they complained that many homes were failing in that role. When Ward Stafford, a young man Morse had befriended and encouraged to prepare for the ministry at Yale, proposed that Morse establish a sabbath school at his church, Morse complied. This school, which began in 1816, was the first linked to a Congregational church in Massachusetts and probably all New England. Soon the sabbath school, relying on women church members for its teachers and promoted by the postwar American Sunday School Union, became an accepted institution, the response to the long-deplored evil of neglect of religious instruction in the home.[31]

Stafford also felt that the rapid growth of America's cities made them proper missionary grounds for the church. With Morse's encouragement, he led the way in the new enterprise of urban missions with his work in New York City. In this way, too, Morse worked to broaden the benevolence movement and enable it to address the entire nation.[32]

Morse had, of course, long been aware of the value of effective means of communication. By 1816 he believed religious newspapers to be essential because, published more frequently than magazines like the *Panoplist,* they would provide quicker and broader dissemination of information on benevolent and moral societies. He persuaded his son Sidney to form the *Boston Recorder,* the first religious newspaper in the United States. Though its circulation grew steadily, Sidney had to give up the paper because it did not provide him an adequate income. It survived under another editor, however, and proved the idea of religious newspapers to be sound. It was soon followed by similar newspapers throughout the nation. One of them was the *New York Observer,* which Sidney and his brother Richard began publishing in 1823 and which soon became the nation's most widely circulated religious newspaper.[33]

The most important aspect of the postwar development of the benevolence movement was the establishment of national societies, and to this Morse also lent his support. Ever since he had entered the ministry, he had wanted orthodox Congregationalists to unite with other evangelicals in promoting their common goals. Before the war he had called for the formation of a national Bible society, arguing that one would be able to print Bibles more cheaply and also collect and disseminate information more efficiently than existing state and local societies could. Morse's hopes were finally fulfilled in 1816 when the American Bible Society was established in New York City. Morse served on the committee that drafted the constitution, and he took great pleasure in his work. He wrote his wife that "a unanimity among so mixed a body of all denominations of Christians, (Quakers & Catholics, among the rest,) so unexpected, perfect, & affectionate, had a surprising effect on the Convention, & drew tears of affectionate joy from many eyes." As Morse's words indicate, this was an interdenominational society. By 1816, though Congregationalists and Presbyterians still regarded Baptists and Methodists with condescension, they could all work together in distributing Bibles and tracts to advance their common faith, even while they competed with each other for church members with their missionary societies.[34]

By the mid-1820s the growth of local societies throughout the country had prepared the way for the formation of other national benevolent societies, and these the Morse brothers promoted in the *New York Observer*. The interdenominational American Tract Society was formed in New York City in March 1825; by June the New England Tract Society (then also called the American Tract Society) agreed to join the national society despite the fact that the headquarters would be in New York City. That was the price of greater efficiency, the major appeal of all national societies.[35]

In 1826 the middle-state United Foreign Missionary Society (UFMS), formed in New York City in 1817 by Presbyterians, Dutch Reformed, and Associate Reformed, merged with the Congregational ABCFM. Again, prospects of greater efficiency and a wider scope of action were the reasons for cooperation among these various denominations, whose religious differences were considered too slight to block close cooperation among them.[36]

The same year, the American Home Missionary Society (AHMS) was formed by these same denominations when various New England Congregational missionary societies joined with New York's United Domestic Missionary Society, which, like the UFMS, had been established after the war by Presbyterians, Associate Reformed, and Dutch Reformed. The belief that only a national society, not the existing regional ones, could provide the western settlements with the educated ministers essential for establishing religious institutions, induced a group of New England ministers to call for the formation of the AHMS, even though the headquarters of this society was also to be in New York City.[37]

Thus, at the time of Morse's death in June 1826, his long-sought goal of a coalition among the educated, Calvinistic clergy had been effected, although, in truth, he and many other Congregationalists were by then only nominally Calvinistic. This clerical alliance, which stretched from New England to Ohio, was advancing farther west and even reached into Virginia, with pockets of support scattered in the deeper South. The alliance was the culmination of those efforts, given great impetus by the war, at making a systematic, organized attempt to provide Bibles, ministers, and schools for all Americans.

As a result of these efforts, the orthodox Congregational clergy in general evinced, by the 1820s, an enterpreneurial outlook much like Morse's. He had always shown a high regard for efficiency and scope of operation, reporting enthusiastically on new inventions and improvements in transportation in his geographical writings. These sped the economic development of the nation, which he regarded as a beneficent process. As one of the New England Tract Society's addresses stated and as Morse believed, the early nineteenth century was an "age of ingenuity," an age of discovery, when Christians should emulate the mechanic and manufacturer in developing new and better ways of spreading the Gospel message.[38]

Morse had always been temperamentally inclined to express his faith in action, and an activist temper came to prevail among the Congregational clergy in general. These ministers believed that action based on system and organization and

aided by technology would soon bring about the evangelization of the world. Their belief in the value of efficiency and
organization was of course the reason they united in national
associations. One minister called "the *associating* plan, that
moral *lever,* by which . . . mighty movements are accomplished; that instrument by which Christianity puts forth some
of its best energies . . . [It is] a kind of modern invention . . .
Barren speculations, indolent sensibilities and wishes give
place to lofty enterprises and vigorous exertions."[39]

As these words suggest, the clergy, as they grew more concerned with action and organization, grew uncomfortable with
even suspicious of abstract thought. Falling under the sway of
Scottish commonsense philosophy, which was working its way
into the American college curriculum as the antidote to both
philosophical skepticism and radical social and political doctrines, ministers endorsed what they called "Baconian philosophy." This, ministers said, concerned itself only with
experience, observation, and fact and eschewed metaphysics.
Metaphysical abstractions, one minister warned, had given rise
to skepticism and then social ruin in France. On the other
hand, a restricted philosophy—by which the clergy sometimes
meant no more than technology—which did not go beyond
the teachings of Christianity or common sense, greatly benefited mankind by producing such inventions as the printing
press and the steamboat, instruments that also enabled missionary societies to keep pace with American growth.[40]

The clergy's confidence in technology was so strong that, at
times, it sounded stronger than their faith in Christian moral
exertion. Sidney and Richard Morse, both graduates of Andover seminary, argued in the *New York Observer* that "as science advances . . . many of those vices, which in spite of all the
efforts of Christians and philanthropists, have been for ages
spreading desolation over the earth will finally vanish at the
touch of some simple improvement in the arts." They went on
to propose that if grapes could be grown inexpensively in the
United States, they could be used to produce cheap wine and
in that way help end the consumption of whiskey. (This was

written before the rise of total abstinence within the temperance movement.) They were suggesting that technology could succeed where moral reform failed.[41]

The clergy's activist spirit developed at the expense of concern with theology and theological consistency. The new mood was evident in the *Panoplist,* which argued that, because it was most important to convert people, the minister should leave "metaphysical divinity" in his study and should follow in the pulpit the example of the "traveling Methodist." Addressing the heart rather than the head, the preacher should "exhibit the simple testimony of the Scriptures, as addressed to common sense, and press the appalling, heart-rending doctrines there inculcated, upon the conscience and the heart." This evangelical concern with winning souls caused the theology of orthodox Congregationalism to take the shape it did. In the search for a "preachable Gospel," some ministers, like Nathaniel William Taylor and Lyman Beecher, consciously played down certain elements of Calvinism. Others, like Morse, simply let the concerns and weapons of the benevolence movement shape the religious message they delivered. The Arminianism implicit in the revival and also in the widely distributed tracts and magazines, stressed human ability at the expense of strict Calvinistic views. Though a minority of orthodox Congregationalists, especially New Divinity ministers, resisted this trend, most gave scant attention to the theological ramifications of their preaching. Sereno Dwight, great-grandson of Jonathan Edwards, reflected the mood of the majority when he expressed the belief that theological speculation was coming to an end. To him this was a happy prospect because then all energies could be devoted to what was most important, evangelizing the world.[42]

Orthodox ministers saw signs all about them that the evangelization of the world would soon be accomplished and the millennial day soon dawn. They believed the economic forces transforming American society, the ever-expanding market system and the emerging industrial order, were forwarding these ends. Like Morse, they greatly admired the technological advances of their day, especially in communications and transportation, realizing how these made it easier to spread their evangelical message. Moreover, the entrepreneur's innovative methods were models for them to emulate in their work of shaping opinion and organizing the public. They were also convinced that the result of economic development would be higher material conditions than man had ever known before, and this too they linked to the coming of the millennium. As early as 1793 Samuel Hopkins had predicted that material abundance would prevail during that happy era. There was broad consensus among the clergy in the 1820s that economic development was realizing part of their millennial expectations of the future.[43]

There were other reasons why ministers were receptive to the new economic order. To them, economic development was a sign of a vigorous, progressive, and morally improving society. New England ministers believed that economic enterprise was part of the legacy handed down by their worthy Puritan forefathers. Proud of the role commerce had long played in New England life, they welcomed the factory as a new force in the economy. The idea of a simple agrarian order held little appeal for them. This is not to say that they imagined that the factory would bring with it the squalid urban slums which it did. Rather, they supported a mixed economy as part of a well-rounded program of both economic and cultural development. To the clergy, industrialization promised to help draw Americans into a truly national community. Linked together by economic and cultural ties, they would enjoy a richness of life far above that of subsistence farmers scattered across isolated frontiers.[44]

In addition, the clergy supported industrialization because they saw it in the prospect of the full expression of the worthiest human qualities and the taming of the worst ones. In the 1793 edition of his geography, Morse welcomed the growth of manufacturers in the United States, contending that this would open new outlets for human ability. Ministers in general believed that economic development allowed the individual to exercise more fully both his intellectual and moral powers. At the same time, the factory was a tool for the moral reformation of the depraved. This point was conveyed in the *New York Observer* in an article about a man who had led a life of drunkenness and idleness until a cotton mill opened in his town. Finding a job there, he began a new life as he became sober and industrious. The factory was at once an expression of the most admirable human traits and a disciplining, morally uplifting force on the weak and sinful.[45]

Thus the clergy regarded the factory as a force for moral order, the embodiment of the laudable values of rationality, self-control, and prudence—values they highly respected and attempted to inculcate through their temperance and other moral reform societies. No wonder, then, that ministers and so many businessmen could work together—clergymen applauding economic development and businessmen contributing their money and encouragement to benevolent societies.

By the mid-1820s, orthodox Congregationalists also vocally expressed a new, patriotic outlook shared with evangelical allies outside New England. This new mood became merged with their national-mindedness and belief in organization from the previous decade. In 1815, in beseeching American Christians to support the evangelical cause, the New England clergy had called on them to cooperate with Britain and the Holy Alliance and had spoken of the great good to come from monarchs' support of Christianity.[46] Since then, the clergy had grown nationalistic and returned to the republican millennialism of the late-eighteenth century, to the idea that the United States served the providential role of introducing liberty as well as Christianity to mankind. This change grew, in part, out of the Era of Good Feelings and the end of that bitter, divisive party spirit many New England clergymen had feared would lead to civil war. The clergy grew more comfortable with American society and less alarmed by the imperfections of democracy. Morse still complained in 1819 that democracy tended "to give importance to mere numbers, and take it away from intelligence and worth." But by now he

180

could accept this failing, remembering "that there is no per-
fection in any thing under the sun." The clergy accepted democracy, finally realizing after considerable success that it
offered them the opportunity to organize a significant proportion of the population and to shape public opinion and
manners.[47]

The clergy now hailed the various republican movements in
the world. In the 1819 edition of *The American Universal Geography*, Morse welcomed the revolutions in Latin America, for
he believed that independence from Spain and republican governments would bring religious liberty and the consequent
growth of Protestantism. By the mid-1820s the Holy Alliance
was denounced as a sham for working against God's millennial
design by suppressing the revolution in Spain but especially
for not aiding Christian Greece against Moselm Turkey.[48]

The clergy argued that the United States, not Britain, was
to lead the world to the millennium. They claimed that
republicanism would gain ascendancy as Christianity prog-
ressed throughout the world, for it was the only form of government compatible with that religion's principles. It was the
United States's mission to be a Christian and republican example for other nations to emulate:

> God designed here to begin the emancipation of the nations of
> the earth from civil bondage, and to give them an example of
> self government, of the enjoyment of equal rights, and of un-
> exampled national prosperity and happiness; to prepare an
> asylum for the oppressed of other nations, and a people signal-
> ly to aid in evangelizing the heathen, and accomplishing His
> great designs of benevolence and mercy towards a lost and
> ruined world.

Beecher insisted that America's independence and growth,
the formation of benevolent societies, and the revivals of the
last thirty years were all aspects of the providential plan in
which the United States was to take the lead in "renovating
the world." The New England clergy returned to the patriotic,
republican millennialism of the early 1790s.[49]

181

Of course Congregational ministers reiterated the familiar claim that republicanism could not succeed without the support of Christianity and education because a republic rested on the character of its people. As worthy as the system of government framed by the Constitution was, Morse argued in 1824, it had not transformed Americans into a virtuous, moral people: "Let us not trust too much to the intelligence and patriotism of our citizens; human passions are the same here as every where else, and patriotism and intelligence are but feeble checks on personal ambition or party spirit." In the end, neither republicanism nor economic development would suffice without the prevalence of religion. Only an enlightened, moral citizenry could assume the responsibilities of self-government. Still citing the French experience, the clergy insisted that the French Republic had failed because the people had made the disastrous mistake of rejecting Christianity. If the United States was to serve its providential role, it must not make the same mistake or allow national expansion to outrun the establishment of religious institutions. An educated clergy, capable of administering benevolent societies and of establishing schools, was essential if religion and morality were to prevail. By 1825 the minister was depicted as a kind of social director whose organizational labors gave to the expanding nation that character which would enable it to fulfill its providential mission.[50]

———— * ————

If the United States was to realize that destiny, many Congregational ministers also insisted, Americans had to concern themselves with the condition of both blacks and Indians. Though the clergy perceived the two races very differently, they believed the condition of each attested to national sins of white Americans, which had to be rectified. They called for efforts to convert and civilize the Indians, and Morse was the leading promoter of this cause. The clergy also supported the colonization of all blacks in Africa, regarding this as the only solution to the problems of slavery and the status of blacks in the United States. Though not actively involved in this cause, Morse, like most of the northern clergy by 1825, had come to support colonization.[51]

Morse had long opposed slavery, having argued in *Geography Made Easy* in 1784 and five years later in *The American Geography* that it was immoral and also had unhappy effects on southern society by making labor seem unworthy of a white man.[52] Morse was confident that American independence, the establishment of the federal government, and national growth would bring about the abolition of slavery. His unstated assumption, like that of many New Englanders at the time, was that slavery must end because it was inconsistent with America's republican principles. These principles, he was certain, were bound to prevail in the world. In 1789 he was not sure what should be done with the slaves when they were emancipated. Colonization in Africa would be cruel to the blacks; in some remote part of America, too dangerous. The only other alternative was according them equal rights in the United States. This would be

disagreeable and unnatural. Deep-rooted prejudices entertained by the whites; ten thousand recollections, by the blacks, of the injuries they have sustained; new provocations; the real distinction which nature had made; besides many other circumstances which would tend to divide them into parties, and produce convulsions, are objections against retaining and incorporating the blacks with the citizens of the several states.

Still, he concluded that "justice and humanity demand that these difficulties should be surmounted."[53]

In 1793, however, in *The American Universal Geography,* Morse, still confident that slavery would be abolished, only said that it remained to be determined whether the blacks would be colonized in Africa or America or integrated into American society. Perhaps his own unfavorable opinions of blacks (he had written in 1789 that southern white children, because of their contact with black slaves, "too often imbibe their low ideas, and vitiated manners and morals"), as well as his hopes for the development of a homogeneous American population, led him to retreat from his claim that integration was the dictate of justice and humanity. In addition, by 1793 the Sierra Leone colony existed. Morse mentioned it in the *Geography* and expressed the hope that it would be successful in introducing civilization to Africa and in making amends for the evils of slavery. Maybe this early he hoped that the colony might provide an example for the United States in dealing with its emancipated slaves when the time came.[54]

By the mid-1790s Morse became fearful of slave revolts in the United States. William L. Smith, Federalist senator from South Carolina and a staunch defender of slavery, pointed out this danger to Morse in complaining of the antislavery remarks in his geographical writings. Attempts to ameliorate slavery and to end the importation of slaves to the West Indies, he insisted, had caused the bloody slave insurrection in Santo Domingo. Smith warned that, within the United States, "any measures calculated to change the state of things, will produce a convulsion, more unfavourable to the blacks than to their owners."[55]

Morse would not go as far as Smith suggested. Again in the 1796 edition of *The American Universal Geography* he condemned slavery and expressed his hope that it would be eliminated. He did, however, warn against hasty action, against calls for immediate emancipation. Referring to the revolutionary French government's pronouncements and actions concerning slavery in Santo Domingo, which had preceded the slave rebellion there, he said that it was to be hoped that in the United States "no measures will be adopted or pursued, which may hazard effects so shocking as have recently taken place in the West India Islands, or which may produce a convulsion as unfavourable to the blacks as to their owners." Morse retreated to his belief that "so rapid is the progress of liberty in the world, that it is probable that the evil of slavery, if left pretty much to its own course, will best cure itself." Smith had written him that the condition of the southern slaves had been improved in recent years and that probably no more slaves would be imported. To Morse, these things suggested that slavery was gradually coming to an end. He regarded them as steps in a course of gradual abolition, of which he expressed his approval while warning against immediate emancipation. He probably hoped that masters would go on to provide basic educational and religious instruction to prepare the slaves for freedom. He continued in his writings to condemn the international slave trade and to call for its end, another measure he believed would speed abolition of slavery itself. It would also reduce the danger of revolts by slowing the increase in the number of slaves.[56]

Morse's fears over slave revolts intensified as the decade wore on. In 1799 he warned that the French might use Santo Domingo as a base from which to stir up a slave revolution in the southern states. Other ministers shared his fear that, French involvement or not, there might be slave insurrections. After 1800, New England Federalists' anger toward their political opponents, whom they considered hypocrites living off of slavery, could sometimes lead them to relish the thought of a slave revolt toppling the southern supporters of "liberty and equality." Part of a New Year's poem in the *Hampshire Gazette* held out such a specter:

> But hark! what rumour strikes the ear,
> 'Tis Afric's sable sons I hear,
> "Infuriate man" begins to rise,
> While freedom sparkles in his eyes,
> "Seeking his long lost liberty"
> Lo! "blood and slaughter" mark his way,
> Unfeeling tyrants are his prey,
> Oppression lifts the scourge in vain,
> New *Gabriels* spurn the galling chain,
> And St. Domingo's awful fate,
> May soon o'ertake the "Antient State!"[57]

Political hostility gave rise to such expressions, but the reality of a slave revolt like that in Santo Domingo was too awful to be welcomed. William Linn, a Dutch Reformed minister in

New York City and a friend of Morse, preached a sermon on the national Fast Day in May 1798 which indicates how great was the fear over the possibility of slave rebellions. Slavery, he said, was a national evil, but even to speak of it might touch off rebellions:

> Prudence may condemn the most distant reference, but conscience remonstrates against an entire silence. We know where we are most vulnerable, and melancholy is the tale of St. Domingo. O thou Judge of the earth! incline us to do all the justice we can, and when visitest "the iniquity of the fathers upon the children," in wrath remember mercy!

Men like Morse and Linn found themselves in a terrible dilemma: they believed that slavery was a sinful institution that had to be eliminated but feared that to act against it might be dangerous.[58]

Fears of slave rebellions were especially strong from 1798 through 1800 because of hostilities with France, but they did not disappear thereafter. Neither did the certainty of the New England clergy that slavery would be eliminated. Ministers and the editors of the *Connecticut Evangelical Magazine* in 1801, reviewing events of the past century, saw slavery gradually giving way. In 1803 an article in the *Balance,* a New England magazine, reflected attitudes and assumptions shared by many people of that region. It argued that slavery was so inconsistent with American republican principles that it could not endure and would be ended either by slave insurrection or gradual abolition. Immediate emancipation was out of the question. If the slaves were simply freed, the southern states "would become another St. Domingo. . . . Liberty to them, until prepared by previous education and discipline, would be a cup of intoxication, and might prove a curse rather than a blessing; while the whole nation would be constantly exposed to their revenge and depredations." Even if the slaves were educated and prepared for freedom, prospects for American society would not be happy. Mixture of whites and blacks was out of the question.

The best that can be hoped, is, that the negroes in this country may always continue a distinct people;—and full bad is this best.—They may probably increase to the number of several millions. Denied the privilege of intermarriage and degraded in society, their views and interests will always clash with those of the white people. Envy, wounded pride, inveterate rancour, and all the dark and dangerous passions, will, from time to time, inflame their breasts; while our nation will, to endless ages, exhibit the deformed, chequered, motley appearance of black and white.[59]

In 1802 Morse became concerned about the unhappy condition of free blacks in the Boston area. One night, hearing some blacks quarreling, he declared that such behavior was not surprising: "'We have given them liberty, but have not taught them to use their liberty for the benefit of themselves or others. We shut them out of our schools, and they are hardly welcome even in our churches. I, for one, am resolved to reform.'" In November 1802 he began a series of Sunday evening lectures on religion which were well attended by blacks from Charlestown and Boston. He helped in 1803 to form a school for black children in Boston, subscribing $100 to it and serving as a trustee. Two years later he assisted a group of black people in Boston in forming their own church.[60]

In appreciation of his efforts in their behalf, Boston blacks invited Morse to preach the sermon at their celebration of the abolition of slave importation in July 1808. Besides condemning slavery as an evil, expressing great joy over the abolition of the slave trade, and alluding to slavery's gradual abolition under the spreading influence of Christianity, Morse touched on two points that later moved many northern ministers to support colonization. First, he insisted that blacks had to accept their low status in the United States and urged them to "be contented in the humble station in which providence has placed you." This idea that blacks, no matter how pious, moral, or well-educated, would never be treated as the equals of whites was later advanced in favor of their colonization in Africa, where they might know true liberty. In addition, Morse spoke enthusiastically of the work of Britain's African Institution and the prospect of missionaries transforming Africa into a Christian continent. Since the 1790s Morse had corresponded with Zachary Macaulay, British leader of the colony at Sierra Leone, and with Wilberforce, leader of the anti–slave-trade forces in Parliament. Earlier than most other Americans, Morse came to regard the conversion of Africa as one of the events that would introduce the millennium. Later the idea that Christian blacks from the United States could assist, and even effect by themselves, the conversion and civilization of Africa was another argument frequently made in behalf of their colonization there.[61]

As early as 1795, Macaulay had written Morse, asking him if he knew of any black families in his area who might want to settle in Sierra Leone. Apparently he did not. In 1811, however, Morse tried to aid Paul Cuffee, a black Massachusetts shipowner, in arranging the emigration of some New England blacks to the colony. The war delayed their departure to the British colony until 1815.[62]

In several ways, the War of 1812 increased concern in New England over slavery. It intensified the persistent fear of slave revolts in the South. Rebellion might be brought on, ministers warned, by Americans' division or by their sins, one of which was slaveholding.[63] Opponents of the war also made polemical use of slavery. Ever since December 1800, New England Federalists had argued that slave representation, the three-fifths clause in the Constitution, had cost John Adams the presidency. Slave representation, Sidney Morse and Serno Dwight argued in their antiwar pamphlets, gave southern slave masters control of the federal government, the power to impose on the nation such sinful, inexpedient measures as the war. In this way, complained Elijah Parish, slave owners used their black slaves to enslave the freemen of New England. For this reason, the Hartford Convention called for the elimination of slave representation.[64]

By 1812 Morse had also become greatly concerned over miscegenation in the South, the effects of which he perhaps had observed during his stay in South Carolina during the winter of 1809/1810. In the 1812 edition of *The American Universal Geography*, he warned "there is more than a possibility that, in the lapse of a century, the whites and the blacks, in the lower country, will constitute a common mass." Miscegenation distressed Morse for several reasons. As he said, it was a matter of masters taking sexual advantage of their women slaves, but also he was repulsed by the idea of the mixture of the two races and was probably fearful that, in increasing the black population, miscegenation heightened the chances of slave revolts.[65]

By December 1816, when the American Colonization Society was established, Morse's feelings toward blacks, which were representative of those of many northern clergymen, were a mixture of sympathy, fear, and revulsion. He believed that slavery was immoral and had all sorts of unfortunate social and political consequences. He was certain that it would come to an end but feared that it might fall by means of a slave insurrection. In addition, though he welcomed the gradual abolition of slavery and sympathized with the plight of free blacks, even trying to aid them, he really was not prepared to admit blacks to American society as equals. The idea of an interracial society distressed him, especially the prospect of miscegenation. Morse believed that, because of white prejudice, some of which he shared, blacks would always remain a separate people within the United States. They would be a source of perpetual danger, even as free men, because of the treatment they had received from whites.

These attitudes tended to make the northern Presbyterian and Congregational clergy (and also those of other denominations) throw their support behind the American Colonization Society. This organization, though conceived by a New Jersey Presbyterian minister, was formed in Washington largely by men from Virginia and Maryland and received its greatest popular support from the people of those states. Both the Presbyterian General Assembly and the General Association of Massachusetts endorsed the society, as did religious journals and newspapers like the *Panoplist, Boston Recorder,* and *New York Observer.* Northern ministers collected contributions to the society at religious services on Independence Day. Young New England ministers offered crucial aid to the society. Samuel J. Mills in 1818 served on the first exploratory mission to Africa, where he died. Leonard Bacon, a student at Andover seminary, wrote a report in behalf of the Colonization Society for Andover's Society of Inquiry on Missions and was invited to attend an emergency meeting of the Colonization Society in July 1823. There, he made some suggestions—to create a national movement by publishing a magazine and to enlist agents throughout the country to form auxiliary societies—that infused new life into the organization.[66]

The northern Presbyterian and Congregational clergy accepted the Colonization Society's claims that the colonization of free blacks in Africa—its only avowed goal—would enable the emigrants to enjoy true freedom and that it would also help to wipe out the slave trade and to effect the conversion of Africa. More important, the clergy believed, as the society sometimes suggested, especially in its journal, that colonization would naturally lead to the abolition of slavery. They believed that the main obstacle to emancipation was the miserable condition of free blacks, whose numbers slave owners did not want to increase. Under a scheme of colonization, however, both free blacks and slaves could be transported to Africa. In this way, Americans could put an end both to the sinful practice of slavery and the dangers arising from the presence of blacks in American society, while also assisting the evangelization of Africa. For these reasons, colonization seemed to the clergy the best means of abolishing slavery.[67]

Colonization, to these northern clergymen, was in fact the key part of a program of gradual abolition supported by them. The other major aspect of it was the education of blacks, both free and slave, to enable them to live in free society. After the war, Sunday schools were organized in a number of northern towns for the instruction of blacks, much in the manner of Morse's work in Charlestown some years before.

The Synod of New York and New Jersey, excited by the idea of converting Africa, established a school to train black ministers and missionaries for that continent. In addition, northern religious periodicals pressured southerners to offer basic educational and religious instruction to their slaves, insisting that the blacks should be able to worship as Christians and to read the Bible, though not telling southerners that they regarded these as measures of gradual abolition.[68]

The program supported by the clergy was most fully described by Evarts in a series of *Panoplist* articles occasioned by the Missouri Compromise. (Evarts, like some other benevolent leaders and clergymen, was outraged by the compromise, considering it inconsistent with republican principles and a measure that tended to perpetuate slavery. Still other clergymen, including Morse, who was in Washington during the debate in February 1820, were unconcerned, apparently not regarding the compromise as assuring the continuance of slavery.[69]) Citing the evils and dangers of slavery, Evarts insisted shortly before the compromise was reached that instead of enlarging the territory open to slavery, the federal government should direct itself to limiting slavery, which it had the power to do under the Constitution, to improving the condition of the slaves, and to colonizing the free blacks with their consent. In June 1820, several months after the compromise was approved, Evarts said that it was certain "that the blacks of our country ought to be immediately furnished with the means of religious instruction—that the most persevering, public-spirited, and unremitted exertions of the best and wisest members of the community should be applied to the mitigation and gradual abolition of slavery." Several months later, he again argued that Americans must immediately turn to improving the condition of the blacks "so that they may become fit to enjoy all the blessings of personal, civil, and religious liberty." Sidney and Richard Morse echoed this call when they began publication of the *New York Observer* in May 1823, explaining that a "system of measures ought to be immediately commenced which shall look ultimately to the utter extinction of the evil, and what shall be continually tending to that result."[70]

The Morse brothers tried to organize national support for colonization, believing that it would be a vast effort that required the support of public opinion throughout the nation. Inasmuch as southern support of colonization was necessary, especially the willingness of slaveholders to emancipate their slaves for them to be colonized, the editors of the *Observer,* like other promoters of colonization, insisted that the South should not be attacked, that slavery should be recognized as a national problem.[71]

In attempting to build up northern support for colonization, the Morses addressed themselves to two objections to it: that it was not feasible and would never lead to the removal of all the slaves as well as free blacks in the country; and that slaveholders did not want to emancipate their slaves. Their favorite reply to the first objection—that not enough slaves could be colonized in one year to match even their annual increase—was a plan by which, as slaves were colonized, the area they were taken from would afterward be closed to slavery. An annual reduction in the area open to slavery must bring about a decline in the slave population, since the land could support only a fixed number of inhabitants. In advancing this scheme, the Morses never explained why they believed Congress might enact such a law after it had refused to keep slavery out of Missouri in 1820.[72] To the second objection, the Morses insisted that slave owners did want to emancipate their slaves. There was a little truth to this claim. Some supporters of colonization in Maryland and Virginia, men like Robert G. Harper, did speak of emancipation. Farther south, however, in Georgia and South Carolina, colonization was vehemently opposed by the mid-1820s.[73]

Richard and Sidney Morse offered such simple assurances and pat formulas in behalf of colonization because they thought the important thing was to organize the public in support of it. Naïve believers in the power of public opinion and or ganization, they undoubtedly were certain that, as the movement proceeded, it would work out these problems. This belief was also bolstered by their religious faith that the world was moving toward a millennium of liberty and Christianity. They assumed this was a force working for the acceptance of colonization. (They suggested that even if southerners did not then support colonization, they would when Sierra Leone and the free republics of Latin America began producing the same goods more cheaply with free labor. Forced to turn to free labor to compete, the South would have to emancipate the slaves, who could then be colonized.)[74]

In addition, promoters of colonization tended to ignore its impracticability because they believed so strongly that it was the only solution to the racial problem in the United States, the only way of abolishing slavery, averting slave insurrections, and insuring that America's future would not be one of racial strife. For the same reasons, they totally ignored the opposition to colonization among most northern free blacks, who called for freedom and equality in the United States.

Clerical supporters of colonization, however, were unable to convince enough white Americans of the desirablility and practicability of colonization to shape a national consensus in support of it. Colonization as a means of gradually abolishing slavery was doomed because the emancipation of the slaves was coming to be less favored and less discussed in the South, especially in the lower South, where colonization even came to be resented as a northern abolitionist plot. More surprisingly, though many New England clergymen supported colonization, laymen of the region never provided the Colonization Society solid support. They were more critical and even tended to suspect that the Colonization Society sought only the removal of free blacks and in no way looked toward the emancipation of the slaves. Statewide auxiliary societies were not organized in Connecticut until 1828 and in Massachusetts until 1831. Soon afterward William Lloyd Garrison effectively attacked the Colonization Society, set it on the defensive, and by publicizing the widespread suspicions about it, destroyed whatever chances it had of gaining broad northern support.[75]

Despite the clergy's confidence in organization and in their ability to mobilize public opinion, they were limited by what the public was prepared to accept. The problems of slavery and race were too divisive, opinion on these issues too fragmented, for the clergy to build the kind of national movement they believed crucial in dealing with them. Eventually, by the mid-1840s, the alliance of Congregationalists, Presbyterians, Dutch Reformed, and Associate Reformed was itself disrupted by differences over slavery, as well as by theological issues and denominational rivalries none of which could longer be glossed over for the sake of cooperation and organization.

# Chapter 7

## The Final Campaign

During the course of his ministry in Charlestown, Morse contributed much to the shaping of the evangelical ministry of the nineteenth century. In part, the evangelical differed from the settled minister of eighteenth century New England in that he was not firmly rooted in a parish. The eighteenth-century minister had derived his authority from his position in the town. He was an elite figure who both represented the ideals of order and harmony and labored to sustain them in the life of the town, the primary political and social unit of colonial New England. With the political, social, and economic changes of the late-eighteenth and early-nineteenth centuries, towns lost their historic primacy. New England towns were drawn into a national society and increasingly into a national market system. Early on in his ministry, Morse understood this well. He was primarily concerned with the development of the new nation. To work only within the old sphere of the parish seemed to him truly parochial, for it would be to ignore the real sources of power and change in American society. Above all, Morse dedicated himself to organizing those in New England and beyond who shared evangelical values in order to shape the national culture.[1]

In focusing on the world beyond his parish in his work as an organizer and opinion molder, Morse slighted his pastoral responsibilities. Visits and conversations with his parishioners, even the preparation of weekly sermons, fell outside the bounds of his real interests. To him these were tiresome and time-consuming chores which detracted from his ability to work in a larger and more important sphere. Morse's ministerial priorities were a source of friction between him and his congregation. Moreover, his involvement with his geographical writings and controversies, all of which he firmly believed served ultimate religious ends, seemed to the congregation but further proof that he was not fulfilling his responsibilities to them.

As early as 1796 there had been uneasiness among Morse's parishioners over his attention to geography. That year the parish refused to increase his settlement salary because many members believed that his writings provided an adequate supplement to his income. The parish's continued refusal finally forced incorporation of the First Society in 1803. Once incorporated, the society was supported only by people who voluntarily belonged to it, no longer by all the citizens of Charlestown who, under the state's religious establishment laws, had previously paid parish taxes. The incorporated society soon voted Morse a salary increase, which put him on a par with the Boston Congregational clergy, who were the best paid ministers in the state.[2]

Morse had blamed his difficulties on the opposition of people who never attended the church, only the parish meetings. He had felt that Democratic-Republicans, who constituted a great majority in Charlestown, were especially responsible. Morse had even considered leaving the Charlestown church for another, a step Deacon Morse had opposed, not wanting his son to live any farther from him than he already did.[3]

There was more to Morse's troubles than the opposition of Democratic-Republicans. A few months after increasing his salary in 1803, the congregation became upset by Morse's absence during his annual summer trip and by his continued attention to his geographical writings. Morse and the society finally agreed in January 1804 that he would prepare no new works, just new editions of the existing ones. This agreement lapsed in 1808 when the society lacked the funds to pay his full salary. It was reduced, and Morse was free to make up the difference with his writings.[4]

Besides the time that he devoted to geography, Morse gave ever greater attention to the growing benevolent societies. He was also at times obsessed with what he believed were liberal efforts to use his difficulties with Hannah Adams to discredit him. Consequently, his performance as a pastor suffered. In 1814, when Morse issued *An Appeal to the Public* on the Hannah Adams controversy, one of his deacons pleaded that he turn his attention to the church. This man complained that, while Morse sought to justify himself before the world, the members of his congregation were "daily sighing, and longing for opportunities for christian conversation, with their minister, not on disputes, and controversies, or Politics, but on *real, internal experimental religion.*" He asked how Morse could allow "months . . . [to] pass away without producing scarcely one, original, well studied discourse" and called upon him to abandon his activities outside the church, to devote himself to preaching "more on the doctrine of the new birth, on regeneration, and the absolute necessity of a thorough change of heart."[5]

Obviously these complaints represented the concerns of the evangelical members of the congregation. In December 1815 some of the liberal minority, angered by Morse's anti-Unitarian campaign and no longer politically divided into Federalist and Democratic-Republican camps, left to form the Second Society of Charlestown, which began meeting for worship in May 1816.[6] This finally stirred Morse to action. In July 1816 he addressed the church on languishing state of religion and called for reformation and the enforcement of church discipline. Fortunately for Morse, by October 1816 a revival was underway, probably caused as much by the general religious climate of the postwar years as by his renewed concern for his parish.[7]

There had once before been a revival in the First Society,

from 1801 through 1803, another great period of revivals in New England. Morse's preaching talents were not those of a rousing evangelist. He was best known for his pleasant manner of delivery, a strength he relied on in the fall of 1801 when he introduced Saturday evening meetings for the young people of his congregation. He in fact read to his audience, taking his texts from the Westminster Assembly's catechism. This strategy proved effective, for the meetings were well attended, and when they concluded in April 1803 more than one hundred people had joined the church.[8]

Morse was enormously uplifted by the new revival of 1816. Characteristically exaggerating, he wrote one of his sons that the "parish, which a few weeks ago was considered, to a great extent on the verge of *dissolution & ruin* is not pronounced the most *prosperous* & happy society in the Commonwealth." By March 1817, as the revival wound down, more than seventy people had joined the church.[9] Morse was dismayed, however, when a number of the most distinguished families in Charlestown now applied for dismission so that they could join the new Unitarian church, which was about to settle its first minister.[10]

By January 1818 Morse once more allowed his attention to the church to lapse, as he began laying plans for a new edition of the *Geography* and some other writings. He proposed to the church that he take on an assistant pastor, with whom he would share his salary. The church would not hear of that. When the new edition of *American Universal Geography* was published in 1819, Morse came under great pressure to resign, as his congregation complained that once more he was ignoring his ministerial duties. Finally, Morse notified his congregation in August 1819 that he would resign. His dismissal was effected in February 1820 by a council of three ministers of Morse's choosing, who cited his various interests, especially his writings, as the reason he "was unable to satisfy his people as to pastoral duties and labours."[11]

Morse was hurt by the opposition of his church members which forced his resignation. He could not understand their complaints and continued to be bitter about his dismissal until his death. His immediate reaction, however, was to turn to organizing in behalf of another cause. When the dismissal council met, Morse was in Washington engaged in another grand enterprise, a campaign to carry Christianity and civilization to all American Indians in order to save them from extinction.

*

Morse had long been interested in Indians. He had written about them in his earliest writings, especially to rebut the charges of their European detractors, like Cornelis de Pauw and Georges Buffon, who depicted them as an inferior race, the product of an inferior environment. In 1790 Morse argued at great length in his article on America in the first encyclopedia published in the United States that Indians were not by nature inferior to Europeans. Their barbarism, he argued somewhat tautologically, was caused by the low state of civilization among them. Morse found much to admire in the Indian character. In one passage he depicted Indians much as he did New Englanders: as a simple people, uncorrupted and undifferentiated by wealth or luxury, who loved liberty and observed equality, while they also honored those of wisdom and experience among themselves.[12]

In these early writings Morse did not address the questions of the need and possibility of Indians accepting Christianity and adopting white civilization. He began to think of these goals afterward, as in 1792 he was elected to membership in the Massachusetts Society for Propagating the Gospel Among Indians and Others in North America. This society supported schools among remnants of New England tribes and aided Samuel Kirkland's mission to the Oneida Indians in New York.[13] Later in the decade he was appointed a commissioner to oversee American operations of the Society in Scotland for Propagating Christian Knowledge, which had been involved in supporting missions to American Indians since its founding in 1709. In 1796 Morse and Jeremy Belknap performed for the Scottish society a tour of inspection of the two missions it supported in New York, the Oneida and the New Stockbridge missions. The two ministers reported that the Indians were reluctant to take up farming and were beset by intemperance and the corrupting influence of immoral whites who lived near them. Still, these findings pointed to the need to press on to civilize them, or like the New England Indians they would all but disappear.[14]

Morse and Belknap made this report at the time when a number of missionary societies were beginning to be established in the United States. In preaching sermons before the members of the societies, ministers often referred to their duty of converting the Indians.[15] Only the New York Missionary Society, however, attempted an ambitious mission to a tribe not already declining because of contact with whites; it was the only society that did not concern itself with missions to white settlers.

In 1799 the New York Missionary Society sent to the Chickasaws of western Georgia a minister and an instructor. With their families they comprised a mission of seventeen people. The Chickasaws, like the other populous tribes of the old southwest—the Cherokees, Choctaws, and Creeks—held vast areas of land in the various southern states and territories. By 1800, under the influence of half-blood members of their tribes, these Indians were prepared to assimilate certain aspects of white culture, especially education and farming though not Christianity, in order to maintain possession of their homelands.[16]

The society was prepared to have its missionaries teach white farming techniques and skille' crafts because it shared the assumption common among whites concerned about the Indians that, to be successful, efforts to convert them had to be accompanied by instruction in white civilized life. Experience had proven, it was said, that civilization would speed the Indians' acceptance of Christianity and that, conversely, retention of traditional ways of life would retard their progress in religion. So the missionaries taught farming to the Chickasaw men and domestic arts to the women. Looking to the future, the missionaries concentrated on the children, whose habits were not set. They instructed them in English, Christianity, and the rudiments of a basic education. Problems arose, however, and by 1802 the instructor had to leave because of a misunderstanding with the Indians. The mission itself was suspended in 1804 because the society could not raise the money to meet the high costs of maintaining it.[17]

The Missionary Society of Connecticut came to support one other mission among distant and populous tribes of Indians, those in the Michigan Territory. Unplanned by the society, the mission evolved in 1800 when David Bacon, who was sent to work among the Indians in the vicinity of New Connecticut in Ohio, learned of far greater numbers of Indians to the northwest. He explored that region and won the society's approval of his establishing a mission there. Encountering opposition from white traders and no interest on the part of the Indians, Bacon labored for two years without success. In 1804 the society decided to abandon the mission and reassigned Bacon to Ohio.[18]

This mission was a small gesture, and it reflects the fact that the New England missionary societies, which enjoyed far greater financial support than those in other parts of the nation, did relatively little for Indians. They largely confined themselves to aiding the remnants of New England tribes and the somewhat larger tribes in New York and to educating a few Indian boys as future missionaries.[19] The New England societies, even the one entitled the Massachusetts Society for Propagating the Gospel Among Indians and Others in North America, concentrated on white settlers. The leaders of the missionary societies were most concerned with establishing religion and order in the new settlements, thinking that these were crucial for the nation's development. They also felt a special obligation to the white settlers, who were often described in missionary literature as the kin, friends, and former neighbors of the societies' supporters.

In addition, the directors of the societies regarded Indian missions as more difficult to conduct and more expensive to support than missions to the new settlements. Almost any minister who was willing to spend several months riding from settlement to settlement could serve as a missionary to whites. It was more difficult to labor among the Indians. As the Missionary Society of Connecticut discovered from Bacon's mission and reported in 1803, the populous tribes were at a great istance, had strange manners with which missionaries had to deal, and tended to be suspicious of efforts to convert them and change their way of life. These observations were less true of the southern tribes than those of the northwest, among whom Bacon had labored. Still, offering oneself as a missionary to the Indians required great dedication and the willingness to learn a strange language and work for years, patiently bearing discouragements, among a distant tribe. Men willing to make such sacrifices were few.[20]

Indian missions were considered expensive because of the belief in the necessity of instruction in civilization as well as in Christianity. The Chickasaw mission of the New York Missionary Society had found it a costly undertaking to supply instructors, tools, and materials to teach farming and skilled crafts. By 1805 ministers in New England began pointing to the growing attention to civilization among the southern Indians as a hopeful sign of their future conversion to Christianity. Still, citing the problems of finding missionaries and money, the New England societies left to the future and the workings of providence the sending of missions to the Indians.[21]

During these years of inaction, however, Morse's thoughts took shape on how missions to the Indians should be conducted. He was greatly influenced by two missions undertaken by individuals. In 1804 Gideon Blackburn, a Tennessee Presbyterian minister, established a mission in his state among the Cherokees. During a fund-raising tour through New England in 1807, he met Morse and stayed for a month at his home in Charlestown. Afterward they corresponded. The other mission was begun by Joseph Badger among the Wyandots of Ohio in 1806. Badger, who had been a Congregational minister in Massachusetts, had dedicated himself to becoming a missionary to the Indians when fear about the Illuminati ran high in 1799. After reading Morse's sermons on the subject, Badger wrote him and expressed his belief that while Christians were contending against infidelity, they must also labor to uplift the heathen.[22]

Badger and Blackburn conducted their missions in the same manner, hoping to lead the Indians to Christianity and civilization by concentrating on the children, teaching them religion and English as well as farming and mechanical arts. They witnessed, however, different results. As Badger complained to Morse, his work was badly impaired by the opposition of white traders among the Wyandots. Badger's experience confirmed Morse's feeling that missions could not succeed if the Indians to whom they were sent were surrounded by whites, the worst of whom were sure to corrupt the Indians with their vices. Despite some white interference, Blackburn enjoyed great success and stated that, although the Cherokees were not taking quickly to Christianity, they were making rapid progress in civilization. He was confident that education of the children, which emphasized instruction in religion and the English language, would speed their complete adoption of white culture and Christianity and their eventual entry into the Union as American citizens. Still, he was forced to abandon the mission in 1810 because he lacked adequate financial support. Blackburn's experience convinced Morse that missions to the Indians could succeed but that they required solid financial backing.[23]

Morse publicized the work of Badger and Blackburn in the *Panoplist* and helped them in raising money. There were other New England ministers who were concerned about the Indians. Some called for immediate action, arguing that the missionary societies could not wait because the Indians were fast disappearing. In 1808 Abiel Holmes insisted before the Massachusetts Society for Propagating the Gospel that it must act.

The New England tribes, he stressed, were all but gone, and missionary societies had to turn quickly to the western tribes and send them schools, tools, and Christian instruction before they too disappeared.[24]

Two developments occurred which promised to render such missions possible. One was the formation in 1808 of Andover seminary, where enthusiastic young men gathered, a significant number of whom were eager to dedicate their lives to missionary work. This commitment on the part of five Andover students led in 1810 to the formation of the American Board of Commissioners for Foreign Missions, an organization which soon was able to raise considerable sums of money, none of which was set aside for the needs of white settlers.

Promising as these events were, neither the prospective missionaries nor the ABCFM turned their first thoughts to dispatching missions to the Indians. The Andover students, somewhat romantically inspired by British writings on missions, wanted to devote themselves to missions in the Far East. The ABCFM decided to make this the seat of its first mission, citing the "many discouragements" of prior missions to the Indians as the reason why it looked to the East. Gordon Hall, an Andover student who became an ABCFM missionary in Bombay, argued in a pamphlet that the American Indians' lack of civilization would make for less impressive results than could be expected among the civilized peoples of the Far East, whose greater number was an additional reason for concentrating on them. The Reverend Manasseh Cutler argued against this position, pointing to Blackburn's success among the Cherokees and insisting that Americans owed a special obligation to the Indians, having taken their land and introduced them to alcohol and the vices destroying so many of them.[25]

Cutler's feelings were shared by other ministers. In 1812 the Massachusetts Society for Propagating the Gospel, finally realizing that the New England Indians were nearly extinct and that it had to turn west, commissioned John F. Schermerhorn to report to it on the western tribes. In 1814 he suggested the

Delawares of the northwest as a tribe among which the society could work, but he strongly recommended that it concentrate on the Cherokees, Chickasaws, and Choctaws of the south. Their larger numbers, their eagerness for civilization, and especially the success of Blackburn's mission made these seem distinctly the most eligible tribes.[26]

Supporters of Indian missions, men like Morse, who was an officer of the Massachusetts Society for Propagating the Gospel as well as a commissioner of the ABCFM, apparently pressed the board in behalf of this cause. They must have been responsible for its growing willingness to assume responsibility for such missions—for its decision in 1811 to establish a mission among a tribe in Lower Canada, which the war prevented; for the vote of the board at its annual meeting in 1814 that missions to Indians within and without the United States were permitted under its act of incorporation; and finally, in 1815, for the call of the prudential committee, on which Morse served for the first time, for the board to enact Schermerhorn's recommendations and send missions to the southern tribes.[27]

The prudential committee of the ABCFM was confident and ambitious in calling for the establishment of missions among the southern Indians. Blackburn had proven what could be done, even though his means had been severely limited. The ABCFM now hoped to follow up with "a combined, well supported, and well conducted effort," to establish schools throughout the Indians' lands so "that in a course of years not very long, the tribe at large . . . [will] . . . become English in their language, Christian in their religion, and civilized in their general habits and manners." In 1816 the ABCFM dispatched its first missionary, Cyrus Kingsbury, a graduate of Andover seminary, and by the beginning of 1817 he had established the Brainerd station among the Cherokees in Tennessee.[28]

Since its inception in 1789, the federal government had practiced dual and contradictory policies of making treaties to remove the Indians to the West while also offering to assist them in becoming civilized so that they could turn to farming and retain their lands. Little had been done to promote this latter policy because the government only made this aid available but did not institute programs in support of it. Now the government was willing to support the efforts of the benevolent societies and assist them in conducting their work. On his journey south, Kingsbury had visited Washington, where President Madison had promised that the War Department would pay for the construction of school buildings and would also supply the mission with tools, farm implements, and spinning wheels. Federal assistance to Indian missions was increased in 1819 when Congress approved the Civilization Fund, an annual $10,000 appropriation for Indian education, which was administered through the benevolent societies that worked among the Indians.[29]

The ABCFM was greatly encouraged by these government actions. It appreciated more than just the money it received, which was much less than it annually spent on Indian missions. Most of all it valued the government's commitment to support the civilizing effort. The ABCFM thought that this was demonstrated by the government's decision in 1819 to renegotiate a treaty that had called for large numbers of Cherokees to cede land east of the Mississippi for land west of it. The Cherokees and the ABCFM had appealed to the government to reconsider the treaty, insisting that removal would disrupt the tribe's progress toward civilization. Government support of the civilization of the Indians was crucial because, as the ABCFM realized, "an opposite disposition or policy would be of dark and disastrous aspect."[30]

By 1821, with this government support and the warm approval (and even some financial assistance) of the southern tribes, the ABCFM had established, in addition to the Brainerd station, two large stations among the Choctaws and one west of the Mississippi in the Arkansas Territory among Cherokees who had emigrated there. The ABCFM was joined in its work by the United Foreign Mission Society, which was to merge with it in 1826. The UFMS established two missions west of the Mississippi among the Osages, one in the Arkansas Territory and the other in Missouri. East of the Mississippi, in 1826, the Synod of South Carolina and Georgia established a mission among the Chickasaws, which was transferred to the ABCFM in 1827. Besides these Congregationalist-Presbyterian efforts, Baptists and Methodists also planted several missions among the southern tribes.[31]

The ABCFM had begun its work among the Cherokees and Choctaws, intending to concentrate on the children, as had Blackburn and Badger, because it was assumed that the adults' habits could not be changed. The converted children were to lead the rest of the tribe to Christianity and civilization. At the large mission stations of Brainerd, Mayhew, and Elliot, Indian children were boarded, away from the distracting influence of their families. All of the instruction was in English, which the missionaries insisted the children speak even among themselves. The boys were taught farming and skilled crafts; the girls, spinning and other domestic arts. The ABCFM had hoped that these stations would be self-supporting, but experience proved them not only to be expensive but to occupy much of the missionaries' time, which would otherwise be spent teaching the Indians. With the Indians making rapid progress in civilization, the ABCFM shifted away from teaching farming and crafts. It dispersed most of the missionaries throughout the tribes at a number of local schools, where they offered basic educational and religious instruction. Missionaries began to learn the Indian languages so that they could itinerate throughout the tribes.[32]

Adapting to conditions in these ways, the ABCFM retained as its ultimate goals the conversion of the Indians, their complete adoption of white culture, and their eventual assimilation into American society. There was some reason to anticipate these things, for the Indians increasingly accepted various aspects of white culture: education, farming, housing, clothing, and even self-government on the white American model. This progress was viewed with growing hostility by southern whites, who wanted the Indians' land and sought their removal.

Morse hoped to have similar missions sent to all Indian tribes in the United States. Especially seeking to have an Indian territory established in the northwest, where the declining remnants of the northern tribes could be gathered and civilized, he left his pulpit in 1819 to devote himself to this goal. He planned first to make an inspection tour of all the tribes and then, working with the federal government, to "form some general, comprehensive *plan* for the benefit of *all* our Indians." If the Indians were instructed in English, Christianity, and the "arts of civilized life," he was certain, they would be prepared "ultimately, to become citizens of the United States, & to enjoy with us all our privileges. They are undoubtedly capable of all this—it is the only way in which they can be saved from misery & extirpation." Morse spent the first two months of 1820 in Washington, where he met and discussed his plans with President Monroe and John C. Calhoun, secretary of war. He received a commission from the War Department to report to it the findings of his tour.[33]

Morse by this time already held a commission from the Society in Scotland for Propagating Christian Knowledge. The origins of his tour lay in some proposals he had made to this society in February 1818. He had suggested then that it transfer its support from the languishing Indian school connected to Dartmouth College to the southern missions and especially to a new mission he proposed among the Delawares in the Indiana Territory. Morse informed the Scottish society that the New Stockbridge Indians were considering moving to the Delawares' territory. He was confident that if they and the other civilized Indians of New York did so, they could rapidly lead the Delaware on to advancement. After receiving the society's commission, and before enlisting the support of the federal government, Morse traveled late in 1819 to New York. There he discussed his plans with officers of the UFMS and received another commission from the upstate Northern Missionary Society, which worked among those New York tribes Morse hoped would emigrate to his proposed mission to the Delawares.[34]

Morse's plans for his Indian tour were extemely ambitious. He intended to travel in the spring of 1820 with his son Richard up the Erie Canal to Buffalo, then along the Great Lakes to the Michigan Territory, southward to Missouri, and then homeward through Illinois, Indiana, Ohio, Pennsylvania, and New York. In the autumn, with his son Sidney, he was to travel south, visiting Georgia, Florida, Alabama, Mississippi, Louisiana, the Arkansas Territory, Tennessee, and Kentucky.[35] He set out with Richard in May 1820. Morse's health was not good. Since childhood he had been afflicted with a respiratory ailment. When he reached Mackinaw an army doctor there told him that he could not continue with his trip. So, instead of going on to Missouri, he began his return to his new home in New Haven, where he and his family had moved earlier that year. He still planned to make the southern tour in the autumn and to complete the rest of the northern tour the next year. He did neither, having spent the $500 the government provided for his traveling expanses and being unable to pay for them himself.[36]

Morse had seen enough during his trip to decide that the Northwest Territory should be made an Indian territory, the colony where the remnants of the northern tribes would be gathered, educated, and prepared for entry into the Union. In August 1820 he proposed this to Secretary of War Calhoun and called on the Northern Missionary Society to establish missions there at Mackinaw and Green Bay.[37]

At home in New Haven Morse set about preparing his report. Besides his own observations, he relied on the records of the ABCFM and government documents, to which he had access through the Department of War. He brought to the report the same thoroughness that he had to his geographical writings, and this made it the best, most accurate study of its kind.

He completed a draft by December 1820 and traveled to

Washington to submit it to Congress, but Calhoun advised him to hold off until later in the session. Morse returned home to continue his work on the report. As the congressional session was nearing its end in February 1821, Calhoun postponed the presentation of the report until the next session. Morse wanted to have it published before Congress convened again in December because he thought it would help to build up public support for missions to the Indians. He also needed money badly. Calhoun persuaded him to wait until Congress called for it.[38]

Morse traveled to Washington again in December 1821 to await the request for the report from the House Committee on Indian Affairs. He expected that he would meet with the committee and in consultation with it would decide which parts of the report would be published. He hoped that together he and the committee would work out official Indian policy from his report. Morse spent several anxious, frustrating months in the capital, upset first by the committee's delay in calling for his report, then its not consulting him when it studied it, and finally its decision to print none of it. When he returned to New Haven in April 1822, he quickly set about having it published.[39]

In his report Morse called upon Americans and the federal government to accept the duty of civilizing the Indians in order to save them from destruction. They were threatened with extinction because of a desperate dilemma. Either they were being forced continually westward to new lands that could barely support them or, staying on their lands, they were surrounded by whites who despised and corrupted them. "In this degraded, most disconsolate and heart sinking of all situations in which man can be placed, they are left miserably to waste away for a few generations, and then to become extinct forever!"[40]

Morse insisted that, although Indian culture was inferior to white culture, Indians were equal to whites in natural abilities. Wherever they had come from, which no one knew, "they are certainly an intelligent and noble part of our race, and capable of high moral and intellectual improvement." They "are of the same nature and origin, and of one blood, with ourselves; of intellectual powers as strong, and capable of cultivation, as ours. They, as well as ourselves, are made to be immortal." Indians, Morse contended, were like children, ignorant but capable of learning. They should therefore be treated as children, educated in Christianity and "the useful arts and sciences," and in this manner "raised gradually and ultimately, to the rank, and to the enjoyment of all the rights and privileges of freemen, and citizens of the United States."[41]

To promote the education of the Indians, Morse proposed that the Northwest Territory, where there were many Indians, be made an Indian territory, a colony where the remnants of the northern tribes could voluntarily emigrate. Experience had proven that "low and depraved white people" interfered with efforts to teach the Indians. The northern tribes, long suffering from such contact, had to be collected and insulated from it. Morse did not, however, call for the removal of the southern tribes, who, he said, "are in situations and circumstances very favorable to be educated where they are, raised to the rank and privileges of citizens, and merged in the mass of the nation. On these tribes we hope the Government will make the experiment of the practicability of a complete civilization of Indians."[42]

Morse cited the work of the ABCFM among the Cherokees and Choctaws and proposed that the government aid benevolent societies in establishing similar "education families" in about twenty additional sites in the South, the Northwest, and west of the Mississippi. The education families would instruct the Indians in Christianity and civilized life, preparing them for assimilation into American society. Once the Indians accepted white culture, "*then* let intermarriage with them become general, and the end which the Government has in view will be completely attained. They would then be literally of one blood with us, be merged in the nation, and saved from extinction."[43]

Morse emphasized the need both of consistency in federal

Indian policy and of cooperation between the agents, missionaries, traders, and soldiers who worked among the Indians. It was especially important, he argued, that the government regulate the Indian trade and exclude from it men who cheated the Indians and sold them whiskey.[44]

To promote cooperation between the federal government and the benevolent societies, which conducted the missions among the Indians, Morse proposed that a national society be formed. This organization, entitled the American Society for Promoting the Civilization and General Improvement of the Indian Tribes in the United States, was to meet annually in Washington at the beginning of the congressional session and, besides collecting information and artifacts, was to make recommendations to the government and the benevolent societies.[45]

Morse conceived the idea of this society earlier in 1822, while he was in Washington awaiting congressional action on his report. He consulted Calhoun on his plans, showed him the society's constitution, which he had drawn up, and won his support. According to the constitution, past United States presidents as well as present cabinet members and state governors would be honorary officers, and ex officio members would include all the clergy in the country, all congressmen, all army officers, and all Indian agents. Anyone else could become a member by contributing five dollars. The real decision-making power, however, would lie with the thirteen-man board of directors. Morse appointed the directors without consulting them, and they included William Wirt, Francis S. Key, Robert Ralston, and other men who served on the boards of other national benevolent societies. It was the board that was to make the recommendations and formulate the policies which, presumably, the government and benevolent societies would enact. This was a daring but impracticable proposal considering both the power this extralegal society was to be granted and the mounting opposition in the southern states to the missionary societies that worked among the Indians.[46]

The society failed to win the support either of the public or of many of its own proposed honorary officers. John Adams declined his position because he felt that the society threatened to interfere in governmental affairs. Thomas Jefferson, too, declined and cited to Morse, certainly with some pleasure, the French Jacobin societies and the Reign of Terror as an example of the evil that could result from extragovernmental associations dictating measures to government. Less abstractly, many southerners resented the work of the ABCFM among the southern tribes, which increasingly promised to prevent their removal. Probably it was a southerner who complained about Morse's proposed society in Washington's National Intelligencer, saying that there already was too much meddling by benevolent societies in Indian affairs. Most important, there was great indifference to the plight of the Indians in Washington, the home of the society.[47]

The first annual meeting did not take place in December 1822 because Morse, perhaps the society's only active supporter, was then confined to bed and did not have the money to make the trip to Washington even if his health had permitted it. He tried to organize a meeting of the Society for December 1823, but a lack of interest among the members forced its postponement to February 1824. Morse could not attend, but he delegated Jeremiah Evarts, secretary of the ABCFM, who was going to Washington on other business, to act as his agent. Few people attended the meeting, and Congressman Stephen Van Rensselaer suggested to Morse that the society be transferred to New York because in Washington Indians were considered "more like wild Beasts than human beings." Morse prepared a report of the first annual meeting, realizing that the society was in serious trouble but hoping that he could excite public support of it. He sent copies of this report to various cities, but its reception was dismal: one copy was sold in Philadelphia and none in Charleston, South Carolina. With that, the society collapsed.[48]

Morse's attempt to set the society on its feet was part of a campaign by the ABCFM and supporters of Indian missions to prevent the repeal of the Civilization Fund and even to increase government aid. In 1824 a bill, supported by southerners, to discontinue the annual $10,000 appropriation was before the House Committee on Indian Affairs. Evarts traveled to Washington to oppose it. He carried with him an ABCFM memorial to Congress written by Morse.[49]

The memorial spoke of Americans' duty to civilize and preserve the Indians and pointed to the success of the ABCFM's southern missions. It also contained several proposals from *A Report to the Secretary of War* but especially called for increased appropriations so that two Indian colonies could be established, one in the South and one in the Northwest. Morse probably mentioned the idea of a southern colony, which he never mentioned either earlier or later and which the ABCFM did not support, for political reasons. He might have thought that this would hold out to southerners the prospect of southern Indian removal and so win some votes for increased appropriations. Morse's real concern was in obtaining more money from the government so that the Northwest colony, his favorite project, could get underway. In 1822 the Northern Missionary Society, acting on his suggestion, had begun a mission at Green Bay. He had tried to persuade the ABCFM to establish a second mission at Mackinaw, but with its funds for Indians tied up in the southern missions, it was unable to do so. The House committee did not vote for an increase in the Civilization Fund, but it at least voted to retain it, pointing to the success and importance of the work being done.[50]

The memorial was Morse's last contribution in behalf of Indian missions. His sons Richard and Sidney carried on the cause in the *New York Observer,* lobbying for public support and, as their father advised them, protesting more and more against demands for removal of the southern tribes. Morse died in 1826, before these demands reached their height. The struggle against removal came to be led by Evarts, Morse's long-time associate.[51]

By 1829, when Andrew Jackson assumed the presidency, the southern Indians, though only a few of them had turned to Christianity, had made great progress in all aspects of civilized life and were determined not to sell their lands. The

Monroe and Adams administrations had respected this decision and withstood the political pressure to force the Indians off. Still, because of southern opinion, both presidents had tried to persuade the Indians to remove to lands west of the Mississippi, where the federal government would liberally finance a program of civilization. In 1826, even Evarts, convinced that the political pressure could not be resisted, had reluctantly approved a plan devised by Secretary of War James Barbour. This plan would have provided liberal support and also would have guaranteed the new western lands to the Indians so that they never again would have to move. Listening to congressional debates in 1828, however, Evarts realized what Congress would not implement such a plan and decided to oppose removal.[52]

In 1830 Evarts organized public opposition to Jackson's Removal Bill, which empowered the government to make removal treaties with the Indians. Evarts correctly contended that Jackson was acting in collusion with Georgia and the other southern states to drive the Indians off their lands by permitting those states to ignore federal treaties with the Indians and to subject them to treatment that would force them to move west. The Removal Bill, which made no provision for aiding the Indians in their new homes, was merely a device to get them out of the way.[53]

Although Evarts organized spirited opposition to the bill in New England and New York, Congress approved it. Southern support of removal was too strong and northern indifference too great for it to be blocked. Gradually, over the next decade, the southern tribes were forced to emigrate. The ABCFM tried to continue its work but was unable to recapture the progress that had been made in the South. Many of the Indians died along the way to their new homes. Among the rest, the hope of finding a place within American society was destroyed.[54]

———— * ————

Had Morse lived to witness the removal of the southern Indians and its disastrous consequences, it would have been a terrible blow to him. As it was, he died believing that prospects were good for the Indians surviving and being assimilated into American society. These hopes and his work in this cause sustained him in the last years of his life, which were not happy ones.

After he retired from his church in 1819, Morse spent much of his time until his death trying to meet his debts and stave off poverty. In 1820, when he and his family moved to New Haven, he bought a house, but in the next several years he had to mortgage and then sell it. To raise money he occasionally preached in a New Haven church, wrote for a local newspaper, and edited a collection of documents on American colonial history and the Revolution. And he continued writing his geographies, especially several more editions of his school book.[55]

Morse blamed his plight on the treachery of others, "the fraud and mismanagement of wicked men," but actually he brought his problems on himself. He was done in by his reckless temperament. Morse had accumulated what he called "an independent fortune" from the sales of his geographical writings, especially in the 1790s with the first several editions. He had invested much of his money in land, banks, canals, and turnpikes, but he had overextended himself and had borrowed money to make some of these investments. He had counted on the future dividends from some of his holdings to pay off the loans. This practice did not cause difficulties for him until the embargo was imposed. Then, with commerce impaired by this policy and afterward by the war, many of his investments yielded no return, while he still had to meet his debts. This did not immediately ruin him, but he made his financial situation even more difficult by attempting to maximize the profits from his writings. He began to have printers publish the books for him, and he negotiated their sale to booksellers. But after twenty years on the market, his writings did not sell as briskly as they once had, and he had to bear the cost of all the unsold copies. Because he had overextended himself and assumed the costs of his writings, Morse faced, when he retired, considerable debts, which he was never able to pay off.[56]

Although Morse tried to be a sharp trader, he did not conserve money. In Charlestown he ran an expensive household, spending more than his salary by regularly entertaining visitors and conducting much of the business of a number of benevolent societies out of his home. He also contributed generously to these societies. In addition, he spent a good deal of money on the education of his sons. All three attended Yale, and Richard and Sidney went on to study theology at Andover seminary. Morse spent $4,000 in four years on Samuel's training as a painter in Britain.[57]

Morse's family life was a source of comfort in a combative life. Morse constantly looked to his wife Elisabeth for comfort and consolation. She conducted a warm and comfortable household. In addition, she pampered him when he was ill, lifted his spirits when he was depressed, and fully sympathized with him in the controversies in which he engaged and in his conflicts with church members. It is impossible to imagine how they could have lived together, had she not agreed that he was correct in all of these and that he suffered as an innocent defender of the truth. She tried to restrain only his recklessness with money but of course was unsuccessful in that.

Morse and his wife exercised a close watch over their sons from early childhood on, as his father had over him, and instilled in them a dedication to piety, morality, and hard work. There was much love between Morse and his sons, but as they reached adulthood, all three complained of his tight reins, manipulation, and fault finding. Of course Deacon Morse, who died a very old man in 1819, had long subjected Morse to such treatment, warning him against spending too much time working on geography and lecturing him against leaving the Charlestown church. Morse had tended to respond by evading his father's criticisms rather than resisting. Samuel, the most independent of Morse's sons, did stand up to his father. He complained about the letters he received from home, while he studied art in England:

> It is true I find a great deal of affectionate solicitude in them, but with it I also find so much complaint and distrust, so much fear that I am doing wrong, so much doubt as to my morals and principles, and fear lest I should be led away by bad company and the like, that, after I have read them, I am miserable for a week. I feel as though I had been guilty of every crime, and I have passed many sleepless nights after receiving letters from you.

Though Samuel resented his father's criticisms, still they had some effect on him.[58]

Morse exerted more control over his other two sons, Sidney and Richard. When they were college students, he enlisted their aid in preparing his geographical writings. After 1823, when they began publishing the *New York Observer,* they told Morse they could no longer help him. Richard, aware that his father's books no longer sold well, advised him not to write any more. Sidney explained to their mother that he and Richard wanted to make a success of their paper and were against any new projects:

> New schemes have been the ruin of the Morses. The rolling stone gathers no moss; and the rolling Morse gathers no gold. If I could see some of the simplest maxims of prudence and economy believed and acted on in the family, I should have hope that the debts would be paid, and something handsome would be earned in a few years, but when these are set aside, and visionary dreams, substituted in their place, I despond.

As Richard told his father, it was time that he and Sidney "shine for ourselves." Nevertheless, Morse made contracts for new books and managed to persuade Richard to spend the winter of 1825/1826 in New Haven helping him. Richard wrote to Sidney that he was at times . . . out of patience at the vexatious detention here a whole winter, with so petty a work, & could hardly help blaming father for controling our arrangements & embarrasing us by engagements made without consultation. I have endeavoured however to be respectful but I think we must avoid being exposed to these evils in future, or they will injure us even more seriously.

Morse died a few months later.[59]

Morse's influence over his sons did have its beneficial aspects for them. With his encouragement and advice, Sidney and Richard made careers for themselves as editors of what became the most important religious newspaper in antebellum America. As editor of the *Panoplist* and director of benevolent societies, Morse was not only a transitional figure between the settled minister of eighteenth-century New England and the new lay religious leader of nineteenth-century America but a model for his sons.

Besides defining careers for Sidney and Richard, Morse set an example of intellectual curiosity, enterprise, and persistence for all three of his sons. He also impressed upon them the importance of science and invention, regarding the growth of scientific knowledge in pietistic terms, as one aspect of man's progress under providence toward the millennium. Speaking before the American Bible Society in 1821, Morse said:

It will be prodigy on prodigy, wonder following wonder, greater as they go, till wonders become the order of the day, wonders on wonders, the steady and established method of Providence. Besides, they will anticipate us, not we them. New resources will be opened. New truth will be learned—new only to us, though old itself as its Eternal Author! For God is our "king of old, working salvation in the midst of the earth!" Like himself always, ever original, as well as supreme, He will do his own pleasure, and illustrate his own word, as equally "wonderful in counsel, and excellent in working."

In 1813 Sidney, interested in discovering a means of "navigating the air," made some experiments with a kite. Several years later, he and Samuel invented an improved piston pump and worked on several other inventions, including some improvements in a steamboat engine. Sidney in later years invented cerography, a process of reproducing maps with a common printing press, and the bathometer, an instrument for measuring the depth of the ocean.[60]

These achievements, of course, were much less important than Samuel's great invention, the telegraph. It took years for him to develop it and win public acceptance, and it required of him the kind of organizational ability and persistence of which his father had provided an example. He bore his difficulties with the same religious faith that Morse had borne his own, finding great comfort in his belief that all things happened as God willed them and so are for the best. In memory of his father, Samuel established at Union Theological Seminary a lectureship on the relation of the Bible to the sciences.[61]

Of the three sons, Samuel was most like his father, ever ready to engage in controversy. In 1811, realizing that Samuel would be happy only as a painter, Morse had accepted that decision and agreed to pay for his education in England. Soon after arriving there, Samuel became a Democratic-Republican, a supporter of Madison's policies and subsequently the war, all because of the contempt with which the British regarded the United States. Confronting his father squarely, Samuel told him that he could not accept the arguments in his Fast Day sermon of July 1812. Morse agreed to disagree with Samuel on politics, which is surprising considering the tenacity with which he usually insisted on his opinions but which indicates his love for his son. (These differences of course became less important after the war. Though Morse considered himself a "Federalist of the New England stamp" until his death, ironically he favored the election of Jackson in 1824. Calhoun had been his first choice, but with the collapse of his candidacy Morse thought the country would be "highly favored" to have

Jackson and Calhoun in the two highest offices. "The advantages in a religious view would be immense.")[62]

Samuel Morse's experiences in Britain, where contempt for the United States forced upon him the painful necessity of breaking politically with his father, made for his developing the most uncritical kind of patriotism. His Democratic faith essentially was a belief that the United States had no real problems of its own making. Like his father, he had a tendency to believe in conspiratorial forces, and to these he attributed America's troubles. Moreover, he was unable to accept changing conditions in the United States and so, though always a Democrat, became a reactionary.

He became a champion of nativism in the 1830s, running unsuccessfully for mayor of New York City. Using the *New York Observer* as one of his forums, he argued that Austria was directing a conspiracy against the United States because American democratic principles threatened it. Austria, he insisted, controlled the Roman Catholic church, which with its influence over the growing immigrant Catholic population, was working to undermine American civil and religious liberty. He called for changes in the naturalization laws so that immigrants would not be permitted to vote. Certainly his anti-Catholicism and probably his nativism can be traced to his upbringing, for his father often had spoken of the Catholic church as the great enemy of liberty and, as a Federalist, had believed that naturalization should be restricted.[63]

Samuel Morse went on to become an important Copperhead Democrat during the Civil War and to fashion a religious defense of slavery. None of Morse's sons approved of abolitionism, though Samuel was the only one to defend slavery. Sidney contended that the abolitionists' harsh denunciations of slavery had destroyed southern support of colonization, which he considered the only acceptable way of abolishing slavery. This was also Richard's position, but by 1864 he decided to vote for Lincoln, which Samuel considered tantamount to becoming an abolitionist.[64]

Samuel Morse fervently believed that abolitionism was the

"logical progeny" of the Unitarian heresy against which his father had struggled. (He also charged that abolitionism was promoted by British aristocrats who wanted to destroy the Union in order to protect their class privileges and wealth.) He was distressed that so many of the northern orthodox clergy, who like his brothers had once been hostile to abolitionism, had been driven to support it by the sectional crisis and finally the war. Samuel Morse argued that abolitionism grew out of William Ellery Channing's false teaching that man is not fallen. Orthodox abolitionists, Morse complained, ignored the Bible, which teaches that, man being lost in sin, God sent Jesus to obey, to atone for man's disobedience. Parallel to Jesus' great mission, he insisted, God had also established the social institutions of government, marriage, the parental relation, and slavery. In each of these as inferior party owes obedience to a superior. In God's providential scheme, the obedience these institutions establish aids in overcoming sin and restoring man in God's sight. As Samuel Morse expressed it, "by a system of redemption devised in the councils of heaven, in which the end is man's salvation from the slavery of sin, man's terrestrial slavery is made one of the wisely-appointed means for giving him celestial and eternal liberty."[65]

More than fifty years earlier, Jedidiah Morse had spoken of the "slavery of sin" in addressing the blacks of Boston who met to celebrate the abolition of the international slave trade. He had insisted then that belief in Christ, which freed man from sin, the worst kind of slavery, was the supreme good, far greater than all temporal blessings. Still, he had contended that chattel slavery was a great evil, which "thrives only on the vices of mankind." Morse's feelings about blacks were inconsistent, but he had expected with pleasure that the ending of the slave trade would lead to the abolition of slavery itself.[66]

In putting orthodoxy to the defense of slavery, Samuel Morse adopted the orthodoxy of the South. He abandoned the millennialist hope with which his father had maintained his faith, his optimism, and his expectation that the world would soon be transformed and made free of sin. Thousands, moved by such hopes and also the perception of themselves as sinners whose only chance for salvation lay in throwing themselves upon the mercy of God, had joined the northern churches during the Second Great Awakening. Later, similar millennial hopes and the same belief that some of the great ends of God's creation would be realized in history led others to become abolitionists. But for Samuel Morse, perhaps in some ways a more consistent Calvinist than his father, the world was fallen and would remain so. At its best, his faith was sad and hard; but it also, as his defense of slavery suggests, tended to make for indifference to injustice.

The millennial vision of the world moving toward universal piety and happiness provided some comfort for Jedidiah Morse in the last years of his life, making up in some ways for personal disappointments. A brief introduction, which he wrote in 1823, to an autobiography that never got any further explained that his ministry took place during

> a period of singular revolutions, & distress of nations; of wars most bloody & desolation throughout the civilized world, of the rise & widespread effects of an Atheistical Species of infidelity, of its remarkable overthrow through the triumphant influence of Christianity & of the rise of an infidel Christianity, out of the ruins of infidel philosophy—a period remarkable for political & religious division, which generated angry contention, affecting, in a great or lesser degree, all the social relations of life.

Morse regarded his life's work, above all, in terms of the development of evangelical Protestantism, which he believed had grown up in response to an atheistic threat and had gone on to defeat it.[67]

Morse could have taken pleasure in recalling the emergence of evangelical Protestantism even if he regarded it just as a matter of Americans finally turning to religion after a long involvement with independence and other political issues. He could also have taken special pleasure in the fact that ministers kept this new spirit alive with their preaching and organizational abilities. But viewing the emergence in the context of a far-reaching conspiratorial threat made it seem grander. This imaginary context also made the defeats he had suffered seem less important.

Certainly there were defeats. During his lifetime he saw the Federalist party and its high-toned elitism fade away as democratic sentiments grew among the American people. But because Morse so badly misunderstood the nature of democracy—even imaging that Jefferson's triumph in 1800 would pose a dire threat to Christianity—when Jefferson's victory did not bring on disaster, defeat in the political battle lost much of its sting.

In religious matters, too, Morse suffered a number of disappointments. He did manage to initiate the separation of orthodox and Unitarian Congregationalists, and this worked to prevent the possibility, which was not very great, of Unitarianism spreading beyond eastern Massachusetts. On the other hand, he witnessed the gradual demise of the Congregational establishments in Connecticut and Massachusetts. In Connecticut the establishment fell in 1817. In 1811, reform of the Massachusetts parish laws denied Congregationalism the advantage it had long enjoyed by making it really possible for other denominations to receive the taxes paid by their members. This, however, did not end their efforts to put an end to the establishment altogether, which they finally managed to do in 1833, several years after Morse's death.[68]

The fate of these establishments, however, was hardly Morse's greatest concern. He had, in several of his geographical writings, pointed to the good effects of the parish laws and made the standard Congregational point that these ensured that the people would always receive necessary religious instruction and that the laws were by no means oppressive. In his correspondence, however, Morse almost never mentioned the issue of establishment, and he did not devote the pages of the *Panoplist* to the defense of the cause. Morse's lack of interest may have stemmed from the fact that his own church had been incorporated in 1803 and was thereafter unaffected by the parish laws. In addition, Morse may have sensed that the apparatus of the Second Great Awakening, to which he devoted so much of his attention, provided a much firmer basis for Congregationalism than did its legal establishment. Though Lyman Beecher struggled to keep the establishment intact in Connecticut, he quickly came to the conclusion that it had hindered, rather than helped, the cause of evangelical Protestantism by dividing Congregationalists and other evangelicals. It had obstructed their cooperating in joint efforts to promote their common faith. In Massachusetts during the 1820s many orthodox Congregationalists even came to conclude that establishment worked much to the benefit of Unitarian churches, and this induced some of them to support disestablishment.[69]

Far more troublesome than disestablishment was one of its principal causes, the impressive growth of the Baptists and Methodists. This cost Congregationalism its dominant position in New England. Yet it, too, could be accepted. By 1820, with Unitarianism looming as the great enemy in the minds of orthodox Congregationalists and with their own drift away from consistent Calvinism, the views of the other evangelical denominations seemed much less distasteful than they once had. Sereno Dwight reported with satisfaction that jealousy was diminishing among the various evangelical denominations: "The line of demarcation which the Church is now drawing, is between those who admit of the doctrines of human depravity, vicarious atonement, regeneration, and the influence of the Holy Spirit, and those who reject them." In addition, the Baptists and Methodists were increasingly emphasizing ministerial education, making them much more respectable to Congregationalists. Then too, the other denominations were willing to join with Congregationalists in moral and some benevolent causes. Though the growth of the Baptists and the Methodists was not the happiest prospect for Congregationalism, they were not regarded as enemies. They were powerful competitors but also valued allies who, in Morse's terms, had helped to overcome an "Atheistic Species of Infidelity."[70]

Because Morse and other Congregationalist ministers believed the national situation was so dire at the close of the eighteenth century, their success within the Second Great Awakening seemed greater and their losses seemed less than they might otherwise have appeared. But by no means was their sense of achievement a delusion. Though Congregationalism was not the dominant denomination that it had been in colonial New England, it had shaken off the lethargy of the late-eighteenth century. More often than not, it initiated new moral and benevolent campaigns and induced the other denominations to cooperate with it. Although its growth did not keep pace with that of other denominations, it still had a solid hold on much of the northern middle class, making it an influential and dynamic force in American society. Morse contributed significantly to the transformation Congregationalism underwent. Despite his natural elitist biases and misgivings, he anticipated the power that public opinion would wield in American society. Above all, Morse managed to forge communication and organizational tools to mold evangelical opinion and bring it to bear in the United States.

While Morse thus had some real and some fanciful reasons for taking satisfaction in the development of evangelical Protestantism, reflection on his career stirred up painful memories. The "political & religious divisions, which generated angry contention, affecting, in a greater or lesser degree, all the social relations of life," certainly affected few lives as much as his own.[71]

Of course his political and religious opponents considered him a laughing stock—either a pathetic fool obsessed by unreal fears or a propagandist and liar. The most accurate view of Morse is that he acted out of honestly held, if overwrought, fears which a deeply suspicious nature drove him to accept. He appeared at his worst in defending his charges and actions, showing an inability to deal honestly with facts. The result was often blatant hypocrisy, with Morse twisting the truth to serve his own purposes or issuing cloying protestations of total innocence.

More surprising, his relations with his associates were seldom close and not very personally satisfying. These men found in Morse many valuable ideas, but they also encountered unappealing personal qualities. Beneath the outward amiability and the genial manners that he had cultivated as a student at Yale, Morse was a man who was extremely difficult to work with. His moods ranged from depression to exaltation and shifted quickly—sometimes, his associates felt, without much relation to reality. In addition, he was overbearing, insisting that others fall into line behind his schemes. He was also at times suspicious of even his colleagues, sometimes imputing reluctance to follow him to ill will or unworthy motives on their part. Morse's correspondence with Elijah Parish, his collaborator for twenty years on various writings and as difficult a man as Morse was, illustrates this side of Morse's personality. Their letters reflect a troubled relationship with almost constant suspicion and mistrust on both sides.

Still, Morse did have engaging qualities, which were reflected in his concern over blacks and especially Indians. His compassion and idealism were evident, even if alloyed with condescension. It was precisely because these groups were regarded and treated as unequal in early national society that Morse could express patronizing attitudes toward them and still work in their behalf. (He more or less felt the same toward all other people, but in expressing his feelings toward other whites, say Democratic-Republicans, he managed only to offend them and win their hostility.) Despite Morse's obvious faults, his concern for blacks and Indians compares favorably with the attitudes of most of his white contemporaries, who viewed these groups either with hostility or indifference.

Retirement from the combative life he had led did little to bring Morse peace. Shortly before he died in June 1826, still bitter about his dismissal from the Charlestown church, Morse complained to one of the ministers who had served on the council that its statement of the grounds of dismissal had injured his character. Morse did not live to read the reply, the ɪninister's candid explanation that he had been surprised that a man of Morse's piety had not confined himself "more within the limits of your office."[72]

Morse also believed that the plan for Indian civilization submitted by Secretary of War Barbour in February 1826 contained suggestions of his for which he received no credit. Barbour unenthusiastically put forward the plan, which called for creating colonies west of the Mississippi and in the Northwest Territory, where the Indians would be civilized, only because of southern pressure for removal of the Indians. Morse, of course, had argued against removal of the southern tribes, but he refused to recognize that that essentially was what Barbour's plan was about. Morse instead regarded it as a pledge that his proposed northwest colony would finally be established and that efforts would be made "to save the remnants of the poor Indians, to compensate them for the injuries done them—to raise our national reputation for justice & humanity." Trying to extort an acknowledgment of his work, Morse wrote Barbour of his approval of the plan, "that it agreed with mine substantially," and sent copies of his *Report to the Secretary of War* and report of the Indian society in proof of that fact.[73]

When Morse died, he was confident that his life's work had not been in vain, that he had helped to overcome dangerous infidel threats to the United States and that the benevolent societies he had helped set in operation would go on to claim all the world for Christianity. He took special delight in the prospect of the preservation of the Indians and their conversion to Christianity, which he was sure would be effected by means of his proposals. His only regret, but a bitter one, was that he was not given credit for his labors. In this way, Morse's feelings during his final days were in keeping with those of his entire life: he was confident that the religious causes he had aided were progressing but bitterly convinced that his contributions went unacknowledged or scorned.

# Notes

## Abbreviations

CHS     Oliver Wolcott, Jr. Papers
          Connecticut Historical Society

HSP     Dreer Collection
          Historical Society of Pennsylvania

NYHS   Morse Papers
          New York Historical Society

NYPL   Morse Papers
          New York Public Library

Yale    Morse Papers
          Yale University

## Introduction

1. Perry Miller, *The New England Mind: From Colony to Province* (Boston, 1953); Richard L. Bushman, *From Puritan to Yankee* (New York, 1967); J. William T. Youngs, Jr., *God's Messengers* (Baltimore, 1976).
2. Bernard Bailyn, *The Ideological Origins of the American Revolution* (Cambridge, Mass., 1967), pp. 301–319; Paul Goodman, *The Democratic-Repulicans of Massachusetts* (Cambridge, Mass., 1964), pp. 1–17.
3. James M. Banner, Jr., *To the Hartford Convention* (New York, 1970), pp. 3–52; David Hackett Fischer, *The Revolution of American Conservatism* (New York, 1965), pp. 1–17.
4. Donald G. Mathews, "The Second Great Awakening as an Organizing Process, 1789–1830," *American Quarterly* 21

(1969):23–43; Perry Miller, *The Life of the Mind in America* (New York, 1965), pp. 3–72.

5. Donald M. Scott, *From Office to Profession* (Philadelphia, 1978).

6. Perry Miller, "From the Covenant to the Revival," in *Nature's Nation* (Cambridge, Mass., 1967), p. 116; Sidney Earl Mead, *Nathaniel William Taylor* (Chicago, 1942).

7. Daniel Walker Howe, *The Political Culture of the American Whigs* (Chicago, 1979).

## Chapter 1

1. Jedidiah Morse [Sr.], *Birthday Reflections of Deacon Jedidiah Morse* (Providence, R.I., 1901), p. 5; Ellen D. Larned, *History of Windham County, Connecticut* (Worcester, Mass., 1874), 1:18–31, 259–263; Clarence Bowen, *Woodstock: An Historical Sketch* (New York, 1886), pp. 12–19.

2. Morse [Sr.], *Birthday Reflections*, pp. 3–4; Larned, *Windham County*, 1:393–395, 401–402; Clarence Bowen, *The History of Woodstock Connecticut* (Norwood, Mass., 1926), p. 99.

3. Morse [Sr.], *Birthday Reflections*, pp. 9, 11; Bowen, *History of Woodstock*, pp. 107–110.

4. Morse [Sr.], *Birthday Reflections*, pp. 9–13; Larned, *Windham County*, 1:206.

5. Larned, *Windham County*, 2:104–128, 143; Bowen, *History of Woodstock*, p. 143.

6. Larned, *Windham County*, 2:137–157.

7. Ibid.:159–183; Bowen, *History of Woodstock*, p. 152.

8. William Buell Sprague, *The Life of Jedidiah Morse* (New York, 1874), pp. 1–2; idem, *Annals of the American Pulpit* (New York, 1857), 2:247.

9. Jedidiah Morse, Jr. to Deacon Morse, April 3, 1782 (quote), March 9, 1781, November 28, 1779, Yale.

10. Morse to Deacon Morse, November 25, 1780, February 20, 1781, Yale.

11. Ezra Stiles, *The Literary Diary of Ezra Stiles*, ed. Franklin B. Dexter (New York, 1901), 2:512, 518, 527, 542–543, 568, 3:14; Morse to Deacon Morse, March 15, 1781, January 6, 1782, June 24, 1783, Yale.

12. Sprague, *Annals*, 2:251 (quote); Bowen, *History of Woodstock*, p.

197; Morse to Deacon Morse, March 19, June 20, 24, November 7, 1783, Yale.

13. Morse to Deacon Morse, October 29, November 7, 1783, Yale; Morse to John Cotton Smith, February 2, 1784, John Cotton Smith Papers, Yale; Morse to Deacon Morse, April 11 (quote), September 8, 1784, Yale; Sprague, *Annals*, 2:247.

14. Sprague, *Morse*, p. 3; Bowen, *History of Woodstock*, p. 196; Morse, notebook 12, April 23, 1784, NYHS.

15. Morse, MS diary for April 28–June 12, 1782, Yale; Morse to Deacon Morse, February 9, 1784, Yale.

16. Sprague, *Annals*, 2:254.

17. Jedidiah Morse, *Geography Made Easy* (New Haven, Conn., 1784), p. 214; Morse to Deacon Morse, January 8, 1785, Yale; Morse to Smith, March 24, 1785, *New England Quarterly* 14 (1941):700–701 (first quote); Morse to Christoph Ebeling, May 27, 1794 (second quote), Yale.

18. Sprague, *Morse*, p. 7; Morse to Deacon Morse, January 7, February 3, 1786 (quote), Yale.

19. Morse to Smith, July 19, 1786, Smith Papers, Yale; Morse to Deacon Morse, September 14, 1786, Yale; Morse to Smith, November 3, 1786, *New England Quarterly* 14 (1941):703.

20. Morse to Deacon Morse, September 20, 1786, June 6, July 15, 1785, February 16, July 28, 1786, Yale.

21. Sprague, *Morse*, pp. 8–9; Morse to Deacon Morse, November 12, 23, 29 (quote), 1786, Yale.

22. Sprague, *Morse*, p. 10; Richard C. Morse, "His Life in the South," MS dated November 19, 1861, Yale.

23. Jeremy Belknap to Ebenezer Hazard, December 8, 1787, *Massachusetts Historical Society Collections*, ser. 5, 2:497; Hazard to Belknap, January 11, 1788, ibid., 3:1, Belknap to Hazard, January 25, 1788, ibid., 3:13.

24. Morse to Belknap, January 18, 1788, *Massachusetts Historical Society Collections*, ser. 6, 4:382; Jedidiah Morse, "To the Friends of Science" (Philadelphia, 1787); idem, "Sir, Whoever. . ." [New York, 1788].

25. Hazard to Belknap, January 11, 1788, *Massachusetts Historical Society Collections*, ser. 5, 3:1; Morse to Belknap, January 18, 1788, ibid., ser. 6, 4:383--384; Morse to Belknap, June 3, 1788, ibid., 4:407; Morse to Belknap, June 26, 1788, ibid., 4:413; Hazard to

Morse, February 14, 1788, NYHS; Hency de Saussure to Morse, February 11, 1788, NYHS; Hazard to Belknap, May 8, 1788, *Massachusetts Historical Society Collections,* ser. 5, 3:34; Hazard to Belknap, May 10, 1788, ibid., 3:39; Jedidiah Morse, *American Gazetteer* (Boston, 1797), p. iii.

26. John Rodgers to Morse, January 19, 1788, HSP; Hazard to Morse, February 14, 1788, NYHS; Morse to Rodgers, January 20, 1788, HSP; Rodgers to Morse, February 11, 1788, HSP; Sprague, *Morse,* pp. 10–12; Hazard to Belknap, May 31, 1788, *Massachusetts Historical Society Collections,* ser. 5, 3:47; Hazard to Belknap, September 9, 1788, ibid., 3:62.

27. Hazard to Belknap, April 16, 1788, *Massachusetts Historical Society Collections,* ser. 5, 3:31.

28. Stiles, *Literary Diary,* 3:262; Morse to his aunt, March 11, 1782, letterbook, Yale; Morse, MS sermons, 1787, Yale.

29. Belknap to Morse, May 24, 1788, HSP; Belknap to Hazard, July 24, 1788, *Massachusetts Historical Society Collections,* ser. 5, 3:53; Belknap to Morse, July 24, 1788, ibid., ser. 6, 4:415–416; Richard Cary to Belknap, November 25, 1788, ibid., 4:428; Morse to Cary, December 6, 1788, HSP.

30. Sprague, *Morse,* pp. 14–16.

31. Morse to Deacon Morse, May 5, 1803, Yale.

32. Morse to Benjamin Trumbull, July 14, 1788 (first quote), Yale; Morse to Deacon Morse, July 22, 1788 (second quote), Yale.

33. Samuel Beach to Morse, April 30, 1789, NYHS.

34. Sprague, *Morse,* p. 285.

35. Morse, *Geography Made Easy,* p. 41.

36. Ibid., pp. 47, 62, 68–69, 73.

37. Morse to Deacon Morse, December 1, 1786, Yale; Morse, MS almanac, 1786, Yale; Morse to Simeon Baldwin, June 19, 1787, Yale.

38. Jedidiah Morse, *The American Geography* (Elizabethtown, N.J., 1789), pp. 145–147, 218, 240, 270.

39. Ibid., pp. 251, 313.

40. Ibid., pp. 352–353, 390–391, 417, 432, 450, 388, 390, 387, 353, 416.

41. Jedidiah Morse, *The American Universal Geography* (Boston, 1793), 1:212 (first two quotes); idem, *American Geography,* pp. 113–125, 67, 81–82, 189, 175, 181, 87–88, 469 (last quote); Morse, MS sermon, delivered November 26, 1789, Yale.

42. Morse, *American Geography*, p. 468; Stiles, *Literary Diary*, 3:364–365; Ezra Stiles, *The United States Elevated to Glory and Honor* . . . (New Haven, Conn., 1783).

43. Morse, *American Geography*, pp. 100, 219, 242.

44. Morse, *American Universal Geography*, 1:212; Morse to the Massachusetts Historical Society, September 1795, NYPL; Christoph Ebeling to William Bentley, April 29, 1796, *American Antiquarian Society Proceedings*, n.s. 35 (1925):290–291.

45. Hazard to Belknap, November 15, 1788, *Massachusetts Historical Society Collection*, ser. 5, 3:73; Abiel Holmes to Morse, April 3, 1789, Yale.

46. Samuel L. Mitchill to Morse, July 4, 1789, NYPL; John Wheelock to Morse, December 19, 1789, Yale; Hazard to Morse, January 2, 1792, NYHS.

47. Morse to Deacon Morse, July 12, 1792, Yale; Morse to Richard Price, January 30, 1789, Yale; Price to Morse, May 18, 1789, HSP; Morse to Price, August 23, 1789, Yale; Price to Morse, March 29, 1790, HSP; Joseph Priestley to Morse, August 24, 1793, HSP.

48. Jedidiah Morse, *Elements of Geography* (Boston, 1795), pp. vi–vii; Ebeling to Bentley, June 31, 1797, Ebeling Papers, Harvard; Ebeling to Belknap, April 28, 1798, *Massachusetts Historical Society Collections*, ser. 6, 4:621–622; Sprague, *Morse*, pp. 214–215.

49. Morse to Ebeling, May 27, 1794, Yale; Ralph H. Brown, "The American Geographies of Jedidiah Morse," *Annals of the Association of American Geographers* 31 (1941):176, 184.

50. Belknap to Hazard, July 13, 1791, *Massachusetts Historical Society Collections*, ser. 5, 3:267; Morse to Deacon Morse, July 30, 1792, Yale; Thomas Dwight to Morse, October 7, 1797, NYPL.

51. Morse to Deacon Morse, July 12, 1792, Yale; Deacon Morse to Morse, October 7, 1792, Yale.

52. Jedidiah Morse, MS sermon delivered May 3, 1798, Yale.

53. Morse to Deacon Morse, August 7, 1789, Yale; Jedidiah Morse, MS sermon delivered November 8, 1789, Yale; Morse to Deacon Morse, December 30, 1789, January 31, 1790, Yale; William Bentley, *The Diary of William Bentley* (Salem, Mass., 1905–1914), 1:187; Jeremy Belknap, *A Sermon, preached at the Installation of the Rev. Jedidiah Morse* . . . (Boston, 1789).

54. Boston *Columbian Centinel*, March 27, 1790; Sprague, *Morse*, pp.

54–55; James King Morse, *Jedidiah Morse: A Champion of New England Orthodoxy* (New York, 1939), pp. 42–44.

55. *Columbian Centinel,* November 17, 27, December 4, 15, 22, 1790; James Freeman, *Remarks on the American Universal Geography* (Boston, 1793), passim; Boston *Independent Chronicle,* November 24, 1793; Conrad Wright, *The Beginnings of Unitarianism* (Boston, 1955), pp. 271–273.

## Chapter 2

1. Jedidiah Morse, MS sermon delivered November 26, 1789, Yale.

2. Joseph Eckley, *A Sermon preached . . . June 4, 1792* (Boston, 1792), pp. 17–18; Theodore Dwight, *An Oration, Spoken before the Society of the Cincinnati . . .* (Hartford, Conn., 1792), pp. 11–12; Joseph Blake, Jr., *An Oration, pronounced July 4th, 1792 . . .* (Boston, 1792), pp. 13–14.

3. Samuel Hopkins, "A Treatise on the Millennium," in *Works* (Boston, 1852), 2:232–233, 296–310; Samuel Langdon, *Observations on the Revelation of Jesus Christ to St. John* (Worcester, Mass., 1791), pp. 266–267.

4. Hopkins, "Treatise," 2:259–267; Langdon, *Observations,* pp. 296–299.

5. Hopkins, "Treatise," 2:271–292; Langdon, *Observations,* pp. 298–299.

6. Hopkins, "Treatise," 2:253, 255; Joseph Bellamy, "The Millennium," in *The Millennium,* ed. David Austin (Elizabethtown, N.J., 1794), pp. 38–41; Jonathan Edwards, "An Humble Attempt to Promote Explicit Agreement . . . ," in *The Millennium,* ed. Austin, pp. 125–127.

7. Hopkins, "Treatise," 2:326–328, 322–323.

8. Ibid., 2:361–364; Langdon, *Observations,* pp. 300–307.

9. Langdon, *Observations,* p. 267.

10. Daniel Foster, *A Sermon preached before His Excellency John Hancock . . .* (Boston, 1790), p. 25 (quote); Eckley, *A Sermon . . . June 4, 1792,* pp. 17–26.

11. *Massachusetts Centinel,* September 19, 23, December 16, 23, 1789, January 6, 8, March 13, 17, 23, August 30, September 3, 10, 1791, May 26, June 23, July 28, August 1, 1792; *Independent Chronicle,* March 24, April 14, 1791.

12. *Centinel,* June 16, 1792.

13. Ibid., January 26, 30, February 2, 6, 1793; *Chronicle*, January 31, February 14, 1793; Chandler Robbins, *An Address, delivered at Plymouth, on the 24th day of January 1793* (Boston, 1793), pp. 6–7.

14. Jeremy Belknap, *A Discourse . . . on the 23rd day of October, 1792 . . .* (Boston, 1792), pp. 42–43; Chandler Robbins, *Address, delivered at Plymouth,* pp. 12–13; Morse to Deacon Morse, October 11, 1792, Yale.

15. David Tappan, *A Sermon, delivered . . . April 11, 1793* (Boston, 1793), pp. 16, 27–29; Joseph McKeen, *A Sermon, preached . . . April 11, 1793* (Salem, Mass., 1793), pp. 11–12; John Lathrop, *A Discourse on the Errors of Popery . . .* (Boston, [1793]), p. 32.

16. *Centinel*, April 13, 1793; *Chronicle*, May 16, 23, June 20, 1793; Samuel Miller, *A Sermon, preached . . . July 4th, 1793 . . .* (New York, [1793]), p. 30.

17. *Centinel*, April 10, May 11, 1793; *Chronicle*, April 19, May 2, 9, 30, July 18, August 1, 1793; Richard Buel, Jr., *Securing the Revolution* (Ithaca, N.Y., 1972), pp. 28–49; Paul Goodman, *The Democratic-Republicans of Massachusetts* (Cambridge, Mass., 1964), pp. 47–69.

18. *Centinel*, July 24, 27, 31, August 3, 14, 17, 21, 24, 28, 31, September 7, 14, 18, 25, October 12, 23, 1793; *Chronicle*, July 25, August 1, 1793.

19. *Centinel*, July 27, August 14, 24, September 11, November 30, December 4, 1793.

20. Morse to Oliver Wolcott, December 16, 1793, CHS; Morse to Deacon Morse, January 15, 1794, Yale.

21. *Chronicle*, January 16, 1794; Morse to Wolcott, February 19, 1794, CHS.

22. *Chronicle*, February 10, 17, 27, March 13, 1794; *Centinel*, February 12, 26, 1794, March 14, 1795.

23. Morse to Deacon Morse, February 28, 1794, Yale.

24. *Centinel*, March 1, 1794; Morse to Deacon Morse, February 28, 1794, Yale.

25. Morse to Christoph Ebeling, May 27, 1794, Yale.

26. Ibid.; William Emerson, *A Discourse, delivered in Harvard, July 4, 1794 . . .* (Boston, 1794), p. 15; Joseph Lathrop, *The Happiness of a Free Government . . .* (Springfield, Mass., 1794), pp. 14, 22–23; Northampton *Hampshire Gazette*, July 23, 1794.

27. *Centinel*, July 16, August 16, 20, 30, September 3, 6, 10, 13, 17, 20, 24, 27, October 1, 4, 1794.

28. Morse to Wolcott, October 15, 1794, CHS.

29. David Osgood, *The Wonderful Works of God* . . . (Boston, 1794), pp. 22–24; Morse to Wolcott, December 7, 1794, CHS.

30. Timothy Dwight, *Virtuous Rulers a National Blessing* . . . (Hartford, Conn., 1791), pp. 34–35; Chandler Robbins, *A Sermon, preached* . . . *May 25, 1791* . . . (Boston, 1791), p. 8; Daniel Foster, *A Sermon, preached* . . . *May 26, 1790* (Hartford, Conn., 1790), pp. 8–11, 18–21; William Morrison, *A Sermon, delivered* . . . *June 7th, 1792* (Exeter, N.H., 1792), pp. 33–37.

31. *Chronicle*, November 24, 27, 1794.

32. Ibid., December 22, 29, 1794; *Centinel*, February 11, 1795.

33. Jedidiah Morse, *The Present Situation of the Other Nations* . . . (Boston, 1795), pp. 10–11, 30.

34. Ibid., p. 14; William Linn, *Discourses on the Signs of the Times* (New York, 1794), p. 19 (quote); David Austin, "The Downfall of the Mystical Babylon," in *The Millennium*, ed. Austin, pp. 382–383.

35. David Osgood, *A Discourse delivered February 19, 1795* . . . (Boston, 1795), p. 17; Benjamin Wadsworth, *America Invoked to Praise the Lord* . . . (Salem, Mass., 1795), pp. 26–27; Samuel West, *A Sermon, delivered* . . . *February 19th, 1795* (Boston, 1795), p. 19; David Tappan, *Christian Thankfulness* . . . (Boston, 1795), pp. 26–29; Abiel Holmes, *A Sermon, on the Freedom and Happiness of America* . . . (Boston, 1795), pp. 21–22; Joseph Dana, *A Sermon, delivered February 19, 1795* . . . (Newburyport, Mass., 1795), p. 15; *Chronicle*, March 12, 1795.

36. *Chronicle*, March 30, 1795; Henry Channing to Morse, April 8, 1795, Yale; Morse to Deacon Morse, April 23, 1795, Yale; *Centinel*, April 4, 1795; *Hampshire Gazette*, April 8, 1795; Morse to Wolcott, July 27, 1795, CHS; John Thornton Kirkland, *A Sermon, preached before the Ancient and Honorable Artillery Company* . . . (Boston, 1795), p. 27.

37. Levi Frisbie, *A Sermon delivered February 19, 1795* . . . (Newburyport, Mass., [1795]), p. 18 (quote); Morse, *Present Situation*, p. 31; Thomas Barnard, *A Sermon, delivered* . . . *February 19, 1795* (Salem, Mass., 1795), pp. 16–17; Ezra Sampson, *A Discourse delivered February 19, 1795* (Boston, 1795), p. 20; Isaac Story, *A Sermon, preached February 19, 1795* (Salem, Mass., 1795), p. 18.

38. Osgood, *Discourse* . . . *February 19, 1795*, pp. 12–13; Holmes, *Freedom and Happiness*, p. 29; Samuel Kendal, *A Sermon, delivered*

... *February 19, 1795* (Boston, 1795), pp. 13–14, 18–19, 22–23; Henry Ware, *The Continuance of Peace* . . . (Boston, 1795), pp. 10–17; Samuel Deane, *A Sermon, preached February 19th, 1795* . . . (Portland, District of Maine, 1795), p. 17; John Mellen, *The Great and Happy Doctrine of Liberty* . . . (Boston, 1795), pp. 15–16.

39. Morse, *Present Situation*, p. 32; John Andrews, *A Sermon, delivered February 19, 1795* . . . (Newburyport, Mass., n.d.), pp. 18–19; Hezekiah Packard, *The Plea of Patriotism* . . . (Boston, 1795), pp. 13–16; John Tyler, *The Blessing of Peace* . . . (Norwich, Conn., 1795), pp. 7–8; Ware, *Continuance of Peace*, p. 20; Frisbie, *Sermon* . . . *February 19, 1795*, pp. 13–14, 19–20; *Centinel*, March 14, 1795.

40. Ebenezer Bradford, *The Nature and Manner of Giving Thanks to God* . . . (Boston, 1795), pp. 9, 17–18; Thomas Thacher, *A Discourse* . . . *February 19, 1795* (Boston, 1795), pp. 16–17; *Chronicle*, March 2, 9, May 25, 1795.

41. *Chronicle*, March 19, 30, April 23, 30, May 11, 18, 21, June 1, 1795; Tappan, *Christian Thankfulness*, p. 36; John S. J. Gardiner, "Remarks on the Jacobiniad," *Federal Orrery*, December 8, 15, 25, 29, 1974; January 1, 5, 12, 15, 19, 22, 1975.

42. *Centinel*, July 8, 1795; *Chronicle*, July 13, 16, 1795.

43. *Chronicle*, July 20, September 3, 1795. See also *Chronicle*, July 23, 27, August 6, November 26, December 3, 1795.

44. John Rodgers to Morse, July 15, 1795, Yale; William L. Smith to Morse, July 17, 1795, Yale; Wolcott to Morse, July 16, 1795, CHS; Morse to Deacon Morse, August 12, 1795, Yale.

45. *Chronicle*, July 23, 1795; *Centinel*, July 27, 1795.

46. Morse to Wolcott, July 21 (first quote), 27, 1795, CHS; Morse to Deacon Morse, August 12, 1795 (second quote), Yale.

47. Morse to Wolcott, July 21, September 10, 1795, CHS.

48. Wolcott to Morse, September 26, 1795, CHS; *Centinel*, September 26, 30, October 7, 14, 21, 31, November 7, 11, 18, 1795; *Chronicle*, September 14, 24, October 1, 1795; Morse to Wolcott, October 19, 1795, CHS.

49. *Chronicle*, September 3, 21, 24, 28, October 5, 26, November 2, 1795; *Centinel*, November 11, 14, 1795.

50. Thomas Worcester, *A Thanksgiving Sermon, delivered November 12, 1795* (Newburyport, Mass., 1796), pp. 21, 27–31; Francis Gardner, *A Sermon, delivered* . . . *November 19, 1795* (Leominster,

Mass., 1796), pp. 17–20; Jonathan Strong, *A Sermon, delivered November 19, 1795* (Boston, n.d.), pp. 10–25; David Osgood, *A Discourse, delivered . . . November 19, 1795* (Boston, 1795), pp. 23, 28–29; *Centinel*, December 12, 1795, February 13, 1796.

51. Morse to Elisabeth Morse, December 11, 21, 26, 1795, NYPL; Morse to Wolcott, December 30, 1795, CHS; Morse to Deacon Morse, January 7, 1796, Yale; Morse to Wolcott, January 13, February 15, March 7, 1796 (quote), CHS; *Centinel*, January 23, 27, February 24, 27, March 5, 1796.

52. *Centinel*, April 23, 25, 27, 1796; *Chronicle*, April 25, 28, 1796.

53. *Centinel*, April 20, May 4, 7, 11, 14, 1796; *Hampshire Gazette*, May 4, 1796.

54. *Chronicle*, May 5, 9, 12, 26, June 2, July 4, 1796.

55. Channing to Morse, June 3, 1796, NYHS.

56. Jedidiah Morse, *The American Geography* (Elizabethtown, N.J., 1789), p. 146; Charles Roy Keller, *The Second Great Awakening in Connecticut* (New Haven, Conn., 1942), pp. 22–25.

57. McKeen, *Sermon . . . April 11, 1793*, p. 17; Dan Foster, *An Election Sermon . . . October 8th, 1789* (Windsor, Vt., 1790), pp. 20–13; Nathan Strong, *A Sermon . . . May 13th, 1790* (Hartford, Conn., 1790), pp. 11–13; Chandler Robbins, *Sermon . . . May 25, 1791*, pp. 9, 35–38; Israel Evans, *A Sermon, delivered at Concord . . .* (Concord, N.H, 1791), pp. 21–22; Charles Backus, *A Sermon, preached . . . May 9th, 1793* (Hartford, Conn., 1793), p. 10; Samuel Deane, *A Sermon, preached . . . May 28th, 1794* (Boston, 1794), pp. 30–31

58. Dwight, *Virtuous Rulers*, pp. 13–15; David Tappan, *A Sermon, preached May 30, 1792 . . .* (Boston, 1792), pp. 16–18; Timothy Stone, *A Sermon, preached . . . May 10th, 1792* (Exeter, N.H., 1792), pp. 20–25; Jonathan Edwards, *The Necessity of the Belief of Christianity* (Hartford, Conn., 1794), pp. 6–9.

59. Morse, *American Geography*, p. 170; Tappan, *Sermon . . . May 30, 1792*, pp. 16–17, 22–23; Backus, *Sermon . . . May 9th, 1793*, pp. 20–26; Timothy Dwight, *The True Means of Establishing Public Happiness . . .* (New Haven, Conn., 1795), pp. 35–36; Henry Cumings, *A Sermon preached . . . December 15, 1796* (Boston, 1797), pp. 14–15; Andrew Lee, *The Origin and Ends of Civil Government . . .* (Hartford, Conn., 1795), pp. 17–18.

60. Simeon Doggett, Jr., *A Discourse on Education . . .* (Newbedford, Mass., 1797), p. 27 (quote); *Centinel*, December 26, 1795; Eli

Forbes, *The Importance of the Rising Generation* . . . (Newburyport, Mass., 1795), p. 10; Clark Brown, *The Importance of the Early and Proper Education of Children* . . . (Newbedford, Mass., 1795), p. 16; Nathaniel Thayer, *A Sermon, delivered . . . April 2, 1795* (Boston, 1795), pp. 9–15; Asa Burton, *A Discourse, delivered . . . October 8th, 1795* . . . (Rutland, Vt., 1795), pp. 13–26.

61. Stone, *Sermon . . . May 10th, 1792*, p. 16 (first quote); Dan Kent, *Electioneering for Office Defended* . . . [Rutland, Vt., 1796], pp. 44–45 (second quote); Josiah Bridge, *A Sermon preached . . . May 27, 1789* (Boston, 1789), pp. 45–46, 52–53, Chandler Robbins, *Sermon . . . May 25, 1791*, pp. 12–25; Dwight, *Virtuous Rulers*, pp. 13–15, 18–19; Jonathan French, *A Sermon preached . . . May 25, 1796* . . . (Boston, 1796), pp. 18–19.

62. Morse, *American Geography*, p. 146; Nathanael Emmons, *A Discourse, delivered November 3, 1790* . . . (Providence, R.I., [1790]), pp. 16, 19–20, 22; Daniel Dow, quoted in Ellen D. Larned, *History of Windham County, Connecticut* (Worcester, Mass., 1874), 2:351 (quote); Ammi Robbins, *The Empires and Dominions of this World* . . . (Hartford, Conn., 1789), pp. 20–21.

63. Andrew Lee, *A Sermon preached at Franklin, July 21, 1793* (Norwich, Conn., 1794), pp. 14–18.

64. Tappan, *Sermon . . . May 30, 1792*, p. 10; Tappan, *Sermon . . . April 11, 1793*, p. 16.

65. [Zephaniah Swift], *The Correspondent* . . . (Windham, Conn., 1793), pp. 7–12. Eliphalet Lyman, *Two Discourses preached at Woodstock* . . . (Norwich, Conn., 1794), pp. 40–63.

66. Swift, *Correspondent*, pp. 11–23, 31–35, 43–44; [idem], *An Address to the Reverend Moses C. Welch* (Windham, Conn., 1794), pp. 53–60 (quote); Lyman, *Two Discourses*, pp. 23–25, 36, 53–55.

67. Larned, *Windham Coutny*, 2:255–257; Swift, *Correspondent*, pp. 122–124.

68. Swift, *Correspondent*, pp. 118–135; idem, *Address*, p. 37; Moses C. Welch, *The Addressor Addressed* . . . (Norwich, Conn., 1796), p. iv; [Zephaniah Swift], *A Second Address, to the Reverend Moses C. Welch* . . . (Windham, Conn., 1796), pp. 20–21, 34–35.

69. Morse to Wolcott, Octover 15, 1794, CHS; Wolcott to Morse, June 22, 1794, NYPL.

70. Gilbert Wakefield, *An Examination of the Age of Reason* . . . (London, 1794), passim; [Ebenezer Bradford], *Mr. Thomas Paine's Trial* (Boston, 1795), pp. 72–77.

71. Mellen, *Great and Happy Doctrine of Liberty*, p. 20; Morse to Deacon Morse, August 12, 1795, Yale; Jedidiah Morse, *Elements of Geography* (Boston, 1795), p. 63; Bradford, *Paine's Trial*, pp. 61–62.

72. *Centinel*, October 19, November 12, 1796; *Chronicle*, November 14, 1796.

73. John Clarke, *An Answer to the Question, Why Are You a Christian?* (Boston, 1795), passim; Jeremy Belknap, *Dissertations on the Character, Death & Resurrection of Jesus Christ* (Boston, 1795), pp. 121–126.

74. Jeremy Belknap, *A Sermon, delivered before the Convention of the Clergy of Massachusetts* . . . (Boston, 1796), pp. 15–16; Tappan, *Sermon* . . . *April 11, 1793*, p. 21; Nathanael Emmons, *National Peace as the Source of National Prosperity* . . . (Worcester, Mass., 1797), pp. 3–15; John Marsh, *Sermon, preached* . . . *May 12, 1796* (Hartford, Conn., 1796), pp. 30–32; William F. Rowland, *A Sermon, delivered* . . . *June 2, 1796* (Exeter, N.H., 1796), pp. 27, 31; John Taylor, *An Oration, delivered on the Fourth of July, 1796* (Greenfield, Mass., 1796), pp. 12–13; Alvan Hyde, *A Sermon delivered* . . . *December 15th 1796* (Stockbridge, Mass., 1796), pp. 14, 22–23.

75. Morse, *Elements of Geography*, p. 126; ibid., 2d. ed. (Boston, 1796), pp. 58, 126, 143.

76. *Centinel*, October 5, 12, November 9, 26, 30, December 3, 7, 21, 1796.

77. Morse to Wolcott, December 23, 1796, CHS.

## *Chapter 3*

1. David Osgood, *Some Facts evincive of the atheistical, anarchical, and, in other respects, immoral Principles of the French Republicans* . . . (Boston, 1798, pp. 21–22; Jeremy Belknap, *A Sermon, delivered on the 9th of May, 1798* . . . (Boston, 1798), pp. 19–22; Joseph McKeen, *Two Discourses, delivered* . . . *May 9, 1798* (Salem, Mass., 1798), pp. 22–28.

2. Nathan Strong, *A Sermon, preached* . . . *April 6, 1798* (Hartford, Conn., 1798), p. 13; David Tappan, *A Discourse, delivered* . . . *April 5, 1798* (Boston, 1798), p. 22.

3. Jedidiah Morse, *A Sermon, delivered* . . . *May 9th, 1798* . . . (Boston, 1798), pp. 17–20; John Robison, *Proofs of a Conspiracy*

*Against All the Governments and Religions of Europe* (London, 1798).

4. Ibid., pp. 21–29.

5. Tappan, *Discourse, delivered . . . April 5, 1798*, pp. 23–24; Thaddeus Mason Harris, *A Sermon preached the 9th of May . . .* (Boston, 1798), pp. 21–22; John Thornton Kirkland, *A Sermon, delivered on the 9th of May . . .* (Boston, 1798), p. 22; Timothy Dwight, *The Duty of Americans, At the Present Crisis . . .* (New Haven, Conn., 1798), pp. 16–19, 24; Thomas Worcester, *An Oration, delivered . . . July 4th, 1798* (Concord, N.H., 1798), pp. 11–16; Samuel Austin, *An Oration, pronounced . . . the Fourth of July . . .* (Worcester, Mass., 1798), pp. 26–28.

6. Nathanael Emmons, "*A Discourse, delivered May 9, 1798 . . . ,*" in idem, *The Works of Nathanael Emmons*, ed. Jacob Ide (Boston, 1842), 3:99–100, 110; John Prince, *A Discourse, delivered . . . May 9, 1798* (Salem, Mass., 1798), pp. 43, 37–38.

7. Nathanael Emmons, *A Sermon . . . April 25, 1799*, in *Works*, 3:145; Elijah Parish, *An Oration delivered at Bayfield, July 4, 1799* (Newburyport, Mass., 1799), p. 16 (quote); Joseph Dana, *The Duty and Reward of Loving our Country . . .* (Boston, 1799), pp. 31–32; John Smalley, *On the Evils of a Weak Government . . .* (Hartford, 1800), p. 11.

8. Address of the Convention of Congregational Ministers of Massachusetts, *Massachusetts Mercury*, June 19, 1798; Nathanael Emmons, "An Election Day Sermon . . . May 30, 1798," in *Works*, 3:125–126; John Wilder, *A Discourse, delivered May 9, 1798 . . .* (Wrentham, Mass., 1798), pp. 8–18.

9. Morse to Oliver Wolcott, May 21, July 13 (quote), 1798, CHS.

10. Morse, *Sermon . . . May 9th, 1798*, p. 20.

11. Morse to Wolcott, July 13, 1798, CHS; Josiah Quincy, *An Oration, pronounced July 4, 1798 . . .* (Boston, 1798), pp. 11–14.

12. Bernard Bailyn, *The Ideological Origins of the American Revolution* (Cambridge, 1967), passim; Gordon S. Wood, *The Creation of the American Republic, 1776–1787* (Chapel Hill, N.C., 1969), pp. 3–124.

13. Lance Banning, *The Jeffersonian Persuasion* (Ithaca, N.Y., 1978), passim; John R. Howe, Jr., "Republican Thought and the Political Violence of the 1790's," *American Quarterly* 19 (1967): 147–165. I do not mean to imply that Morse and other ministers who warned of the Illuminati were speaking out of the

Commonwealth tradition that stressed the danger of governmental abuse of power and was essentially an opposition outlook. Morse, of course, spoke of the Illuminati in order to bolster support of the Adams administration. I mean to suggest only that many ministers retained the habit of thinking in terms of conspiracies even after they had abandoned the political outlook that had given rise to it.

14. See letter by Morse in *Independent Chronicle*, June 18, 1798.

15. Jedidiah Morse, *A Sermon, preached . . . November 29, 1798 . . .* (Boston, 1798), pp. 13–15; Nathan Strong, *Political Instruction From the Prophecies of God's Word . . .* (Hartford, Conn., 1798), pp. 9, 14, 25–29; Joseph Buckminster, *A Discourse delivered . . . November 15, 1798 . . .* (Portsmouth, N.H., 1798), pp. 10–11; Dwight, *Duty of Americans,* pp. 5–14.

16. Henry Cumings, *A Sermon, preached . . . November 29, 1798 . . .* (Boston, 1798), pp. 16–29; Jonathan French, *A Sermon, delivered . . . November 29, 1798 . . .* (Andover, Mass., 1798), pp. 21, 24; Samuel Camp, *Thanksgiving and Praise due to God . . .* (Danbury, Conn., 1799), pp. 9–12; Robert Gray, *A Discourse delivered . . . November 15th, 1798 . . .* (Dover, N.H., [1798]), p. 17.

17. Joseph Eckley, *A Discourse, delivered . . . November 29, 1798* (Boston, 1798), p. 14 (quote); Morse to Deacon Morse, November 20, 1798, Yale; Samuel Spring, *A Thanksgiving Sermon, preached November 29, 1798 . . .* (Newburyport, Mass., 1798), pp. 21–22; Asa McFarland, *A Sermon, delivered . . . November 15, 1798* (Concord, Conn., n.d.), pp. 13–19; John Taylor, *A Sermon, delivered . . . November 29, '98* (Greenfield, Mass., [1798]), pp. 8–14.

18. Morse to Timothy Pickering, January 22, 1799, Pickering Papers, Massachusetts Historical Society; Morse, *Sermon . . . November 29, 1798,* pp. 32–56.

19. Morse, *Sermon . . . November 29, 1798,* pp. 73–74.

20. George Washington to G. W. Snyder, September 25, October 24, 1798, in Washington, *Writings . . . ,* ed. John C. Fitzpatrick (Washington, D.C., 1939), 36:453, 518–519.

21. Washington to Morse, February 20, 1799, NYPL; Dwight Foster to Morse, February 6, 26, 1799, Yale; John Lang to Morse, March 16, 1799, NYHS; Morse to Pickering, February 11, 1799, Pickering Papers, Massachusetts Historical Society; Morse to Deacon Morse, February 15, 1799, Yale.

22. Morse to Wolcott, October 19, 1795, CHS.
23. Jedidiah Morse, MS New Year sermon delivered in January 1799, Yale.
24. Jedidiah Morse, *A Sermon . . . delivered at Charlestown, April 25, 1799* . . . (New York, 1799), pp. 11–12, 24–35.
25. Ibid., pp. 12–15, 35–36, 21.
26. Morse to Wolcott, April 22, 1799, CHS; Wolcott to Morse, May 2, 1799, HSP.
27. Boston Association of Ministers, *Circular Letter, April 15, 1799* (n.p., n.d.); Convention of Congregational Ministers of Massachusetts, "Address to the Clergy," *Chronicle*, July 4, 1799; Morse to Deacon Morse, [April, 1799], Yale.
28. Morse to Wolcott, April 22, June 11 (quote), 1799, CHS.
29. Joseph Buckminster to Morse, April 24, 1799, Yale; Samuel Phillips to Morse, April 26, 1799, Yale; Morse to Elisabeth Morse, May 9, May 15, 1799, Yale; John Abeel to Ashbel Green, May 18, 1799, HSP.
30. Augustin Barruel, *Memoirs, Illustrating the History of Jacobinism* (London, 1797); Morse to Wolcott, June 5, 1799, CHS.
31. Levi Frisbie, *The Nature and Effects of the Works of Darkness . . .* (Newburyport, Mass., 1799), pp. 46–53; Hezekiah Packard, *Federal Republicanism, displayed in two discourses . . .* (Boston, 1799), pp. 18–20; Abiel Abbot, *A Discourse, delivered . . . July 4th, 1799* . . . (Hartford, Conn., 1799), pp. 7–8; Daniel Dana, *Two Sermons, delivered April 25, 1799* . . . (Newburyport, Mass., 1799), pp. 7–8; Ezra Weld, *A Discourse, delivered April 25, 1799 . . .* (Boston, 1799), 11–21.
32. Paul Coffin, *A Sermon, preached before His Honor Moses Gill . . .* (Boston, 1799), p. 26 (quote); Joseph Buckminster, *A Sermon, preached . . . June 5, 1799* (Concord, N.H., 1799), pp. 28–30; Nathanael Emmons, "Sermon on the National Fast, April 25, 1799," in *Works*, 3:138.
33. Address of the Grand Lodge of Massachusetts to Adams, *Massachusetts Mercury*, August 21, 1798; Josiah Bartlett's letters, *Massachusetts Mercury*, August 7, September 7, 1798; William Bentley, *A Charge delivered before the Morning Star Lodge . . . June 25, 1798* (Worcester, Mass., 1798), pp. 23–31; *Chronicle*, May 28, 1798; *Massachusetts Mercury*, July 27, August 10, 28, 1798. See also William Bentley, *An Address delivered in the Essex Lodge . . .*

(Salem, Mass., 1799), pp. 9–13; and [idem], *Extracts from Professor Robison's "Proofs of a Conspiracy,"* . . . (Boston, 1799), pp. 3–4, 7–8, 11–14, 21–23, 28–29.

34. *Chronicle,* June 4, 18, 1798.

35. *Massachusetts Mercury,* August 3, 10, 14, 17, 21, 18, 1798.

36. Ibid., August 31, September 18, 1798.

37. Christoph Ebeling to William Bentley, March 13, 1799, in *American Antiquarian Society Proceedings,* n.s. 35 (1925):307–333; Ebeling to Morse, March 20, 1799, Yale.

38. Walter King to Morse, August 22, 1799, Yale.

39. Morse to King, August 16, 1799, Yale; Morse to Ezekiel Williams, October 16, 1799, copy in MS letter book, Yale.

40. Hartford *American Mercury,* September 26, November 7, 14, 1799; Hartford *Connecticut Courant,* November 4, 1799; Morse to Charles Babcock, October 31, 1799, MS copy in letter book, Yale.

41. Worcester *Massachusetts Spy,* October 9, 1799; *New London Bee,* November 20, 27, 1799.

42. Morse to Deacon Morse, November 30, 1799, Yale; Morse to C. Holt, December 2, 1799, MS copy in letter book, Yale.

43. *Chronicle,* January 10, April 25, 29, May 2, 9, 30, 1799; [John Cosens Ogden], *A View of the Calvinistic Clubs in the United States* [Litchfield, Conn., 1799], passim; [idem], *A View of the New-England Illuminati* (Philadelphia, 1799), passim; idem, *An Appeal to the Candid: Upon the Present State of Religion and Politics in Connecticut* [Stockbridge, Mass., 1799], passim; Morse to Wolcott, November 29, 1799, CHS; Dwight Foster to Morse, January 8, 1800, Yale.

44. Morse to William Wilberforce, December 11, 1799, MS copy in letter book, Yale; Theodore Dwight to Morse, [January 1800], Beinecke Library, Yale.

45. Morse to Wolcott, June 11, November 8, 1799, CHS; Jedidiah Morse, *A Prayer and Sermon on the Death of George Washington* (Charlestown, Mass., 1800), p. 18. For other sermons that expressed the fear that Washington's death was an ominous sign for the United States, see David Osgood, *A Discourse, delivered December 29, 1799* (Boston, 1800), pp. 12–17; Nathanael Emmons, *A Sermon, on the Death of Gen. George Washington* . . . (Wrentham, Mass., 1800), pp. 15–17, 20–21; Joseph Buckminster, *A Sermon, delivered in the First Church in Portsmouth* . . .

(Portsmouth, N.H., 1800), pp. 6, 9–11; John Foster, *A Discourse, delivered December 29, 1799* . . . (Boston, 1800), pp. 15–20.

46. Morse to Samuel Breese, March 24, 1800, NYPL; Abiel Abbot, *Traits of Resemblance in the People of the United States to Ancient Israel* . . . (Haverhill, Mass., 1799), p. 15; Joseph Sumner, *A Sermon, preached at Shrewsbury, November 28, 1799* . . . (Brookfield, Mass., 1800), p. 17; Peter Eaton, *A Sermon, preached at Boxford, November 28, 1799* . . . (Haverhill, Mass., 1799), pp. 18–19.

47. Jedidiah Morse, MS sermon delivered on Thanksgiving Day, November 28, 1799, Yale; Morse to Breese, March 24, 1800, NYPL.

48. Morse to Phillips, March 28, 1800, Yale; Morse to Wolcott, April 4, 1800, CHS; Morse to Charles Nisbet, April 4, 1800 (quote), MS copy in letter book, Yale; Morse to John Jay, May 23, 1800, MS copy in letter book, Yale; Morse to John Adams, May 23, 1800, MS copy in letter book, Yale.

49. Morse to Moses Fisk, June 22, 1800, Tennessee State Library and Archives.

50. [William Linn], *Serious Considerations on the Election of a President* (New York, 1800), pp. 6–13, 24–27, 35; Thomas Jefferson, *Notes on Virginia*, ed. William Peden (Chapel Hill, N.C., 1955).

51. Jedidiah Morse, MS sermon preached in Charlestown on March 24, 1799, Yale; *Chronicle*, July 21, August 11, September 3, 15, 1800.

52. Morse to Nisbet, April 4, 1800, MS copy in letter book, Yale; Morse to Josiah Parker, April 4, 1800, MS copy in letter book, Yale; *Connecticut Courant*, May 19, 1800; Morse to Pickering, May 15, 1800, CHS.

53. Morse to Wolcott, April 4, 1800, CHS; Morse to Samuel Phillips, March 28, 1800, Yale.

54. Morse to Wolcott, October 27, December 10, 1800, CHS; Robert Edson Lee, "Timothy Dwight and the *Boston Palladium*," *New England Quarterly* 35 (1962):229–239.

55. Morse to Wolcott, December 10, 1800, CHS; George Cabot to Wolcott, October 5, 1800, in Henry Cabot Lodge, ed., *The Life and Letters of George Cabot* (Boston, 1877), p. 295; Goerge Cabot to Alexander Hamilton, October 11, 1800, in ibid., p. 294; Dwight to Morse, November 7, 1800, HSP; Wolcott to Morse, November 28, 1800, CHS.

56. William Bentley, *The Diary of William Bentley* (Salem, Mass.,

1905–1914), 2:302; Dwight to Morse, December 13, 19, 1800, Yale.

57. Morse to Deacon Morse, December 22, 1800, January 1, 1801, Yale.

58. *National Intelligencer,* January 23, 1801; *Chronicle,* February 12, 1801.

59. *Chronicle,* February 16, 19, March 2, 1802.

60. Morse to John Lettsom, January 26, 1801 (first quote), Yale; Morse to Fisk, February 10, 1801, MS copy in letter book (second quote), Yale.

61. Morse to Ebeling, March 5, 1801, Yale.

62. Dwight to Morse, March 31, 1801, HSP; Morse to Dwight, April 17, 1801, Yale; Seth Payson to Morse, January 31, 1802, HSP; Seth Payson, *Proofs of the Real Existence, and Dangerous Tendency, of Illuminism* (Charlestown, Mass., 1802), passim; John Codman to Morse, January 1806, Yale.

63. *Chronicle,* April 16, 1801; *New England Palladium,* April 21, 1801.

64. Abraham Bishop, *Oration delivered in Wallingford, on the 11th of March 1801* . . . (New Haven, Conn., 1801), pp. 27–31, 36–40, 45–47, 83–89; idem, *Proofs of a Conspiracy, against Christianity, and the Government of the United States* . . . (Hartford, Conn., 1802), pp. 34–39, 42–47, 50–52, 59–61, 64–67, 81–87, 95–97; *Chronicle,* June 22, July 30, August 10, 17, 24, 1801; Pittsfield *Sun,* July 14, 1801; Worcester *National Aegis,* December 2, 1801.

65. *Centinel,* December 23, 30, 1801; *New England Palladium,* December 29, 1801, January 22, 1802; Morse to Deacon Morse, November 24, 1802, Yale.

66. Elijah Waterman, *A Century Sermon preached . . . December 10, A.D. 1800* . . . (Windham, Conn., 1801), pp. 36–37; Charles Backus, *A Sermon, delivered January 1, 1801* . . . (Hartford, Conn., 1801), pp. 11–13; Moses Welch, *A Century Sermon* . . . (Hartford, Conn., 1801), pp. 22–24; Nathanael Emmons, "God Never Forsakes His People . . . ," in *Works,* 3:170–180; Benjamin Trumbull, *A Century Sermon* . . . (New Haven, Conn., 1801), pp. 8–9; *Connecticut Evangelical Magazine* 1 (1800–1801):249–250, 294–298.

67. Jedidiah Morse, *A Sermon delivered before the Ancient and Honourable Artillery Company* (Charlestown, Mass., 1803), pp. 9, 12–14, 24–28.

68. Aaron Bancroft, *A Sermon, preached . . . May 27, 1801* . . . (Bos-

ton, 1801), pp. 7–13; Benjamin Trumbull, *The Dignity of Man* . . . (Hartford, Conn., 1801), pp. 21–24; Rufus Anderson, *Two Discourses, delivered . . . April 8, 1802* (Portland, District of Maine, 1802), pp. 16–17; Zephaniah Moore, *An Oration . . . July 5, 1802* (Worcester, Mass., 1802), pp. 5–23; Reuben Puffer, *A Sermon, delivered . . . May 25, 1803 . . .* (Boston, 1803), pp. 19–26; Samuel Kendal, *Religion the only sure Basis of Free Government . . .* (Boston, 1804), pp. 9–20; Eliphalet Gillet, *A Discourse delivered . . . November 29, 1804* (Augusta, District of Maine, 1804), pp. 10–14, 22, 24–25.

69. Joseph Strong, *A Sermon, preached . . . May 13, 1802* (Hartford, Conn., 1802), pp. 11–13; Nathaniel Porter, *A Discourse, delivered . . . June 7th, 1804* (Concord, N.H., 1804), pp. 6–8, 14–16.

70. William Emerson, *An Oration pronounced July 5, 1802 . . .* (Boston, [1802]), pp. 20–24; Jeremiah Atwater, *A Sermon, preached . . . October 14, 1802* (Middlebury, Vt., 1802), pp. 6–24; Samuel Taggart, *An Oration: Spoken at Colrain, July 4, 1803 . . .* (Greenfield, Mass., 1803), pp. 13–17; Jonathan Strong, *A Sermon, delivered . . . December 22, 1803 . . .* (Boston, 1804), pp. 21–26.

71. John Foster, *Infidelity exposed, and Christianity recommended . . .* (Cambridge, Mass., 1802), 33; Leonard Worcester, *A Sermon, preached . . . April 28th, 1802 . . .* (Peacham, Vt., 1802), pp. 25–30; John Crane, *An Oration, delivered . . . July 5th, 1802 . . .* (Worcester, Mass., 1802), pp. 9–11; Joseph Lathrop, *The Constancy and Uniformity of the Divine Government . . .* (Springfield, Mass., [1803]), pp. 12–16; Nathanael Emmons, "Religious Instructers Useful to Civil Society . . . ," in *Works*, 2:235–241; Eli Smith, *The Signs of the Times . . .* (Amherst, N.H., 1804), pp. 26–29; Jotham Waterman, *National Righteousness National Security . . .* (Boston, 1804), pp. 14–19.

72. Thomas Crafts, *A Sermon, delivered . . . April 5, 1804* (Boston, 1804), pp. 7–13; Zebulon Ely, *The Wisdom and Duty of Magistrates . . .* (Hartford, Conn., 1804), pp. 12–16, 26–32; Elijah Parish, *A Discourse, delivered . . . Nov. 29, 1804* (Salem, Mass., 1805), pp. 3–10; Joseph Lyman, *The Two Olive-Trees . . .* (Northampton, Mass., 1804), pp. 6–12; Seth Payson, *An Abridgement of two discourses . . .* (Keene, N.H., 1805), pp. 9–18; Solomon Williams, *Three Sermons, preached at Northampton . . .* (Northampton, Mass., 1805), pp. 13–14; Isaac Braman, "*The Union of All Honest Men*" . . . (Newburyport, Mass., 1805), pp. 14–17.

73. Morse to Manasseh Cutler, February 3, 1803, in Manasseh Cutler, *Life, Journals and Correspondence of Rev. Manasseh Cutler,* ed. William P. Cutler and Julia P. Cutler (Cincinnati, 1888), 2:129.

74. Morse to Dwight Foster, February 3, 1802 (first two quotes), Yale; Morse to William Plumer, December 12 (third quote), November 16, (fourth quote), 1803, Plumer Papers, New Hampshire State Library. For similar fears on the part of other Federalists, see Richard Buel, Jr., *Securing the Revolution* (Ithaca, N.Y., 1972), pp. 265–266.

## Chapter 4

1. Jedidiah Morse, MS sermon delivered on November 28, 1799 in Charlestown, Yale; Timothy Dwight, *A Discourse on Some Events of the Last Century . . .* (New Haven, Conn., 1801), pp. 25–29, 35–41, 43, 49–51; Nathan Strong, *On the Universal Spread of the Gospel . . .* (Hartford, Conn., 1801), pp. 6–8, 35–41; Joseph Lathrop, *The Works of God in Relation to the Church in General . . .* (Springfield, Mass., 1801), pp. 21–22; Oliver W. Elsbree, *The Rise of the Missionary Spirit in America* (Williamsport, Pa., 1928), pp. 122–130.

2. Morse to Deacon Morse, August 7, 1789, Yale; Jedidiah Morse, MS sermon delivered in Charlestown, November 8, 1789, Yale; David Austin, *The Voice of God to the People of the United States* (Elizabethtown, N.J., 1794), pp. 107–113, 128, 131; Elsbree, *Rise of the Missionary Spirit,* p. 36.

3. Jedidiah Morse, MS sermon delivered on April 4, 1799 in Charlestown, Yale; idem, MS sermon delivered on November 28, 1799 in Charlestown, Yale.

4. Jedidiah Morse, MS sermon delivered on New Year, January 1799 in Charlestown, Yale; Nathan Perkins, *Two Discourses on the Grounds of the Christian's Hope . . .* (Hartford, Conn., 1800), p. 40; *Connecticut Evangelical Magazine* 1 (1800–1801):22, 56, 342; 2 (1801–1802):24.

5. Deacon Morse to Morse, October 21, 1800, Yale: *Connecticut Evangelical Magazine* 1 (1800–1801):19–21, 23, 101, 104, 133, 342, 382–383; 2 (1801–1802):25 (quote); *Panoplist* 5 (1808–1809):149; 7 (1811–1812):490–491; 9 (1813):333; Charles Roy Keller, *The Second Great Awakening in Connecticut* (New Haven, Conn., 1942), pp. 53–54.

6. Ebenezer Porter, *Letters on the Religious Revivals Which Prevailed about the Beginning of the Present Century* (Boston, 1858), pp. 17–20, 29–32, 75–78; *Connecticut Evangelical Magazine* 1 (1800–1801):57, 58, 100, 132, 133, 136, 140, 157–158, 217–218, 269–270, 344, 462–463; 2 (1801–1802):24–25; *Panoplist* 7 (1811–1812):114–115.

7. Archibald Alexander to Morse, December 2, 1801, HSP; Samuel L. Campbell to Morse, March 1802, Yale; Henry Kollock to Morse, March 24, 1802, HSP; Morse to Geoge Burder, June 1, 1805, Yale.

8. Lyman Beecher, *The Government of God Desireable* (New York, 1809), passim; Sidney Earl Mead, *Nathaniel William Taylor* (Chicago, 1942), passim.

9. William Buell Sprague, *The Life of Jedidiah Morse* (New York, 1874), pp. 128–129.

10. Keller, *Second Great Awakening in Connecticut*, pp. 70–94; *Panoplist* 9 (1815):222–224; General Association of Connecticut, *An Address to the Inhabitants of the New Settlements . . .* (New Haven, Conn., [1793]), pp. 3–5; idem, *A Narrative of the Missions to the New Settlements . . .* (New Haven, Conn., 1794), pp. 4, 15; idem, *A Continuation of the Narrative . . .* (New Haven, Conn., 1795), pp. 17–19.

11. John H. Livingston, *A Sermon, delivered before the New York Missionary Society . . .* (New York, 1804), p. 46; Timothy Dickinson, *A Sermon, delivered before the Massachusetts Misionary Society . . .* (Boston, 1811), p. 14; General Association of Connecticut, *An Address . . . on the subject of a Missionary Society . . .* (Norwich, Conn., 1797), pp. 10–30; New York Missionary Society, *The Address and Constitution . . .* (New York, 1796), pp. 3–4, 22–23, 26–28; Timothy Dwight to Morse, June 29, 1797, Yale; John Erskine to Morse, March 7, 1796, Yale; Charles I. Foster, *An Errand of Mercy* (Chapel Hill, N.C., 1960), pp. 61–100.

12. Morse, MS sermon delivered on November 28, 1799 in Charlestown, Yale; Nathanael Emmons, *A Sermon, delivered before the Massachusetts Missionary Society . . .* (Charlestown, Mass., 1800), pp. 26–29; Joseph Lyman, *A Sermon, preached at Northampton . . .* (Northampton, Mass., 1801), pp. 10–15; Enoch Hale, *A Sermon, preached before the Hampshire Missionary Society . . .* (Northampton, Mass., 1804), pp. 14–16; Elijah Parish, *A Sermon,*

*preached before the Massachusetts Missionary Society* . . .(Newbury-port, Mass., 1807), pp. 8–16; Missionary Society of Connecticut, *An Address from the Trustees* . . . (Hartford, Conn., 1807), pp. 11–12; John M. Mason, *Hope for the Heathen* (New York, 1797), pp. 7–18, 29–38; John Blair Smith, *The Enlargement of Christ's Kingdom* . . . (Schenectady, N.Y., 1797), pp. 31–35.

13. Abiel Holmes, *A Sermon, delivered before the Massachusetts Missionary Society* . . . (Cambridge, Mass., 1804), p. 27; Missionary Society of Connecticut, *An Address from the Trustees* . . . (Hartford, Conn., 1801), pp. 3–6; Hampshire Missionary Society, *Instructions of the Trustees* . . . (Northampton, Mass., 1802), pp. 10–13; Levi Frisbie, *A Discourse, before the Society for Propagating the Gospel* . . . (Charlestown, Mass., 1804), p. 27.

14. Jedidiah Morse, "Journal of a Mission to the Isle of Shoals . . ." (unpublished MSS) NYPL; *Massachusetts Historical Society Collections* 8 (1800):259–260.

15. Solomon Williams, *A Sermon, preached at Northampton* . . . (Northampton, Mass., 1802), pp. 17, 3–6; Missionary Society of Connecticut, *A Narrative on the Subject of Missions* . . . (Hartford, Conn., 1802), p. 4; Samuel Spring, *A Sermon, delivered before the Massachusetts Missionary Society* . . . (Newburyport, Mass., 1802), pp. 25–27; Samuel Taggart, *Knowledge Increased by Travelling to and Fro* . . . (Northampton, Mass., 1807), pp. 18–21; Samuel Worcester, *The Wisdom of God* . . . (Boston, 1809), pp. 19–25; Leonard Woods, *A Sermon delivered before the Massachusetts Missionary Society* . . . (Boston, 1812), pp. 11–15.

16. Thomas Robbins, quoted in Missionary Society of Connecticut, *An Address from the Trustees* (1807), p. 5; Daniel Dorchester, *Christianity in the United States* (New York, 1895), p. 373.

17. Jedidiah Morse, *The American Geography* (Elizabethtown, N.J., 1789), p. 387; Morse to Jackson Kemp, October 17, 1804, Yale.

18. Jonathan Ward, *A Brief Statement and Examination of the Sentiments of the Wesleyan Methodists* (Hallowell, District of Maine, 1799), passim; idem, *A Vindication of A Brief Statement and Examination* . . . (Hallowell, District of Maine, 1801), passim; Samuel Taggart, *A Scriptural Vindication of the Doctrine of the Final Perseverance* . . . (Northampton, Mass., 1801), passim.

19. Convention of Congregational Ministers of New Hampshire, *An Address to the Inhabitants* . . . (Concord, N.H., 1791), pp. 6–13; Noah Worcester, *Impartial Inquiries, respecting the progress of the*

*Baptist denomination* (Worcester, Mass., 1794), pp. 15–16; Joshua Taylor, *A Reply to Rev. Jonathan Ward's Vindication* . . . (Augusta, District of Maine, 1801), pp. 87, 14, 74.

20. Taggart, *Scriptural Vindication*, pp. 132–139; Stephen West, *Sermon, delivered on the public fast* . . . (Stockbridge, Mass., 1801), pp. 11–12, 16–17; Ezra Witter, *Two Sermons on the party spirit and divided state of the country, civil and religious* . . . (Springfield, Mass., 1801), pp. 18–19; Joseph Woodman, *The Substance of Two Discourses* . . . (Concord, N.H., 1801), pp. 30–31; Eli Smith, *The Signs of the Times* . . . (Amherst, N.H., 1804), pp. 11–12; Walter King to Morse, April 10, 1806, Yale.

21. *Connecticut Evangelical Magazine* 1 (1800–1801):324, 399–400; Hampshire Missionary Society, *Report of the Trustees* . . . (Northampton, Mass., 1804), pp. 12–14; General Association of New Hampshire, *Extracts from the Minutes* . . . Charlestown, Mass., 1810), p. 7; Missionary Society of Connecticut, *A Narrative* . . . (Hartford, Conn., 1811), pp. 6, 11, 14–15.

22. Thaddeus Osgood to Morse, February 7, 1809, Yale; missionary quoted in John Emerson, *The Duty of Christians* . . . (Northampton, Mass., 1809), p. 30; Keller, *Second Great Awakening in Connecticut*, pp. 88–91.

23. Hampshire Missionary Society, *Report of the Trustees* . . . (Northampton, Mass., 1806), p. 5; Abiel Holmes, *A Discourse, delivered before the Society for Propagating the Gospel* . . . (Boston, 1808), pp. 53–60; William Jenks, *The True Spirit of Missions* . . . (Hallowell, District of Maine, 1809), p. 25; Jonathan Ward, *A Sermon delivered before the Maine Missionary Society* . . . (Hallowell, District of Maine, 1811), pp. 21–25.

24. Sprague, *Morse*, pp. 150–157; Sidney E. Morse, *Memorabilia in the Life of Jedidiah Morse* (Boston, 1867), p. 11; William B. Sprague, *Anals of the American Pulpit* (New York, 1857), 2:250, 256; Massachusetts Society for Promoting Christian Knowledge, *An Account of the Massachusetts Society* . . . (Cambridge, Mass., 1811), pp. 17–18; Keller, *Second Great Awakening in Connecticut*, pp. 117–118.

25. Morse to Burder, October 8, 1802, Yale; Erskine to Morse, December 23, 1802, Yale.

26. [Jedidiah Morse], *An Address to Christians recommending the distribution of cheap religious tracts* (Charlestown, Mass., 1802), p. 23; Eliphalet Pearson, *A Sermon delivered . . . before the Massachusetts*

*Society for Promoting Christian Knowledge* . . . (Cambridge, Mass., 1811), pp. 22–24.

27. Massachusetts Society for Promoting Christian Knowledge, *Account*, p. 21. [Morse], *Address to Christians*, pp. 3–14; Marshfield Steele to Morse, December 24, 1806, HSP; Sidney Earl Mead, *Nathaniel William Taylor* (Chicago, 1942).

28. Sprague, *Morse*, p. 280; Sidney Morse, *Memorabilia*, p. 12; Robert Ralston to Morse, June 27, 1809, Yale; James Gray to Morse, June 30, 1809, Yale; Ralston to Morse, September 4, December 16, 1809, Yale.

29. *Connecticut Evangelical Magazine* 1 (1800–1801):233.

30. Deacon Morse to Morse, December 9, 1800, Yale; Keller, *Second Great Awakening in Connecticut*, p. 55.

31. Morse, MS sermon delivered November 28, 1799, Yale.

32. Porter, *Letters on the Religious Revivals*, p. 9; *Connecticut Evangelical Magazine* 1 (1800–1801):27, 58, 133, 314.

33. Deacon Morse to Morse, October 21, 1800, Yale; *Connecticut Evangelical Magazine* 1 (1800–1801):22; *Panoplist* 7 (1811–1812):473–474; 9 (1813):332.

34. *Panoplist* 9 (1813):42, 93; Thomas Snell, *Women ministering to Christ* . . . (Brookfield, Mass., 1815), p. 14; American Board of Commissioners for Foreign Missions, *Report* . . . (Boston, 1817), p. 21; *The Recorder*, December 10, 1816; Elsbree, *Rise of the Missionary Spirit*, pp. 58, 63–64; Keith Melder, "Ladies Bountiful: Organized Benevolence in Early 19th Century America," *New York History* 48 (1967):234–237. For women's support of the Hampshire Missionary Society, see Hampshire Missionary Society, *Report of the Trustees* (1804), pp. 21–22; idem, *Report of the Trustees* . . . Northampton, 1805), p. 7; idem, *Report of the Trustees* . . . (1806), pp. 12–13; and the appended reports to these sermons: Taggart, *Knowledge Increased by Travelling*, p. 35; Timothy Cooley, *The Universal Spread of the Gospel* . . . (Northampton, Mass., 1808), pp. 36–38; John Emerson, *Duty of Christians*, pp. 39–40; Jonathan Grout, *A Sermon, preached* . . . *before the Hampshire Missionary Society* (Northampton, Mass., 1810), pp. 28–29; Rufus Wells, *A Sermon, preached* . . . *before the Hampshire Missionary Society* . . . (Northampton, Mass., [1811]), pp. 30–32.

35. Timothy Dwight, *The Charitable Blessed* . . . (New Haven, Conn., 1810), pp. 17–18; Moses Stuart, *A Sermon, delivered by request on*

*the Female Charitable Society in Salem . . .* (Andover, Mass., 1815), pp. 19–20; Samuel Worcester, *Female Love to Christ* [Salem, Mass., 1809], pp. 7–15; Joseph Lathrop, *The Importance of Female Influence in the Support of Religion . . .* (Springfield, Mass., 1810), pp. 5, 9–11; David T. Kimball, *The Obligation and Disposition of Females to Promote Christianity . . .* (Newburyport, Mass., 1819), pp. 7–9; Nancy F. Cott, *The Bonds of Womanhood* (New Haven, Conn., 1977), pp. 126–159; Melder, "Ladies Bountiful," pp. 240–250; Keller, *Second Great Awakening in Connecticut,* pp. 233–235.

36. Porter, *Letters on the Religious Revivals,* p. 10; Nathan Strong to Morse, February 21, 1799, Yale; Morse, MS sermon delivered April 4, 1799, Yale; *Connecticut Evangelical Magazine* 1 (1800–1801):19, 22, 27–28, 58, 102, 133, 2 15, 265, 344; 2 (1801–(1802):26, 61.

37. *Panoplist* 6 (1810–1811):380.

38. Porter, *Letters on the Religious Revivals,* p. 9; *Panoplist* 2 (1806–1807):237; 8 (1812–1813):187–188, 366–367; Kiah Bayley to Morse, November 2, 1811, NYPL; Thomas Andros, *Zion enlarged by her own Energy . . .* (Boston, 1812), passim; Benjamin Wood, *Labourers needed in the harvest of Christ . . .* (Worcester, Mass., 1812), passim; Keller, *Second Great Awakening in Connecticut,* pp. 124–125.

39. Gardiner Spring, *Memoirs of the Rev. Samuel J. Mills* (New York, 1820), 29–40; Joseph Tracy, *History of American Missions to the Heathen* (Worcester, Mass., 1840), pp. 28–30; *Panoplist* 7 (1811–1812):174–178, 221–229, 323–327, 431; Elijah Waterman to Morse, August 24, 1809, Yale.

40. American Board of Commissioners for Foreign Missions, *Report* (Boston, 1811), pp. 27–28; *Panoplist* 7, (1811–1812):332–333, 380, 427, 479, 570–571; 8 (1812–1813):47, 228, 285–286.

41. Stanley Faber, *A Dissertation on the Prophecies* (New York, 1811), 1:30–36, 87–91, 235–248, 253–256; 2:69–78, 203–261; Elijah Parish, *A Sermon . . . on the annual fast, April 11, 1811* (Boston, 1811), p. 3.

42. Ethan Smith, *A Dissertation on the Prophecies relative to Antichrist and the Last Times . . .* (Charlestown, Mass., 1811), pp. 17–98, 104–142, 145–154; *Panoplist* 4 (1808–1809):35–40; 7 (1811–1812):32–38, 75–84.

43. Ethan Smith, *Dissertation on the Prophecies,* p. 362; Parish, *Sermon*

... *Massachusetts Missionary Society* ..., pp. 17–22; Elijah Parish, *Ruin or Separation from Anti-Christ* ... (Newburyport, Mass., 1808), pp. 4–23; Mighill Blood, *A Discourse, delivered* ... *on the annual fast* ... (Buckstown, Mass., [1808]), pp. 5–19; Joseph Lathrop, *The Signs of Perilous Times* ... (Springfield, Mass., 1808), pp. 3–9; Asa McFarland, *Signs of the Last Times* ... (Concord, N.H., 1808), pp. 3–31; Joseph Lathrop, *The Prophecy of Daniel* ... (Springfield, Mass., 1811), passim; *Panoplist* 3 (1807–1808):305–306.

44. Amos Bassett, *Advantages and Means of Union in Society* ... (Hartford, Conn., 1807), pp. 3–6, 16–29; Nathan Perkins, *The Benign Influence of Religion on Civil Government and National Happiness* ... (Hartford, Conn., 1808), pp. 8–32, 40–41, 44–51; William F. Rowland, *A Sermon, delivered before the Honorable General Court* ... (Concord, N.H., 1809), pp. 9–20, 22–26; Eliphalet Gillet, *The Patriot: A Sermon delivered on the Annual Fast* ... (Hallowell, District of Maine, 1811), pp. 6–10; Samuel Nott, *Prayer, Eminently the Duty of Rulers, in the Times of Trial* ... (Hartford, Conn., 1809), pp. 17–20, 23–26.

45. King to Morse, February 10, 1809, Yale; Blood, *A Discourse*, p. 21 (quote); Samuel Spring, *Two Sermons* ... *Fast Day, April 6, 1809* (Newburyport, Mass., 1809), pp. 5–18, 22–26; David Osgood, *A Discourse, delivered before the Lieutenant-Governor* ... (Boston, 1809), pp. 25–26; Issac Braman, *Union with France a greater evil than union with Britain* ... (Haverhill, Mass., 1810), pp. 15–19; Festus Foster, *The Watchman's Warning to the House of Israel* ... (Worcester, Mass., 1811), pp. 17–19; Moses Welch, *An Excellent Spirit Forms the Character of a Good Ruler* ... (Hartford, Conn., 1812), pp. 22–23.

46. William Ellery Channing, *A Sermon, preached* ... *April 5, 1810* ... (Boston, 1810), pp. 11–20; John Lathrop, *Peace and War* ... (Boston, 1811); *Monthly Anthology* 6 (1808):414–415; John Romeyn, *Two Sermons, delivered* ... *September 8, 1808* ... (Albany, N.Y., 1808), pp. 59–64.

47. William Bentley, *A Sermon, before the Governor* ... (Boston, 1807), p. 22; Thomas Thacher, *A Sermon preached* ... *April 7, 1808* ... (Dedham, Mass., 1808), pp. 19–20; Thomas Allen, *A Sermon, preached before His Excellency, James Sullivan* ... (Boston, [1808]), pp. 14–16; Solomon Aiken, *A Letter, addressed* ... *to the Rev. Samuel Spring* ... (Haverhill, Mass., 1809), pp. 7–11; Edmund Fos-

ter, *A Sermon, preached before His Excellency the Governor* . . . (Boston, 1812), pp. 15–17; Solomon Aiken, *The Rise and Progress of the Political Dissension in the United States* . . . (Haverhill, Mass., 1811), passim.

48. Jedidiah Morse, *Signs of the Times* . . . (Charlestown, Mass., 1810), pp. 29–31; Samuel Taggart to Morse, January 28, 1811, Yale; *Panoplist* 8 (1812–1813):3–4.

## *Chapter 5*

1. Morse to Deacon Morse, January 31, 1790, Yale. See also Morse to Deacon Morse, July 12, October 7, 1792, Yale.

2. Morse to Ashbel Green, [October 1791], April 9, September 1, 1792, HSP; Green to Morse, November 14, 1792, Ashbel Green Papers, Princeton University Library; General Convention of Massachusetts to the General Assembly, May 8, 1794, Yale; Green to Morse, June 9, 1794, Yale; Morse to Green, December 8, 1794, HSP.

3. David Tappan, *A Sermon, delivered before the annual convention of the Congregational Ministers of Massachusetts* . . . (Boston, 1797), pp. 29–33.

4. William Wilberforce, *A Practical View of the Prevailing Religious System of Professed Christians* . . . (Boston, 1815), passim; *Massachusetts Mercury*, April 16, 1799.

5. Eli Forbes, *The Inoffensive Ministry Described* . . . (Charlestown, Mass., 1799), pp. 8–9, 12; Convention of Congregational Ministers of Massachusetts, *An Address* . . . [Boston, 1799]; Joseph Dana, *The Duty and Reward of loving our Country* . . . (Boston, 1799), pp. 23–25, 41; Joseph Buckminster, *A Sermon, preached . . . before the Ecclesiastical Convention of New Hampshire* . . . (Concord, N.H., 1799), pp. 17–21, 30–31; Joseph Buckminster to Morse, April 24, 1799, Yale.

6. *Mercury*, April 23, 30, May 3, 1799; *Independent Chronicle*, May 3, 1799.

7. Morse to William Wilberforce, October 15, 1799, Yale; *Chronicle*, September 16, December 9, 1799; *Mercury*, October 11, December 6, 1799.

8. Joseph Dana, *A Sermon, delivered before the Annual Convention of the Congregational Ministers of Massachusetts* . . . (Boston, [1801]), pp. 5–32; Timothy Dwight, *A Discourse on Some Events of the Last*

*Century* . . . (New Haven, Conn., 1801), pp. 24–25; Seth Payson, *Proofs of the Real Existence, and Dangerous Tendency, of Illuminism* (Charlestown, Mass., 1802), pp. 281–284; Joseph Strong, *A Sermon, preached* . . . *May 13, 1802* (Hartford, Conn., 1802), pp. 9–10; Jonathan French, *A Discourse, delivered* . . . *December 1, 1803* . . . (Newburyport, Mass., 1804), pp. 18–19; Jonathan Strong, *A Sermon, delivered at* . . . *December 22, 1803* . . . (Boston, 1804, pp. 20–21; Samuel Stillman, *Sacred Performances at the Dedication of the Baptist Meeting-House in Charlestown* . . . (Boston, 1801), pp. 15–18; Jedidiah Morse, *A Sermon, preached at the Ordination of the Rev. Hezekiah May* . . . (Charlestown, Mass., 1803), pp. 5–6.

9. Morse to Jackson Kemp, October 17, 1804, Yale.
10. Samuel Eliot Morison, *Three Centuries of Harvard* (Cambridge, Mass., 1936), pp. 187–189; Sidney Willard, *Memories of Youth and Manhood* (Cambridge, Mass., 1855), 2:173.
11. *Columbian Centinel*, September 22, November 10, 14, 21, 1804.
12. *Centinel*, November 24, 28, December 1, 12, 1804, January 16, 26, February 13, 1805; *New England Palladium*, December 18, 1804.
13. Morse to Joseph Lyman, December 4, 27, 1804, February 9, 1805, Yale.
14. Jedidiah Morse, *The True Reasons* . . . (Charlestown, Mass., 1805), pp. 9–12, 19–20.
15. *Monthly Anthology* 2 (1805):152–157, 206, 211–212.
16. Morse to Lyman, June 15, 1805, Yale.
17. Nathanael Emmons, *Unity of Sentiment among Christians, necessary to Unity of Affection* . . . (Boston, 1804), passim; Samuel Spring, *Two Discourses on Christ's Selfexistence* . . . (Newburyport, Mass., 1805), p. 52.
18. William Buell Sprague, *The Life of Jedidiah Morse* (New York, 1874), pp. 27–28; Jedidiah Morse, MS sermon preached on July 26, 1789, Yale; idem, MS sermon preached on April 10, 1789, Yale; Nathan Williams to Morse, February 1, 1792, NYPL; Joseph Lathrop to Morse, July 9, 1792, HSP; Nathan Perkins to Morse, September 16, 1792, HSP; Lathrop to Morse, October 19, 1792, HSP; Morse to Lathrop, October 22, 1792, HSP; Nathan Williams, *An Enquiry Concerning the Design and Importance of Christian Baptism and Discipline* . . . (Boston, 1792), pp. 20–21; Joseph Lathrop, *A Church of God described* . . . (Hartford,

Conn., 1792), pp. 10–26, 47–51; idem, *Sermons on the Mode and Subjects of Christian Baptism* . . . (Boston, 1793), pp. 24–50; Moses Hemmenway, *A Discourse Concerning the Church* . . . (Boston, 1792), pp. 44–59, 72, 117–118.

19. Nathanael Emmons, *A Dissertation on the Scriptural Qualifications for Admission and Access to the Christian Sacraments* . . . (Worcester, Mass., 1793), pp. 70–73, 116–133.

20. Moses Hemmenway, *Remarks on the Reverend Mr. Emmons Dissertion on the Scriptural Qualifications* . . . (Boston, 1794), pp. 23–28.

21. *Semi-Centennial Celebration of the First Sabbath School Society in Massachusetts* . . . (Boston, 1867), p. 87; Leonard Woods to Morse, April 20, 1806, Yale; Elijah Parish to Morse, May 3, 1806, Yale; Woods to Morse, March 11, 1808, in Leonard Woods, *History of the Andover Theological Seminary* (Boston, 1885), p. 575; Woods to Morse, April 4, 1808, ibid., p. 582.

22. Willard, *Memories*, 2:175–179; Morse to Lyman, February 19, 1806, Yale.

23. Woods, *Andover Theological Seminary*, pp. 54–62, 72–94; Samuel Spring to Woods, April 1, 1807, ibid., p. 471; Morse to Joseph Lathrop, November 18, 1807, Yale; Morse to Timothy Dwight, February 22, 1808, Yale.

24. Timothy Dwight, *A Sermon preached at the opening of the Theological Institution in Andover* . . . (Boston, 1808), pp. 11–14, 23–27; *Panoplist* 3 (1807–1808):306–316.

25. Sprague, *Morse*, pp. 112–115; William B. Sprague, *Memoir of the Rev. Edward D. Griffin* (New York, 1839), pp. 119–124.

26. Daniel Chaplin, *A Sermon, delivered May 26, 1808* . . . (Boston, 1808), pp. 17, 19–22; John Foster, *A Sermon, preached before the Ancient and Honourable Artillery Company* . . . (Boston, 1809), p. 12.

27. William Bentley, *The Diary of William Bentley* (Salem, Mass., 1905–1914), 3:346.

28. William Emerson, right hand of fellowship address in Joseph Buckminster, *A Discourse, delivered at the Ordination of the Rev. Joseph S. Buckminster* . . . (Boston, 1805), p. 35; Henry Ware, *A Sermon, delivered at Hingham, Lord's-Day, May 5, 1805* . . . (Boston, 1805), pp. 13–14; John Reed, *A Sermon, preached before the Convention of the Congregational Ministers in Boston* . . . (Boston, 1807), passim; *Monthly Anthology* 5 (1808):609–613; 8 (1810):133–134.

29. Samuel Worcester, *The Knowledge of Jesus Christ supremely important* . . . (Salem, 1808), pp. 22, 24; Paul Litchfield, *A Sermon, preached before the Massachusetts Missionary Society* . . . (Salem, Mass., 1805), p. 13; Joseph Lyman, *A Sermon, preached before the Convention of the Clergy of Massachusetts* . . . (Boston, 1806), pp. 17–19; Jedidiah Morse, *A Sermon, delivered* . . . *at the Ordination of the Rev. Joshua Huntington* (Boston, 1808), pp. 6–8; *Panoplist* 3 (1807–1808):174–178; 4 (1808–1809):125–131.

30. George Punchard, *History of Congregationalism* (Boston, 1881), 5:615–616; Williston Walker, *A History of the Congregational Churches in the United States* (New York, 1894), p. 337; Joseph Eckley, *A Sermon, delivered at the Installation of the Rev. Horace Holley* . . . (Boston, 1809), pp. 25–26; John Lathrop, charge to Holley, in Eckley, *A Sermon*, pp. 43–46.

31. *Christian Monitor,* no. 1, pp. 7–8; List of ministers who received subscriptions in *Christian Monitor,* no. 4, pp. 183–186; Morse to Lyman, June 15, 1805, Yale; Joseph Lathrop to Morse, July 20, 1805, HSP.

32. Joseph Lathrop, *Damnable Heresies Defined and Described* . . . (Springfield, Mass., [1808]), pp. 3–6; Lathrop to Morse, May 20, 1808, Yale.

33. Jedidiah Morse, *The American Geography* (Elizabethtown, N.J., 1789), p. 219; Jedidiah Morse, *The American Universal Geography* (Boston, 1793), 1:253; Morse to Green, September 1, 1792, May 8, 1794, HSP; Morse to Lyman, February 17, 1804, Yale.

34. Judah Nash to Simeon Howard, July 29, 1799, NYHS; Judah Nash and Joseph Lee, MS plan for church discipline [1799], Yale; Morse to Nash, October 21, 1799.

35. Henry Channing to Morse, April 8, 1795, Yale; Channing to Morse, June 3, 1796, NYHS; Channing to Morse, November 12, 1796, Yale.

36. Sprague, *Morse,* pp. 78–82; Hamilton A. Hill, *History of the Old South Church* (Boston, 1890), 2:281–283; Joseph S. Clark, *A Historical Sketch of the Congregational Churches in Massachusetts, 1620–1858* (Boston, 1858), pp. 238–241; Morse to Deacon Morse, January 1, 1801, Yale; Morse to Lyman, April 8, 19, 1803, Yale; Jedidiah Morse, *A Sermon delivered before the Ancient and Honourable Artillery Company* (Charlestown, Mass., 1803), pp. 31–32; Morse to Lyman, November 15, 1803, February 17, April 10, 1804, Yale; Bentley, *Diary,* 3:89, 91, 122; Morse to

Lyman, June 22, December 4, 1804, February 9, May 2, June 15, 1805, Yale; Convention of Congregational Ministers of Massachusetts, "Reverend Sir, I am . . ." (broadside) (Boston, 1804).

37. *Panoplist* 1 (1805–1806):480–483; 2 (1806–1807):15–17, 167–173, 210–216, 269–274, 313–318, 358–365, 404–412, 504–512.

38. Sprague, *Morse*, pp. 82–84; *Panoplist* 3 (1807–1808):444–448; Joseph Lathrop to Morse, May 20, 1808, Yale.

39. Sprague, *Morse*, p. 89; Morse to Lyman, February 18, 1808, Yale; Edward Griffin to Morse, March 27, 1809, HSP; Morse to Henry Kollock, April 3, 1809, HSP; Morse to Lyman, January 21, 1811, HSP; Griffin to James Richards, March 13, 1811, HSP.

40. *Monthly Anthology* 5 (1808):609–613; 6 (1809):205, 251–252; 8 (1810):128–134; 9 (1810):266–280.

41. John Sherman, *A View of Ecclesiastical Proceedings in the County of Windham, Connecticut* (Utica, N.Y., 1806), pp. 50, 67, 79–82; Moses Welch, *Misrepresentation Detected . . .* (Hartford, Conn., 1807), pp. 9–31.

42. General Association of Connecticut, *Proceedings . . .* (Hartford, Conn., 1812), pp. 8–29; Abiel Abbot, *A Statement of Proceedings in the First Society in Coventry, Connecticut . . .* (Boston, 1811), passim.

43. Abbot, *Statement*, p. 50.

44. Eliphalet Porter, *The Simplicity that Is in Christ, and the Danger of its being Corrupted . . .* (Boston, 1810), pp. 7–10, 14, 19–20; *Panoplist* 6 (1810–1811):79–80, 135; 4 (1808–1809):170–177, 363–368, 461–471; *Monthly Anthology* 5 (1808):18–21, 636–638; 6 (1809):349; 10 (1811):107–114, 403–421; *Panoplist* 6 (1810–1811):264–274, 310–319, 502–515, 538–549; 7 (1811–1812):118–133; Joseph S. Buckminster, *Sermons by the late Rev. J. S. Buckminster . . .* (Boston, 1814), pp. xxxi–xxxii; Bentley, *Diary*, 3:431; *Panoplist* 6 (1810–1811):20–21; Daniel Dana, *The Deity of Christ . . .* (Haverhill, Mass., 1810), pp. 20–22; Samuel Worcester, *The Foundation of God Sure and Sealed . . .* (Boston, 1811), p. 27.

45. Punchard, *History of Congregationalism*, 5:629–630; Earl Morse Wilbur, *Our Unitarian Heritage* (Boston, 1925), pp. 409–410; Eliza Buckminster Lee, *Memoirs of Rev. Joseph Buckminster, D.D., and of his son, Rev. Joseph Stevens Buckminster* (Boston, 1849), pp. 128–129.

46. John S. J. Gardiner, *A Sermon, delivered . . . Christmas Day, . . .* (Boston, 1811), pp. 3–19; idem, *A Preservative Against Unitarianism . . .* (Boston, 1811), pp. 22–23.

47. Jedidiah Morse, *A Sermon, delivered before the Convention of Congregational Ministers . . .* (Boston, 1812), pp. 7–10, 16, 20.

48. Samuel Taggart, *God's Visitation of Sinful Nations . . .* (Greenfield, Mass., 1812), p. 43; *Panoplist* 9 (1813):2–4; Huntington Porter, *The Present Distressed Situation of Our Country . . .* (Portsmouth, N.H., [1812]), p. 8; *Panoplist* 8 (1812–1813):502–506.

49. *General Repository* 3 (1813):349–378.

50. *Panoplist* 9 (1813):168; *General Repository* 2 (1812):1–6.

51. Henry Ware, Jr., *Memoirs of the Rev. Noah Worcester* (Boston, 1844), pp. 51–57; William Ellery Channing, *Memoirs . . . ,* ed. William Henry Channing (London, n.d.), 1:269–270.

52. Jedidiah Morse and Elijah Parish, *A Compendius History of New England* (Charlestown, Mass., 1804); Jedidiah Morse, *An Appeal to the Public . . .* (Charlestown, Mass., 1814), pp. 22–23; Hannah Adams, *A Narrative of the Controversy . . .* (Boston, 1814), pp. 2–8.

53. Morse, *Appeal,* pp. 60–65.

54. *Monthly Anthology* 2 (1805):538–544, 670–674.

55. Morse, *Appeal,* pp. 78–79; Elijah Parish to Morse, February 26, 1809, Yale; Dwight to Morse, April 22, 1809, HSP.

56. Morse, *Appeal,* pp. 81–94.

57. Ibid., p. 104.

58. Ibid., pp. 106–115; Adams, *Narrative,* pp. 15–18.

59. Morse, *Appeal,* pp. 115–116, 188–190; Dwight to Morse, December 21, 1812, Yale; *General Repository* 3 (1813):387; 4 (1813):221–222; Moses Stuart to Morse, June 17, 1813, Yale; Bentley, *Diary,* 4:241–242.

60. Morse, *Appeal,* pp. 121–126; Adams, *Narrative,* pp. 21–27.

61. Morse, *Appeal,* pp. 178–185, 57.

62. Adams, *Narrative,* passim; [John Lowell], *Review of Morse's 'Appeal to the Public' . . .* (Boston, 1814), pp. 5–7; [Sidney Edwards Morse], *Remarks on the Controversy Between Doctor Morse and Miss Adams,* 2d ed. (Boston, 1814), pp. 20–25.

63. Morse to Deacon Morse, October 19, 1814, Yale; Enoch Hale to Morse, March 1, 1815, NYPL; Lyman to Morse, March 17, 1815, NYPL; *Panoplist* 10 (1814):256–281, 289–307.

64. Thomas Belsham, *Memoir of the Life of Theophilus Lindsey* (Lon-

don, 1812); idem, *American Unitarianism*, 3d ed. (Boston, 1815), pp. 37–46.

65. *Panoplist* 11 (1815):265–266. This review was published as a pamphlet entitled *Review of American Unitarianism*.

66. Morse to Samuel F. B. Morse, July 19, 1815, Yale; William Channing, *A Letter to the Rev. Samuel C. Thacher . . .* , 3d ed. (Boston, 1815), passim; idem, *Remarks on the Rev. Dr. Worcester's Letter . . .* (Boston, 1815), passim; idem, *Remarks on the Rev. Dr. Worcester's Second Letter . . .* (Boston, 1815), pp. 15–16.

67. Samuel Worcester, *A Letter to the Rev. William E. Channing . . .* (Boston, 1815), passim; idem, *A Second Letter to the Rev. William E. Channing* (Boston, 1815), passim; idem, *A Third Letter to the Rev. William E. Channing* (Boston, 1815), pp. 19–34.

68. William Wells to Thomas Belsham, March 12, 1812, in Belsham, *American Unitarianism*, pp. 45–46.

69. General Association of Massachusetts, *Extracts from the Minutes . . .* (Boston, 1814), pp. 2–3, 5–20; idem, *Extracts from the Minutes . . . 1815* (n.p., n.d.), pp. 3–17; idem, *Extracts from the Minutes . . .* (Boston, [1816]), pp. 2–3; Lyman to Morse, March 17, 1815, NYPL; Hale to Morse, July 23, 1816, HSP. See [Samuel Spring], *An Essay on the Discipline of Christ's House* (Newburyport, Mass., 1816) for expression of opposition to consociations by an important member of the General Association.

70. Channing, *Remarks on . . . Worcester's Second Letter*, pp. 34–40; Worcester, *Third Letter*, p. 78; [John Lowell], *An Inquiry into the Right to Change the Ecclesiastical Constitution of the Congregational Churches of Massachusetts* (Boston, 1816), pp. 22–24, 77–78.

71. *Panoplist* 12 (1816):234; Williston Walker, *A History of the Congregational Churches in the United States* (New York, 1894), pp. 341–343; Jacob C. Meyer, *Church and State in Massachusetts from 1740 to 1833*, rev. ed. (New York, 1968 [1930]), pp. 172–181; Punchard, *History of Congregationalism* 5:642–644.

## Chapter 6

1. The prowar sermons included these: Titus Barton, *A Fast Sermon, preached . . . July 23, 1812* (Leominster, Mass., 1812), passim; Reed Paige, *Obedience to the Laws of Civil Rulers . . .* (Concord, N.H., 1812), passim; John Giles, *Two Discourses, delivered . . . August 20, 1812* (Haverhill, Mass., 1812), passim.

Morse, March 24, 1814, Yale; Elijah Parish to Morse, January 28, 1814 (first quote), HSP; Morse to Deacon Morse, October 19, 1814 (second quote), Yale.

10. Samuel Worcester to Morse, January 9, 1815, NYPL; Morse to Deacon Morse, November 7, 1814, Yale.

11. William Wilberforce to Morse, September 9, 1815, NYPL; Morse to Deacon Morse, March 14, 1815, Yale; Abel Flint, *A Discourse, occasioned by the news of peace* . . . (Hartford, Conn., 1815), pp. 5–11; William Miltimore, *A Discourse, delivered* . . . *March 1, 1815* (Portland, District of Maine, 1815), pp. 9–12; Nathan Bradstreet, *Peace: A Discourse, delivered* . . . *April 13, 1815* (Concord, N.H., 1815), pp. 12–15; John Smith, *The goodness of God in restoring peace to the United States* (Haverhill, Mass., 1815), p. 14; Jonathan Curtis, *Two Sermons, delivered* . . . *April 13, 1815* (Concord, N.H., 1815), pp. 26–28; Otis Thompson, *A Sermon preached on the National Thanksgiving* . . . (Providence, R.I., 1815), pp. 17–19; Silas Churchill, *A Sermon, delivered* . . . *April 13, 1815* . . . (Pittsfield, Mass., 1815), pp. 18–22; John R. Bodo, *The Protestant Clergy and Public Issues* (Princeton, N.J., 1954), pp. 204–205.

12. *Panoplist* 8 (1812–1813):3–4; Timothy Dwight, *A Discourse* . . . *delivered August 20, 1812* (New York, 1812), pp. 46–55; Jacob Catlin, *Alarm to the Churches* (Stockbridge, Mass., 1812), p. 9; Samuel Taggart, *God's Visitation of Sinful Nations* . . . (Greenfield, Mass., 1812), p. 68; Samuel Austin, *A Sermon, preached* . . . *July 23rd, 1812* (Worcester, Mass., 1812), pp. 21–27; Moses Dow, *A Sermon, preached* . . . *August 20, 1812* . . . (Salem, Mass., 1813), pp. 13–14; Perkins, *National Sins and National Punishment*, pp. 27–30.

13. Jedidiah Morse, *The Gospel Harvest* . . . (Boston, 1815), pp. 12–14; Deacon Morse to Morse, November 22, 1814, Yale; Timothy Dwight, *A Discourse* . . . *delivered July 23, 1812* . . . (New Haven, Conn., 1812), passim; idem, *Discourse* . . . *delivered August 20, 1812*, passim; Asa McFarland, *A Sermon, delivered before the New Hampshire Missionary Society* . . . (Concord, N.H., 1812,), pp. 3–11; Samuel Worcester, *The Kingdom of the Messiah* . . . (Salem, Mass., 1813), passim; Joseph Lyman, *God's judgments upon the wicked the salvation of his Church* . . . (Northampton, Mass., 1813), p. 25; Joseph Lathrop, *A Sermon, preached in Springfield* . . . (Springfield, Mass., 1814), pp. 10–11; Joseph Harvey, *A Sermon,*

*preached . . . February 15, 1815* (New Haven, Conn., 1815), passim.

14. *Panoplist* 8 (1812–1813):416; 6 (1810–1811):211–214; Charles Roy Keller, *The Second Great Awakening in Connecticut* (New Haven, Conn., 1942), pp. 138–152. For a very interesting discussion of alcoholic consumption in the early national period, see W. J. Rorabaugh, *The Alcoholic Republic* (New York, 1979).

15. *Panoplist* 7 (1811–1812):18–21; 8 (1812–1813):183–190, 442–446, 536–538; 9 (1813):23–28, 97–103, 309–314, 440–443; 10 (1814):22–23; General Association of Connecticut, *Proceedings . . .* (Hartford, Conn., 1812), pp. 7–8, 31–33; Samuel Miller, *The Life of Samuel Miller* (Philadelphia, 1869), pp. 315–316; Kiah Bayley, *Wine-Bibbers Dangerous Companions . . .* (Boston, 1812), passim; Joseph Emerson, *Christian Economy* (Boston, 1813), pp. 14–19; *Remarks on the Baneful Effects of Intemperance in Drinking* (Boston, 1813), passim; [Heman Humphrey], *Intemperance* (Hartford, Conn., 1813), passim.

16. Nathanael Emmons, *A Discourse, delivered November 3, 1790 . . .* (Providence, R.I., [1790]), pp. 16–27; Lyman Beecher, *The Practicability of Suppressing Vice . . .* (New London, Conn., 1804), passim; Charles I. Foster, *An Errand of Mercy* (Chapel Hill, N.C., 1960), pp. 133–136.

17. Lyman Beecher, *The Autobiography of Lyman Beecher,* ed. Barbara M. Cross (Cambridge, Mass., 1961), 1:189–191; Donald M. Scott, *From Office to Profession* (Philadelphia, 1978), chap. 2.

18. Beecher, *Autobiography,* 1:176.

19. *The Charlestown Association for the Reformation of Morals: A Tract . . .* (Boston, 1813), pp. 14–15; Josiah Bartlett, *An Historical Sketch of Charlestown* (Boston, 1814), p. 21. For similar expressions of ministers; confidence, see Lyman Beecher, *A Reformation of morals practicable and indispensable . . . ,* 2d ed. (Andover, Mass., 1814), pp. 25–26; Heman Humphrey, *The Efficacy and Importance of Combined and Persevering Action . . .* (New Haven, Conn., 1815), p. 8; Jesse Appleton, *A Discourse, delivered at Bath, May 11th, 1813* (Boston, 1813), pp. 3–15.

20. *Panoplist* 8 (1812–1813):480; 9 (1813):370; 10 (1814):4, 159–162, 512–519. For a series of articles on the Sabbath, see *Panoplist* 10 (1814):198–203, 241–246, 345–354, 433–440, 481–485; 11 (1815):6–11, 107–111, 201–206, 448–454; 12 (1816):6–13, 111–118.

21. *Panoplist* 10 (1814):314–316, 382; *Christian Disciple* 2 (1814):219; Ebenezer Porter, *Great Effects Result from little Causes* . . . (Andover, Mass., 1815), p. 21.

22. William Bentley, *The Diary of William Bentley* (Salem, Mass., 1905–1914), 4:306, 358; Gribbin, *Churches Militant*, pp. 135–155. On the county conventions of moral societies, see Bentley, *Diary*, 4:329; *Panoplist* 10 (1814):431–432, 503, 524; 11 (1815):92–94, 374; 12 (1816):21–25; Walter Harris, *A dis-Course, at Londonderry East-Parish* . . . (Concord, N.H., 1814), pp. 21–28; Abiel Abbot, *An Address, delivered before the Massachusetts Society for Suppressing Intemperance* . . . (Cambridge, Mass., 1815), pp. 21–22; Daniel Sanders, *A Sermon, preached . . . before the Convention of Norfolk County* . . . (Dedham, Mass., 1816), pp. 19–20.

23. For the finances of the Missionary Society of Connecticut, see *Panoplist* 7 (1811–1812):474–475; Missionary Society of Connecticut, *A Missionary Address* . . . (Hartford, Conn., 1813), pp. 19–21; idem, *Fifteenth Annual Account* . . . (Hartford, Conn., 1814), pp. 23–25; *Connecticut Evangelical Magazine*, n.s. 8 (1815):46–48. For the Hampshire Missionary Society, see *Panoplist* 8 (1812–1813):283; 10 (1814):341; 11 (1815):91. For the Massachusetts Missionary Society, see *Panoplist* 8 (1812–1813):99–100; 9 (1813):89–90; 10 (1814):30; 11 (1815):565. For the American Board of Commissioners for Foreign Missions, see idem, *First Ten Annual Reports* (Boston, 1834), pp. 34, 65, 92, 125, 177.

24. Morse to Ashbel Green, March 14, 1812, HSP; Andrew Flinn to Morse, March 18, 1812, NYPL.

25. John F. Schermerhorn and Samuel J. Mills, *A Correct View of that Part of the United States which lies West of the Allegany Mountains* . . . (Hartford, Conn., 1814), passim; Samuel J. Mills and Daniel Smith, *Report of a Missionary Tour* . . . (Andover, Mass., 1815), pp. 19–20, 47.

26. Charitable Society for the Education of Indigent Young Men for the Ministry of the Gospel, *An Address* . . . (n.p., [1814]), pp. 8–11, 13, 19–20.

27. Heman Humphrey, *A Sermon, preached at Lenox . . . July 6, 1818* (Pittsfield, Mass., n.d.), passim; Eliphalet Pearson, *A Sermon delivered in Boston . . . October 26, 1815* (Andover, Mass., 1815), pp. 7–8, 13–19; American Society for Educating Pious Youth, *Constitution & Address* . . . (n.p., [1816]), pp. 10–13; Daniel Dana,

*The Importance of the Christian Ministry* . . . (Andover, Mass., 1818), pp. 19–21.

28. *Panoplist* 13 (1817):416, 133–137; Daniel Chaplin, *A Sermon, delivered* . . . *before the Massachusetts Society for Promoting Christian Knowledge* . . . (Boston, 1815), p. 20; New Hampshire Missionary Society, *The Fourteenth Report* . . . (Concord, N.H., 1815), pp. 7–14, 22; Massachusetts Society for Promoting Christian Knowledge, *An Account* . . . (Andover, Mass., 1815), pp. 25, 32, 37, 71; General Association of Massachusetts, *Minutes* . . . (Boston, 1818), pp. 3–5, 9–17; Massachusetts Domestic Missionary Society, circular letter, January 3, 1818, Yale.

29. *Panoplist* 12 (1816):242–243. See also *Boston Recorder,* April 20, May 8, July 10, 1816; *Panoplist* 12 (1816):467–468; J. A. Merrill to Morse, January 27, 1817, NYPL; Joshua Bradley, *Accounts of Religious Revivals in Many Parts of the United States from 1815 to 1818* (Albany, N.Y., 1818), passim.

30. Jedidiah Morse et al., circular letter, March 1814, Yale; American Tract Society (Boston), *Proceedings of the First Ten Years of the American Tract Society* (Boston, 1824), pp. 5, 42–46; Gideon Blackburn to Morse, August 16, 1815, NYPL; Charles Coffin to Morse, May 16, 1817, Yale; James Hall to Morse, February 4, 1818, HSP.

31. Sidney E. Morse, *Memorabilia in the Life of Jedidiah Morse* (Boston, 1867), pp. 5–7; William Buell Sprague, *The Life of Jedidiah Morse* (New York, 1874), pp. 269, 272; *Semi-Centennial Celebration of the First Sabbath School Society in Massachusetts* . . . (Boston, 1867), pp. 27–30, 50–58; Charles I. Foster, *Errand of Mercy,* pp. 157–167; Keller, *Second Great Awakening in Connecticut,* pp. 128–135.

32. Ward Stafford, *New Missionary Field* . . . (New York, 1817), passim.

33. *Semi-Centennial Celebration,* pp. 90–93; *Boston Recorder,* January 3, 1816, April 1, 1817.

34. *Panoplist* 9 (1813):356–358; 10 (1814):117–124; 12 (1816): 90–92, 269–270; *Boston Recorder,* March 27, 1816; Morse to Elisabeth Morse, May 10, 1816, Yale; Charles I. Foster, *Errand of Mercy,* pp. 108–115.

35. *New York Observer,* January 22, 29, March 19, May 14, 28, June 4, 1825; Keller, *Second Great Awakening in Connecticut,* pp. 118–120; Clifford S. Griffin, *Their Brothers' Keepers* (New Brunswick, N.J., 1960), pp. 33–36.

36. *Panoplist* 13 (1817):427–428; American Board of Commissioners for Foreign Missions, *Report* (Boston, 1824), p. 15; idem, *Report* (Boston, 1825), pp. 19–22; *Missionary Herald* 21 (1825): 332–333; 22 (1826):260–261.

37. *New York Observer*, August 13, 1825, March 25, May 20, 1826.

38. American Tract Society, *Proceedings of the First Ten Years*, p. 20.

39. Daniel Dana, *A Discourse addressed to the New Hampshire Auxiliary Colonization Society* . . . (Concord, N.H., 1825), p. 5.

40. Joshua Bates, *Influence of Christian Truth* . . . (Boston, 1825), pp. 8–9. On the acceptance of commonsense philosophy in the United States and its relation to clerical political and social views, see Theodore Dwight Bozeman, *Protestants in an Age of Science* (Chapel Hill, N.C., 1977), pp. 3–31; Henry F. May, *The Enlightenment in America* (New York, 1976), especially pp. 341–350; Henry F. May, *Protestant Churches and Industrial America* (New York, 1949), pp. 3–25.

41. *New York Observer*, December 19, 1823.

42. *Panoplist* 14 (1818):364–365; Sereno Dwight, *The Kingdom Come* . . . (Boston, 1820), pp. 18–19; Sidney Earl Mead, *Nathaniel William Taylor* (Chicago, 1942), passim; Sidney Earl Mead, *The Lively Experiment* (New York, 1963), pp. 123–125; Perry Miller, *The Life of the Mind in America* (New York, 1965), pp. 59–66.

43. John Codman, *An Oration on the Fiftieth Anniversary of American Independence* (Boston, 1826), p. 20; Sereno Dwight, *Kingdom Come*, p. 15; Samuel Hopkins, "A Treatise on the Millennium," in idem, *Works of Samul Hopkins, D. D.* (Boston, 1852), 2:271–292.

44. Heman Humphrey, *The Character and sufferings of the Pilgrims* . . . (Pittsfield, Mass., 1821), pp. 5–6; Drew R. McCoy, *The Elusive Republic* (Chapel Hill, N.C., 1980), pp. 86–90.

45. Jedidiah Morse, *The American Universal Geography* (Boston, 1793), 1:245; *New York Observer*, December 6, 1823; Daniel Walker Howe, *The Political Culture of the American Whigs* (Chicago, 1979), pp. 150–167.

46. *Panoplist* 12 (1816):185–186, 370; *Boston Recorder*, April 3, 24, June 12, 1816; Alexander Proudfit, *Tidings of Great Joy For All People* . . . (Salem, Mass., 1816), p. 16; Samuel Austin, *Religion the Glory of a Community* . . . (Montpelier, Vt., 1816), p. 24; Samuel Spring, *A Sermon, preached* . . . *September 10, 1818* (Boston,

1819), pp. 12–13; Jedidiah Morse, *The American Universal Geography*, 7th ed. (Boston, 1819), 2:24, 177–178, 468–469.

47. Morse, *American Universal Geography*, 7th ed., 1:123. For his earlier, more extreme concern about the effects of democracy and party spirit, see ibid., 6th ed. (Boston, 1812), 1:209–210, 370–371.

48. Morse, *American Universal Geography*, 7th ed., 1:780; *New York Observer*, November 22, December 19, 1823, February 4, 1826; Sereno Dwight, *The Greek Revolution* (Boston, 1824), pp. 25–34; *Missionary Herald* 22 (1826):20–22, 248.

49. Jonathan Ward, *A Sermon, delivered . . . July 4, 1825 . . .* (Plymouth, N.H., 1826), pp. 13–14 (first quote); Lyman Beecher, *A Sermon, addressed to the Legislature of Connecticut . . .* (New Haven, Conn., 1826), pp. 6–13; Joshua Bates, *A Sermon, preached on the day of General Election . . .* (Montpelier, Vt., 1821), p. 13; John Nelson, *A Sermon, delivered . . . December 5, 1822* (Leicester, Mass., 1822), p. 16; Samuel Austin, *An Address, Pronounced . . . on the Fourth of July, 1825 . . .* (Worcester, Mass., n.d.), p. 22; *New York Observer*, August 23, 1823.

50. Jedidiah Morse, *Annals of the American Revolution* (Hartford, Conn., 1824), p. 398; Henry Nixon, *An Oration . . . on the 4th of July, 1821* (New Haven, Conn., 1821), pp. 19–20; Samuel Austin, *An Oration, pronounced . . . July 4, 1822 . . .* (Newport, R.I., 1822), pp. 4–5; John Codman, *Home Missions: A Sermon delivered . . . May 31, 1826* (Boston, 1826), p. 11; Nathaniel Taylor, *A Sermon, addressed to the Legislature of Connecticut . . .* (Hartford, Conn., 1823), pp. 8–9, 17; Alexander Proudfit, *A Knowledge of the Bible . . .* (Salem, N.Y., 1824), pp. 28–29; Edward D. Griffin, *An Address delivered before the American Education Society . . .* (Boston, 1825), pp. 11–13.

51. *New York Observer*, November 1, 1823; *Panoplist* 13 (1817):3–4.

52. Jedidiah Morse, *Geography Made Easy* (New Haven, Conn., 1784), pp. 68–70; idem, *The American Geography* (Elizabethtown, N.J., 1789), pp. 65, 353, 432.

53. Morse, *American Geography*, p. 67.

54. Morse, *American Universal Geography*, 1st ed., 1:211–212; 2:310; idem, *American Geography*, p. 65. The passage quoted is from *American Geography* and closely follows a section of Thomas Jefferson, *Notes on Virginia*. It comes just after a lengthy direct

quote from *Notes*. See *Notes*, ed. William Peden (Chapel Hill, N.C., 1955), p. 138.

55. William L. Smith to Morse, May 5, 1792, Yale.

56. Jedidiah Morse, *The American Universal Geography*, 2d ed. (Boston, 1796), 1:231, 686; ibid., 1st ed., 2:515–516; ibid., 3d ed. (Boston, 1801), 2:616–619; ibid., 4th ed. (Boston, 1805), 2:535–536.

57. Jedediah Morse, *A Sermon . . . delivered at Charlestown, April 25, 1799 . . .* (New York, 1799), pp. 10–11; Joseph Dana, *The Duty and Reward of Loving our Country . . .* (Boston, 1799), pp. 21–22; Daniel Dana, *Two Sermons, delivered April 25, 1799 . . .* (Newburyport, Mass., 1799), p. 41; *Hampshire Gazette*, January 6, 1802.

58. William Linn, *A Discourse on National Sins . . .* (New York, 1798), pp. 33–34.

59. Quotes are from the *Balance* article that was reprinted in the *Hampshire Gazette*, June 29, 1803. See also Charles Backus, *A Sermon, delivered January 1, 1801 . . .* (Hartford, Conn., 1801), p. 10; James Dana, *Two Discourses . . . delivered in New Haven . . .* (New Haven, Conn., 1801), pp. 38–39; *Connecticut Evangelical Magazine* 1 (1800–1801):248.

60. Sidney Morse, *Memorabilia*, p. 9; Morse to Deacon Morse, November 4, 1802, May 5, 1803, Yale; Morse to Joseph Lyman, April 19, 1803, Yale; Sprague, *Morse*, pp. 143–144.

61. Jedidiah Morse, *A Discourse, delivered at the African Meeting-House . . .* (Boston, 1808), passim.

62. Zachary Macaulay to Morse, October 20, 1795, HSP; Sidney Morse, *Memorabilia*, p. 10; Early Lee Fox, *The American Colonization Society, 1817–1840* (Baltimore, 1919), pp. 42–43; P. J. Staudenraus, *The African Colonization Movement, 1816–1865* (New York, 1961), pp. 9–11.

63. Timothy Dwight, *Discourse . . . delivered July 23, 1812*, pp. 49–50; Austin, *Sermon, preached . . . July 23rd, 1812*, pp. 13, 20–21; Perkins, *National Sins and National Punishment*, pp. 16–18; Strong, *Fast Sermon, delivered . . . July 23, 1812*, p. 17; Andros, *Grand Era of Ruin to Nations*, pp. 14–15.

64. *Columbian Centinel*, December 24, 27, 1800; *New England Palladium*, January 20, 1801; [Sidney Edwards Morse], *New States*, pp. 32–33; [Sereno Dwight], *Slave Representation*, passim; Parish, *Discourse, delivered . . . April 7, 1814*, pp. 16–17; *The Proceedings*

*of a Convention of Delegates . . . convened at Hartford,* pp. 15–16. Linda K. Kerber, *Federalists in Dissent* (Ithaca, N.Y., 1970), chap. 2 ably discusses northern Federalists' attitudes about slavery and its political and social consequences.

65. Morse, *American Universal Geography,* 6th ed., 1:210, 204–205, 477–478, 505.

66. Fox, *American Colonization Society,* pp. 57, 64, 78–79; Staudenraus, *African Colonization Movement,* pp. 77–81, 122–124; *Boston Recorder,* June 16, 1818, August 19, 1820; *Panoplist* 14 (1819):241; *New York Observer,* July 31, 1824; Theodore D. Bacon, *Leonard Bacon: A Statesman in the Church* (New Haven, Conn., 1931), pp. 55–59; Bodo, *Protestant Clergy and Public Issues,* pp. 112–132.

67. *Panoplist* 13 (1817):180–182; *African Repository* 1 (1825): 161–164, 225–228; *New York Observer,* July 12, November 1, 1823; *Christian Spectator* 5 (1823):492–494, 540–550; *North American Review* 18 (1824):59–90; Samuel Miller, *A Sermon, preached at New-Ark, October 22d, 1823* . . . (Trenton, N.J., 1823), pp. 13–15; Leonard Bacon, *A Plea for Africa* (New Haven, Conn., 1825), pp. 12–22; Dana, *Discourse . . . New Hampshire Auxiliary Colonization Society,* pp. 7–8.

68. *Boston Recorder,* July 24, October 1, November 12, 19, 1816; June 9, 16, 23, 30, 1818; May 6, 1820; E. C. Tracy, *Memoir of the Life of Jeremiah Evarts* (Boston, 1845), pp. 252–253; Edward D. Griffin, *A Plea for Africa* (New York, 1817), pp. 32–33; Miller, *A Sermon, preached . . . October 22nd, 1823,* pp. 7–10.

69. Morse to Lucretia Morse, February 5, 1820, Yale. For sermons criticizing the Missouri Compromise, see Josephus Wheaton, *The Equality of Mankind and the Evils of Slavery* (Boston, 1820), pp. 23–24; Thaddeus Mason Harris, *A Discourse delivered before the African Society in Boston, 15th of July, 1822* . . . (Boston, 1822), pp. 9–12, 20. See also *Christian Spectator* 2 (1820):52–53, 108, 165–166, 278, 440–441.

70. *Panoplist* 16 (1820):17–24, 59–72, 241–245, 484–492; *New York Observer,* May 31, September 27, 1823.

71. *New York Observer,* November 1, 1823; April 24, 1824.

72. Ibid., November 1, 8, 15, 1823; July 24, 1824.

73. Ibid., August 16, 1823; April 3, 1824; July 7, 1825. See the letter by Robert G. Harper in American Colonization Society, *The First Annual Report* . . . (Washington, D.C., 1818), pp. 14–22.

271

74. *New York Observer*, December 13, 1823; July 10, 1824.
75. Staudenraus, *African Colonization Movement*, pp. 86–87, 126–128, 133–135; Fox, *American Colonization Society*, p. 78; American Colonization Society, *The Sixth Annual Report* . . . (Washington, D.C., 1823), pp. 48–51; idem, *The Seventh Annual Report* . . . (Washington, D.C., 1824), p. 109; idem, *The Eighth Annual Report* . . . (Washington, D.C., 1825), pp. 14–15, 47–50.

## Chapter 7

1. Donald M. Scott, *From Office to Profession* (Philadelphia, 1978), chap. 1, provides an excellent discussion of the eighteenth-century ministerial office.
2. William Buell Sprague, *The Life of Jedidiah Morse* (New York, 1874), pp. 33–34; Morse to Ebenezer Hazard, September 30, 1796, Yale. For the act of incorporation, see *New England Palladium*, March 15, 1803.
3. Morse to Manasseh Cutler, February 3, 1803, in Manasseh Cutler, *Life, Journals, and Correspondence of Rev. Manasseh Cutler*, ed. William P. Cutler and Julia P. Cutler (Cincinnati, 1888), 2:130; Morse to Deacon Morse, February 22, 1803, Yale.
4. Sprague, *Morse*, pp. 36–37; Ralph H. Brown, "The American Geographies of Jedidiah Morse," *Annals of the Association of American Geographers* 31 (1941):199–200; Morse to the Parish Committee, January 4, 1804, Yale; Morse to the First Parish in Charlestown, January 20, 1804, Yale.
5. Issac Warren to Morse, April 1814, Yale.
6. *History of the Harvard Church in Charlestown* . . . (Boston, 1879), pp. 54–55, 60–63.
7. Sprague, *Morse*, pp. 39–42; Morse to the First Society, July 11, 1816, Yale; Elisabeth Morse to Richard Morse, August 10, 1816, Yale.
8. *Semi-Centennial Celebration of the First Sabbath School Society in Massachusetts* (Boston, 1867), p. 81; Sprague, *Morse*, p. 273; Morse to Deacon Morse, December 10, 1801, February 4, April 22, November 4, 1802, May 5, 1803, Yale.
9. Morse to Samuel F. B. Morse, January 31, 1817, Yale; Morse to S. V. S. Wilder, August 5, 1817, Yale.
10. Morse to Richard Morse, March 22, 1817, Yale; Dr. Josiah Bartlett to Morse, February 18, 1817, NYPL; Morse to Bartlett,

July 16, 1807, Yale; Joseph Badger to Morse, July 8, 1799, HSP; Missionary Society of Connecticut, *A Narrative on the Subject of Missions* (Hartford, Conn., 1806), pp. 1–12; Western Missionary Society, *A Brief View of the Missionary Proceedings in the Western Country* (Washington, Pa., 1807), pp. 5–6, 9–11, 18–19.

23. Badger to Morse, July 1, 1809, Yale; *Panoplist* 4 (1808–1809):427–428; 5 (1809–1810):184–186; 6 (1810–1811):228–231; Badger to Morse, February 6, 1811, NYPL; *Panoplist* 11 (1815):86–89; 3 (1807–1808):39–40, 84–86; 4 (1808–1809):85, 137–139, 325–326, 519; 5 (1809–1810):474–475; Gideon Blackburn to Morse, June 27, 1809, Yale; Blackburn to Morse, May 16, 1811, HSP.

24. Abiel Holmes, *A Discourse, delivered before the Society for Propagating the Gospel* . . . (Boston, 1808), pp. 29–32; Elijah Parish, *A Sermon, preached before the Massachusetts Missionary Society* . . . (Newburyport, Mass., 1807), pp. 24–26; Jacob Norton, *Faith on the Son of God* . . . (Boston, 1810), pp. 28–29.

25. American Board of Commissioners for Foreign Missions, *First Ten Annual Reports* (Boston, 1834), p. 18; Gordon Hall, *The Duty of the American Churches in Respect to Foreign Missions* . . . , 2d ed. (Andover, Mass., 1815), pp. 18–20; Manasseh Cutler, *A Discourse, delivered in Salem* . . . *April 21, 1813* (Salem, Mass., 1813), pp. 14–18.

26. John F. Schermerhorn, "Report Respecting the Indians, Inhabiting the Western Parts of the United States," *Collections of the Massachusetts Historical Society*, ser. 2, 2 (1814), passim. Elijah Parish, *A Sermon preached at Boston, November 3, 1814* . . . (Boston, 1814), pp. 33–34.

27. American Board of Commissioners for Foreign Missions, *First Ten Annual Reports*, pp. 26, 124; idem, *Report* (Boston, 1814), p. 4.

28. American Board of Commissioners . . . , *First Ten Annual Reports*, pp. 123–124.

29. Francis P. Prucha, *American Indian Policy in the Formative Years* (Cambridge, Mass., 1962), pp. 214–224; R. Pierce Beaver, *Church, State, and the American Indians* (St. Louis, 1966), pp. 63–73; *Panoplist* 12 (1816):431–432, 451–453; S. C. Bartlett, *Historical Sketches of the Missions of the American Board* (Boston, 1876), pp. 3–4; American Board of Commissioners . . . , *First Ten Annual Reports*, p. 161.

30. Samuel M. Worcester, *The Life and Labors of Rev. Samuel*

*Worcester* (Boston, 1852), 2:413–417; Joseph Tracy, *History of American Missions to the Heathen* (Worcester, Mass., 1840), pp. 76–77, 128–131; *Panoplist* 15 (1819):137; American Board of Commissioners for Foriegn Missions, *Report* (1819), pp. 38–50; idem, *Report* (Boston, 1820), pp. 109–113.

31. Malone, *Cherokees,* pp. 106–113; Gibson, *Chickasaws,* pp. 109–113.

32. Worcester, *Samuel Worcester,* 2:323–324; American Board of Commissioners for Foreign Missions, *Report* (Boston, 1822), pp. 44–54; *Missionary Herald* 19 (1823):285; American Board of Commissioners for Foreign Missions, *Report* (Boston, 1823), pp. 81–82, 17, 95–96, 101–102; Berkhofer, *Salvation and the Savage,* pp. 16–43.

33. Sprague, *Morse,* pp. 173–176; Morse to Richard Morse, January 28, 1820 (first quote), Yale; Morse to Lucretia P. Morse, February 5, 1820 (second quote), Yale.

34. Sprague, *Morse,* pp. 168–173; Morse to John Campbell, February 23, 1818, Yale; David Ogden to John C. Calhoun, December 10, 1819, in John C. Calhoun, *The Papers of John C. Calhoun,* ed. W. Edwin Hemphill (Columbia, S.C., 1964), 4:475.

35. *Religious Intelligencer* 4 (1820):686; *Panoplist* 16 (1820):189–190.

36. Morse to Calhoun, June 22, 1820, in Calhoun, *Papers,* 5:203–205; Morse to Calhoun, August 15, 1820, ibid., 5:331; Morse to Calhoun, October 3, 1820, ibid., 5:372; Morse to Calhoun, October 16, 1820, ibid., 5:398–399.

37. Morse to Calhoun, August 15, 1820, *Papers,* 5:332; Morse to John Chester, August 28, 1820, HSP.

38. Sprague, *Morse,* pp. 185–186; Morse to Calhoun, January 8, 1821, *Papers,* 5:452; Morse to Calhoun, February 26, 1821, ibid., 5:648–649; Morse to Calhoun, March 3, 1821, ibid., 5:694; Calhoun to Morse, April 2, 1821, Yale.

39. Sprague, *Morse,* p. 187; Morse to Calhoun, January 19, 1822, Yale; Morse to Elisabeth Morse, January 19, 1822, Yale; Morse to Calhoun, January 27, February 26, 1822, Yale; Morse to Elisabeth Morse, February 26, March 5, 1822, Yale.

40. Jedidiah Morse, *A Report to the Secretary of War . . . On Indian Affairs . . .* (New Haven, Conn. 1822), p. 66.

41. Ibid., pp. 73, 79–82.

42. Ibid., pp. 24–27, 32–33, 82–83; app., pp. 12, 20, 313.

43. Ibid., pp. 74–75, 78–79, 82.

44. Ibid., pp. 61–64, 87–89.

45. Ibid., pp. 75–76.
46. Morse to Calhoun, January 27, 1822, Yale; Calhoun to Morse, January 28, 1822, Yale; Morse to Elisabeth Morse, January 28, 1822, Yale; Calhoun to Morse, February 1, 1822, Yale, Morse to Elisabeth Morse, February 3, 1822, Yale; Morse to Calhoun, February 7, 1822, Yale; American Society for Promoting the Civilization and General Improvement of the Indian Tribes in the United States, *The First Annual Report* (New Haven, Conn., 1824), pp. 3–9.
47. For Adams's and Jefferson's letters, see American Society for Promoting the Civilization . . . , *First Annual Report*, pp. 20–22; Washington *National Intelligencer*, March 4, 1822.
48. Morse to Calhoun, October 30, 1822, Calhoun, *Papers*, 7:322; Morse to Calhoun, December 31, 1822, ibid., 7:399; Morse to Jeremiah Evarts, January 24, 1824, Yale; Stephen Van Rensselaer to Morse, March 3, 1824, Yale; Morse to Joseph Lyman, March 17, 1824, Yale; Jackson Kemper to Morse, December 28, 1824, HSP; Thomas Legare to Morse, November 16, 1824, NYHS.
49. American Board of Commissioners for Foreign Missions, *Report* (1824), pp. 93–96; Morse to Lyman, March 17, 1824, Yale.
50. American Board of Commissioners for Foreign Missions, *Memorial of the ABCFM*, March 3, 1824; U.S., House of Representatives, *Executive Papers*, no. 102, 18th Cong., 1st sess., vol. 5 (1824) passim; *Missionary Herald* 20 (1824):93, 150–153; Evarts to Morse, September 10, 1821, Yale.
51. Richard Morse to Sidney Morse, December 5, 1825, Yale; *New York Observer*, December 11, 25, 1824, January 22, March 12, May 21, June 4, August 6, 27, September 3, December 10, 1825.
52. Malone, *Cherokees*, pp. 116–170; Debo, *Choctaw Republic*, pp. 45–49; R. S. Coterill, *The Southern Indians* (Norman, Okla., 1954), pp. 224–230; Woodward, *Cherokees*, pp. 139–146; Gibson, *Chickasaws*, pp. 122–123; Beaver, *Church, State, and the American Indians*, pp. 104–109; Prucha, *American Indian Policy*, pp. 227–233; Arthur H. De Rosier, Jr., *The Removal of the Choctaw Indians* (Knoxville, Tenn., 1970), pp. 98–99; U.S. Secretary of War, *Preservation and Civilization of the Indians* . . . , U.S., House of Representatives, 19th Cong., 1st sess., doc. no. 102, passim; E. C. Tracy, *Memoir of the Life of Jeremiah Evarts* (Boston, 1845), pp. 267–275, 306–308.
53. Tracy, *Jeremiah Evarts*, pp. 336–339, 348–361, 382–383; [Jere-

miah Evarts], *Essays on the Present Crisis in the Condition of the American Indians* (Boston, 1829), passim; Gibson, *Chickasaws,* pp. 153–155; Prucha, *American Indian Policy,* pp. 233–238, 243; Debo, *Choctaw Republic,* pp. 49–55; De Rosier, *Removal of the Choctaw Indians,* pp. 103–105.

54. Bartlett, *Missions of the American Board,* pp. 20–21; William E. Strong, *The Story of the American Board* (Boston, 1910), pp. 42–47.

55. Morse to Lyman, March 17, 1824, Yale; Carlton Mabee, *The American Leonardo: A Life of Samuel F. B. Morse* (New York, 1943), p. 81.

56. Morse to Lyman, March 17, 1824 (quotes), Yale; Morse to William Woodward, January 9, 1823, HSP.

57. Edward Lind Morse, *Samuel F. B. Morse, His Letters and Journals* (Boston, 1914), 1:155.

58. Ibid., 1:159–160.

59. Richard Morse to Morse, August 24, 1824, Yale; Sidney Morse to Elisabeth Morse, August 11, 1824, Yale; Morse to Richard Morse, January 26, 27, 1825, Yale; Richard Morse to Sidney Morse, February 4, 1826, Yale.

60. Morse quoted in Samuel I. Prime, *The Life of Samuel F. B. Morse* (New York, 1875), pp. 5, 10, 103–108, 115; Morse to Richard Morse, July 26, 1813, Yale.

61. Prime, *Samuel F. B. Morse,* pp. 730–734, 751; Mabee, *American Leonardo,* p. 360.

62. Edward Lind Morse, *Samuel F. B. Morse,* 1:21–22, 70–88; Morse to Samuel F. B. Morse, April 16, 1824, Yale.

63. Mabee, *American Leonardo,* pp. 162–180; [Samuel F. B. Morse], *Foreign Conspiracy Against the Liberties of the United States* (New York, 1835), passim; [idem], *Imminent Dangers to the Free Institutions of the United States through Foreign Immigration* (New York, 1835), passim.

64. Sidney Morse, *Premium Questions on Slavery* (New York, 1860), passim; idem, *Letter on American Slavery* (New York, 1847), pp. 7–8; Edward Lind Morse, *Samuel F. B. Morse,* 2:429–430.

65. Samuel F. B. Morse, *An Argument on the Ethical Position of Slavery in the Social System,* Papers from the Society for the Diffusion of Political Knowledge, no. 12 (New York, 1863), passim; [idem], *The Present Attempt to Dissolve the American Union, a British Aristocratic Plot* (New York, 1862), pp. 41–42. Samuel F. B. Morse's religious defense of slavery and his general religious outlook are

very similar to those of antebellum southern evangelicals as described by Donald G. Mathews, *Religion in the Old South* (Chapel Hill, N.C., 1977).

66. Jedidiah Morse, *A Discourse, delivered at the African Meeting-House in Boston* . . . (Boston, 1808), passim.

67. Jedidiah Morse, introduction to autobiography, March 1823, Yale.

68. Jacob C. Meyer, *Church and State in Massachusetts from 1740 to 1833*, rev. ed. (New York, 1968 [1930]), pp. 155–156.

69. Ibid., pp. 172–180, 201–220; Lyman Beecher, *The Autobiography of Lyman Beecher*, ed. Barbara M. Cross (Cambridge, Mass., 1961), 1:336–337. For Morse's remarks on Congregational establishment in New England, see Morse, *Geography Made Easy*, p. 32; Morse, *American Geography*, p. 170; Jedidiah Morse, *The American Universal Geography*, 6th ed. (Boston, 1812), 1:209. In his Fast Day sermon of April 1799, Morse did cite efforts in Massachusetts to have the parish laws reformed as part of the Illuminati's campaign to undermine religion in the United States. In making this charge, his main intention was to convince people of the existence of the conspiratorial order rather than to stave off such reform.

70. Sereno Dwight, *The Kingdom Come* . . . (Boston, 1820), pp. 21–23.

71. Morse, introduction to autobiography, March 1823, Yale.

72. William Greenough to Morse, June 8, 1826, HSP.

73. Morse to James Barbour, March 1, 1826, Yale; Morse to Van Rensselaer, March 3, April 10, 13, 1826, HSP.

# Note on Sources

Jedidiah Morse has been the subject of two other biographies, William Buell Sprague, *The Life of Jedidiah Morse* (New York, 1874) and James King Morse, *Jedidiah Morse: A Champion of New England Orthodoxy* (New York, 1939). Sidney E. Morse, *Memorabilia in the Life of Jedidiah Morse* (Boston, 1867) is brief but contains some very interesting information. Morse's geographical publications are discussed in Ralph H. Brown, "The American Geographies of Jedidiah Morse," *Annals of the Association of American Geographers* 31 (1941):145–217.

The most important sources for understanding Morse are his many publications and especially his vast correspondence. His published works include sermons, geographies, histories, and polemical writings. With the exception of Morse's address before the Charlestown moral society, which is listed under *Charlestown Association for the Reformation of Morals* (Boston, 1813), all his writings are entered under his name in the Evans and the Shaw and Shoemaker bibliographies of early American imprints. I have also made much use of the *Panoplist*, which Morse founded and edited, and of the *Boston Recorder* and the *New York Observer*, the religious newspapers his sons edited.

The largest collection of Morse's correspondence is at Yale University Library, but the Pennsylvania Historical Society, the New York Historical Society, and the New York Public Library also hold major collections. In addition, the Connecticut Historical Society's collection of Oliver Wolcott, Jr.'s papers includes some very important letters from Morse.

In order to understand the context in which Morse worked,

I have tried to read as many as I could of the Congregational clergy's sermons and addresses bearing on the issues that concerned him. William B. Sprague, *Annals of the American Pulpit* (New York, 1857) is invaluable for its biographical sketches of many of the most important ministers. For an understanding of the politics of the 1790s, I have read several newspapers, especially Boston's *Columbian Centinel* (originally the *Massachusetts Centinel*) and *Independent Chronicle,* that Morse read and sometimes referred to in his correspondence.

In preparing this book I relied on a large number of works and here list only those of most importance to me. For the general New England religious background I relied on Frank Hugh Foster, *A Genetic History of the New England Theology* (Chicago, 1907) and Joseph Haroutunian, *Piety versus Moralism* (New York, 1932). My understanding of the ministry has been influenced by David D. Hall, *The Faithful Shepherd* (Chapel Hill, N.C., 1972); Richard L. Bushman, *From Puritan to Yankee* (New York, 1967); Daniel H. Calhoun, *Professional Lives in America* (Cambridge, Mass., 1965); J. William T. Youngs, Jr., *God's Messengers* (Baltimore, 1976); and Donald M. Scott, *From Office to Profession* (Philadelphia, 1978). My thinking about millennialism has been stimulated by Ernest Lee Tuveson, *The Redeemer Nation* (Chicago, 1968); Alan Heimert, *Religion and the American Mind* (Cambridge, 1966); James W. Davidson, *The Logic of Millennial Thought* (New Haven, Conn., 1977); and Nathan O. Hatch, *The Sacred Cause of Liberty* (New Haven, Conn., 1977).

For the development of Unitarianism I am most indebted to Conrad Wright, *The Beginnings of Unitarianism* (Boston, 1955), which traces the rise of religious liberalism during the eighteenth century. Daniel Walker Howe, *The Unitarian Conscience* (Cambridge, Mass., 1970) is most valuable for its discussion of the intellectual and social outlooks of Morse's liberal antagonists. I have also been aided by Jacob C. Meyer, *Church and State in Massachusetts from 1740 to 1833* (New York, 1930); George W. Cooke, *Unitarianism in America* (Boston, 1910); George Punchard, *History of Congregationalism* (Boston, 1881);

Williston Walker, *A History of the Congregational Churches in the United States* (New York, 1894); Earl Morse Wilbur, *A History of Unitarianism* (Cambridge, Mass., 1955); and Earl Morse Wilbur, *Our Unitarian Heritage* (Boston, 1925).

Many historians have addressed the issues of the causes and nature of the Second Great Awakening. In understanding the rise of the movement I am especially indebted to Perry Miller, *The Life of the Mind in America* (New York, 1965); Rowland Berthoff, *An Unsettled People* (New York, 1971); and Whitney R. Cross, *The Burned-over District* (New York, 1965).

Sidney Earl Mead, *Nathaniel William Taylor* (Chicago, 1942) has been most important for my understanding of the impact of the Awakening on orthodox Congregational theology. But also important are Sidney Earl Mead, *The Lively Experiment* (New York, 1963) and Perry Miller, "From the Covenant to the Revival," in idem, *Nature's Nation* (Cambridge, Mass., 1967).

My thinking about other aspects of the Second Great Awakening, especially the issue of social control, has been informed by Lois Banner, "Religious Benevolence as Social Control," *Journal of American History* 60 (1973):23–41; Richard D. Birdsall, "The Second Great Awakening and the New England Social Order," *Church History* 39 (1970):345–364; John R. Bodo, *The Protestant Clergy and Public Issues* (Princeton, N.J., 1954); Oliver W. Elsbree, *The Rise of the Missionary Spirit in America, 1790–1815* (Williamsport, Pa., 1928); Charles I. Foster, *An Errand of Mercy* (Chapel Hill, N.C., 1960); Dixon Ryan Fox, "The Protestant Counter-Reformation," *New York History* 16 (1935):19–35; Evarts B. Greene, "A Puritan Counter-Reformation," *American Antiquarian Society Proceedings*, n.s., 42 (1932):17–46; Clifford S. Griffin, *Their Brothers' Keepers* (New Brunswick, N.J., 1960); Charles Roy Keller, *The Second Great Awakening in Connecticut* (New Haven, Conn., 1942); W. David Lewis, "The Reformer as Conservative: Protestant Counter-Subversion in the Early Republic," in Stanley Coben and Lorman Ratner, eds., *The Development of an American Culture* (Englewood Cliffs, N.J., 1970); Donald G. Mathews, "The Second Great Awakening as an Organizing Process, 1789–1830: An Hypothesis," *American Quarterly* 21 (1969):23–43; and Paul R. Johnson, *A Shopkeeper's Millennium* (New York, 1978).

Several works were suggestive for understanding the intellectual and social outlooks taking shape among evangelical Congregationalists about the time of Morse's death. Daniel Walker Howe, *The Political Culture of the American Whigs* (Chicago, 1979) gives particular attention to evangelicals' concerns and their attraction to the Whig party. Although Carl Siracusa, *A Mechanical People: Perceptions of the Industrial Order in Massachusetts, 1815–1880* (Wesleyan, Conn., 1978) does not examine clerical attitudes, this book is important for those interested in the clergy's response to industrialization. Charles C. Cole, Jr., *The Social Ideas of the Northern Evangelical Clergy* (New York, 1954) and the early chapters of Henry F. May, *Protestant Churches and Industrial America* (New York, 1949) both have much to say about the social concerns of the clergy in antebellum America. Theodore Dwight Bozeman, *Protestants in an Age of Science* (Chapel Hill, N.C., 1977) is important for its discussion of the relation between evangelical Protestantism and the pursuit of scientific knowledge.

A number of books have influenced my treatment of Morse's involvement in politics. Like other historians, I am indebted to Bernard Bailyn, *The Ideological Origins of the American Revolution* (Cambridge, Mass., 1967) and Gordon S. Wood, *The Creation of the American Republic, 1776–1787* (Chapel Hill, N.C., 1969). In particular, these works helped me to understand the role that the Commonwealth concepts of conspiracy and corruption had played in the decades preceding the 1790s. Two recent books, Lance Banning, *The Jeffersonian Persuasion* (Ithaca, N.Y., 1978) and Drew R. McCoy, *The Elusive Republic* (Chapel Hill, N.C., 1980), follow up on the work of Bailyn and Wood, demonstrating the impact of the Commonwealth outlook on Democratic-Republicans' views and policies. Paul Goodman, *The Democratic-Republicans of Massachusetts* (Cambridge, Mass., 1964) is the most important work on the origins and development of the opposition party in New England.

Both James M. Banner, Jr., *To the Hartford Convention* (New York, 1970) and David Hackett Fischer, *The Revolution of American Conservatism* (New York, 1965) are most helpful in explaining what attracted men to the Federalist party and what happened to the party after 1800. Another very important book, on the political struggle of the 1790s, is Richard Buel, Jr., *Securing the Revolution* (Ithaca, N.Y., 1972). Other valuable books which deal with the same topic are Joseph Charles, *The Origins of the American Party System* (New York, 1961); Manning Dauer, *The Adams Federalists* (Baltimore, 1953); and Stephen Kurtz, *The Presidency of John Adams* (Philadelphia, 1957).

Two good books which deal with very different aspects of the War of 1812 are Roger H. Brown, *The Republic in Peril: 1812* (New York, 1812), which provides the best account of the Democratic-Republicans' decision to go to war, and William Gribbin, *The Churches Militant* (New Haven, Conn., 1973), which examines the various denominations' response to the war.

I have also benefited a good deal from several older books, especially Anson Ely Morse, *The Federalist Party in Massachusetts to the year 1800* (Princeton, N.J., 1909) and Richard J. Purcell, *Connecticut in Transition, 1775–1818* (Washington, 1918). Vernon Stauffer, *New England and the Bavarian Illuminati* (New York, 1918) was the starting point and very helpful for my research into Morse's charges about the conspiracy.

The most important article for me was Gary B. Nash, "The American Clergy and the French Revolution," *William and Mary Quarterly*, ser. 3, 22 (1965):392–412, which emphasizes the Congregational clergy's early support of the French Revolution and suggests that they turned against it in 1795 when they also expressed public opposition to the Democratic-Republicans. I differ in thinking that the clergy did not finally reject the Revolution until late in 1796 when the French announced their opposition to the Jay treaty and interfered in the presidential election.

My discussion of Morse's and the Congregational clergy's attitudes toward blacks, slavery, and colonization has been influenced by Winthrop D. Jordan, *White over Black* (Chapel Hill, N.C., 1968); Linda K. Kerber, *Federalists in Dissent* (Ithaca, N.Y., 1970); John R. Bodo, *The Protestant Clergy and Public Issues* (Princeton, N.J., 1954); Early Lee Fox, *The American Colonization Society, 1817–1840* (Baltimore, 1919); and P. J. Staudenraus, *The African Colonization Movement, 1816–1865* (New York, 1961).

Bernard W. Sheehan, *Seeds of Extinction* (Chapel Hill, N.C., 1973) provides an excellent discussion of those Americans who, like Morse, sought to assimilate the Indians into American society. Robert F. Berkhofer, Jr., *Salvation and the Savage* (Lexington, Ky., 1965) discusses the assumptions and approaches of missionaries to the Indians. My understanding of the federal government's Indian policies and of conditions among the Indians is based on R. Pierce Beaver, *Church, State, and the American Indians* (St. Louis, 1966); R. S. Coterill, *The Southern Indians* (Norman, Okla., 1954); Angie Debo, *The Rise and Fall of the Choctaw Republic* (Norman, Okla., 1934); Arthur H. De Rosier, Jr., *The Removal of the Choctaw Indians* (Knoxville, 1970); Arrel M. Gibson, *The Chickasaws* (Norman, Okla., 1971); Henry Thompson Malone, *Cherokees of the Old South* (Athens, Ga., 1956); Francis P. Prucha, *American Indian Policy in the Formative Years* (Cambridge, Mass., 1962); Grace Steele Woodward, *The Cherokees* (Norman, Okla., 1963); and Robert S. Walker, *Torchlights to the Cherokees* (New York, 1931).

# Index